COMFORT
ZONE

COMFORT ZONE

A NOVEL BY

CHRISTOPHER G.MOORE

Heaven Lake Press

Distributed in Thailand by:
Asia Document Bureau Ltd.
P.O. Box 1029
Nana Post Office
Bangkok 10112 Thailand
Fax: (662) 260-4578
www.heavenlakepress.com
email: editorial@heavenlakepress.com

First published in 1995 by White Lotus
Second printing in 1997 by BookSiam
Third edition in 2001 by Heaven Lake Press
Forth edition in 2011 by Heaven Lake Press

Jacket design: K. Jiamsomboon
Cover photograph: Ralf Tooten © 2010

ISBN 978-616-7503-06-6

For David Jacobson and Phuong Anh Nguyen
and
Les Stein

Man is a rope stretched between the animal and the Superman—a rope over an abyss.

Friedrich Nietzsche

CHAPTER 1

THE FOURTH OF JULY PICNIC

CALVINO HAD A law for Fourth of July which went something like this: no American should be caught dead or alive wearing a safari suit to the Fourth of July picnic in Bangkok. The hardship of concealing a handgun wasn't a valid exception to the rule. Every year Calvino wore the same all-American outfit of New York Yankees T-shirt, blue jeans, baseball cap, and Reeboks to the Fourth of July picnic in Bangkok. Being the first one to follow his own law, he always left his gun at home. This was also the twentieth year of the liberation of Saigon; or if you were on the losing side, the twentieth year of the fall of Saigon. One of those tiny details which Calvino knew would give the Fourth picnic a certain edge.

Lt.Col. Prachai Chongwatana—"Pratt" as he was called by Calvino and one or two other close friends—arranged his weekly schedule at the Crime Suppression Department, Royal Thai Police, so he would be free to attend the Fourth of July picnic with Calvino. Pratt slipped into civilian clothes and covered his head with a New York Yankees baseball cap. The annual ritual began with Pratt driving to Vincent Calvino's apartment in Sukhumvit Road. Like many rituals it was based more on faith in a simpler past before all the construction on Sukhumvit Road made driving like having sex in a bad marriage. But Pratt was too Thai ever to point out this hardship to Calvino, and the test of a friendship was the tolerance for a certain level of discomfort and pain.

"The Fourth of July comes only once a year," Pratt told himself as he turned down Soi 27, slowed his new powder gray BMW at the T-intersection in front of the private members club called Pegasus, turned left and a few seconds later pulled into the broken driveway of Calvino's broken down apartment house. Calvino climbed in, feeling chilled air inside, he smiled, slamming the door.

Pratt sneezed once, then again. "What are you wearing?"

"What? You're allergic to my shirt?" asked Calvino. He lowered his designer sunglasses.

"What's that smell?"

"It's cologne. Imported."

"I'm afraid to ask imported from which hill tribe."

"Paris," said Calvino.

"I thought the Fourth of July picnic was for business," said Pratt.

"It is," said Calvino, a little too quickly.

"Does this cologne mean you are going after a new clientele?"

"I'll roll down the window."

Pratt shook his head. "The air-conditioner's on."

A long silence fell like a rope ladder between them, each waiting for the other to volunteer to go first. They sat in a traffic snarl, motorcycles finding the narrow gap between the immobilized cars streaked past on both sides of the car. Pratt was right about the new contact aspect of the picnic. A Bangkok private eye trolled official functions for the walking wounded who stumbled into a party, looking for someone to help them once the fireworks ended and the food was gone and they were back on the streets.

Their destination was one and a half kilometers to the old International School grounds where the picnic was held every year.

"There is this possibility, I might meet someone who is not a client. A middle-class woman, someone normal, for instance," said Calvino, breaking the silence.

"This is Bangkok," said Pratt. "There's always an expectation of a possibility."

"Now, who is cynical?" asked Calvino, as the traffic light changed and the cars started to move as in a military convoy.

"And normal women like this smell?" asked Pratt.

"For Christsakes, it cost six hundred baht for this tiny bottle. I mean it has to be good," Calvino said, as they crossed the Asoke intersection.

"You are only supposed to put on a little," said Pratt. Calvino didn't say anything.

"You put on the whole bottle," said Pratt.

"Half," said Calvino.

"But it was tiny." He gestured with his thumb and forefinger the size of a bottle less than an inch high.

"You've got no sense of smell."

"My nose has filtered so much Bangkok air that even bacteria can't survive inside it."

"Then why did you buy the cologne?"

"The salesgirl recommended it."

"She saw you coming."

"No, she sold me the foul smelling cologne."

"Very funny," said Pratt.

As a university student Pratt had gone to New York with the intention of studying business but spent most of his time hanging out at the Pratt Institute, taking art lessons, and keeping his passion a secret from his parents in Bangkok. He had first met Calvino walking through Washington Square on his way to Greenwich Village. At the time, Calvino had been a law student at NYU. Calvino had taken Pratt to his parents' house in Brooklyn for his first Fourth of July picnic. He had stood on the roof of the building along with fifty or sixty neighbors, kids, women, old people. When the fireworks arc terminated with a burst of light, he saw the faces of these Americans and saw something he had never seen before, something between reverence and awe. The face of a Thai going into a Buddhist temple. This was a sacred moment for them, a ritual of remembering, of hope, of rebirth. It was about the future as much as about the past. Pratt never forgot the faces looking heavenward, illuminated as the fireworks filled the night sky with a flash of white light. Near the end, Calvino's mother had taken his hand, squeezed it. She looked at him, "Welcome to America, Mr. Pratt." Calvino had a crooked smile on his face as he watched his friend from Thailand shake hands with his mother and then his father. Pratt never forgot the power of that experience. Years later in Bangkok, Pratt had a number of friends in the American expat community. But none of them went back as far as Vincent Calvino. Calvino had been the one he had shared that first Fourth of July with, twenty years ago, and the memory was as fresh as if it had happened the day before.

"What's her name?" asked Pratt.

"Meow. That means cat in Thai," said Calvino.

"Thanks for the translation."

"She's beautiful, intelligent, able, so Harry says. She's not from the Zone."

Zone was short-hand for Comfort Zone, expat-speak for the vast archipelago of go-go bars, massage parlors, restaurants, barbershops, discos, clubs, cafes clustered like floating icebergs stretching from horizon to horizon in the sea of a Bangkok night.

"And you believe Harry?"

"His wife is not, you know, made out of lego bricks. The woman has substance. Meow's her younger sister."

"So the picnic is more than business this year," said Pratt, rubbing it in, and rolling down his window.

"You hate the cologne," said Calvino.

"It's distinctive."

"What's the Thai translation for distinctive?"

Pratt didn't miss a beat.

"*Men.*" The Thai word of choice for any bad smell like one of those gaseous farts from a patch of badly cooked fish from a street vendor.

Pratt, who had dressed in a light brown Mao-style shirt buttoned down the front and trousers, received the salute of the two Thai police officers checking people as they walked toward the main gate. This year Calvino had ironed the New York Yankees T-shirt himself, the jeans were fading to a bluish gray. He sported one new accessory: a pair of aviator sunglasses. He looked like a hitman who had taken a wrong turn on a Federal Witness Protection program and ended up on a permanent tropical holiday, thought Pratt.

There was a security checkpoint, one of those airport doorframes wired to pick up house keys, rings, loose change, and guns. Everyone walked through the frame and waited to see if they set off the alarm bell. Well, almost everyone waited. Thailand ran on the basis of the salute or run theory, meaning if you lack power don't question those in authority. If you had the power, then no one had authority over you. No one could scan you, make you wait. The guards at the gate had to check out when they could exercise power and when they had to salute. The Americans going to the picnic, they were used to being screened for weapons; it seemed a natural state and there was no constitutional right to get in the way of authority. Bangkok was one of the few places where Americans could control their own people.

Control you needed in Bangkok. All that heat, broken roads and traffic caused a lot of people to arrive angry, doubled up with swollen bladders and cranky kids. Enough to turn a quiet American into a serial killer claiming at his subsequent trial that the heat, dust, and aggro had turned him loco and mean. Turning off Sukhumvit Road and onto Soi 15 Pratt had found himself bumping along on a twisted, torn strip half-submerged under a foot of muddy water; it was as if some machine had slashed and destroyed the surface of the land, cut it hard, hurt it, made it bleed tons of hot mud that you needed a four-wheel vehicle to get through. Pratt's car looked like it had been vandalized by the time he entered the parking lot.

As they walked into the main grounds, the Thai military band struck up—not all at the same time—a big band tune. Jersey Bounce, one of those Benny Goodman songs from World War II. Calvino bought five hundred baht of coupons and headed straight for the beer and hot dogs. He returned a moment later and gave Pratt a beer. Pratt snapped the tab off the can of Bud.

"Here, take this," said Calvino, holding out a hot dog for Pratt. Pratt looked at it, wrinkled his nose.

"Once a year, you can eat a hot dog," Calvino said. "And don't tell me you've decided to become a vegetarian. You used that line last year."

"Afterwards, you will eat fried grasshoppers or red ants. Your choice," said Pratt. They had driven down Sukhumvit Road past a vendor with a cart with a small mountain of fried grasshoppers, stuffing them in a plastic bag.

Calvino took back the hot dog. "Head, wings, tail. The

whole animal," he said. This was part of the diet of the girls working inside the Zone.

"You keep looking at the shirt," said Calvino taking a bit from the hot dog.

"It makes you look like…"

"A tourist," said Calvino, knowing the outfit had troubled Pratt from the moment he had arrived at his apartment. *Farang* who dressed like a tourist were an embarrassment to their Thai friends.

"Relax, Pratt. Everyone looks like a tourist at the Fourth of July picnic. Besides it's our national dress."

Inside the grounds everyone was herded together into one large enclosure. Some of the expat families, kids with mouths open, eyes squinting in the bright sunlight, looked like they had just taken a wrong step out of a shopping mall time-warped video game and walked straight into Bangkok. Blank faces staring at the hot dog in one hand and a can of Bud in the other, wondering how all this had happened. Mormons roamed the grounds in white shirts, black name tags, and black trousers. A group of Hell's Angels, beards flecked with gray, sweat drenched bandannas, had ridden their Harleys from Korat. They walked into the grounds, their Thai mommas following; the whole group was dressed in black and wore leather cowboy boots. Earnest young men and women watched the Hell's Angels parade past their "Overseas Americans for Republicans" booth. There was no eye contact. Every nationality and race gathered on the green, lush grass to celebrate a revolutionary war which the Americans had won; no one was talking about Vietnam which they had lost. Near the band was a table of middle-aged expats drinking beer who had come to lurk around the teenaged Amerasian girls.

A World War II vet, his sunken face creased with age and watery eyes, came up to Pratt and Calvino with a box of red poppy pins for sale. His assistant was a Thai bar girl in cut-off jeans and a T-shirt which read "I like to smoke." She had teamed up in the name of free enterprise to help the old vet on his rounds with the box of red poppies for sale.

"Who's your helper, Ed?" asked Calvino, recognizing the *farang* from the Washington Square bars.

"You buying to help disabled vets or not, Calvino?" The old man squinted against the sunlight.

"How much this year?"

"Thirty baht," said the bar girl.

"Ten baht, or whatever you want to give."

There was the difference between a bar girl and a war vet. No bar girl ever left a customer the option of giving what he wanted. This was Comfort Zone pricing rules.

"What's her cut, Ed?"

"Lek has a good heart. She just wants to help."

Calvino's law was that any time a bar girl just wanted to help was the same time you made contingency plans as to where to hide the wallet. He bought two red poppies and gave one to Pratt who pinned it to his shirt.

Calvino watched Ed and the bar girl Lek head for the next group a couple of feet away.

"Makes you homesick for Times Square," he said.

Before he could finish his sentence someone from the American Embassy ran over and whispered if he might have a private word with Pratt. His name was Fred Harris and he was wearing black Bermuda shorts with yellow stripes. Harris was mid–40s, thinning gray hair, wide shoulders like he had once played football and a gut that hung over the top of his Bermuda shorts like he had retired to the bar.

"Nice shorts, Mark," said Calvino.

"Float like a butterfly, sting like a bee," said Harris.

"Until you hit the age when you start to float like a bee and sting like a butterfly," said Calvino.

Harris forced a smile. "Calvino, I'd like to borrow the

Colonel for a couple of minutes," he said.

That meant one thing: an American was in trouble with the authorities. Calvino exchanged a glance with Pratt.

"I think I'll get another hot dog. Catch up with you later."

"I hope she likes it," said Pratt.

Calvino turned around, cocked his head. "You know, that smell," he added.

The Fourth of July picnic was supposedly his new start. A week earlier he had been upcountry with a go-go dancer named Daeng. Someone he had been seeing for about two weeks which translated into two years in the Zone. They had gone to Daeng's village for a few days to unwind, get out of Bangkok, slip free of the Zone. One morning as he lowered his head so as not to bang it on the midget-sized doorway, he watched as Daeng dragged a green hose across the dirt yard, then she filled the concrete trough used for bath water, another concrete pool used for toilet water. After she turned off the hose, she squatted on the dirt floor of the kitchen and tore up a plastic bag and started eating red ants mixed with garlic and onions. She called on him to join her. He walked over and squatted down next to her and watched her use two fingers to pinch a batch of dead ants and pop them into her mouth. She smiled and reached back into the bag with thousands of bodies and squeezed her fingers around a man- sized portion for him. At the same time, her younger brother, Haeng, arrived and squatted down holding a grill over the flames of the wood fire; inside the grill was a fried rat. Daeng explained how the rat came from the forest. They were clean rats. Not like the garbage eating rats in Bangkok which no one in Isan would ever stoop so low as to eat. He looked at the squashed, flattened rat body, the head of the rat looked like a child's drawing, a snaggled tooth, one inky, smudged black eye, as if the brother had taken a hammer and hit the rat until it was thin as the gold leaf someone put onto the back of a wooden elephant at Erawan Shrine. Calvino watched Haeng eating rat and Daeng eating ants for a couple of minutes, got up, walked straight for the road and took a bus back to Bangkok, swearing he was finished with Zone women. He had had enough. He put the word out that he wanted a non-Zone lady. Harry Markle said he would deliver at the picnic. The Fourth of July was a new start, a revolutionary event to be celebrated, an event almost as great as breaking free of the Zone.

§ § § §

WITH the overhead sun beating down, Calvino headed in the direction of hundreds of people who huddled around a long row of concession stands with volunteers hawking everything from lotto tickets, hot dogs, hamburgers, to Budweiser beer. Kids rode on the ferris wheel and the merry-go-round. An image of his own daughter, Melody, flashed through his mind, leaving some guilt, some pain as it screamed on through his consciousness. A few feet away, an American Chamber of Commerce guy in baggy shorts and Washington University T-shirt pressed a bullhorn to his mouth and announced that substituting boiled eggs was, once again this year, against the rules. And no rolling of eggs. You had to toss them in the air. This guy was obviously a veteran of a number of Bangkok Fourth of July celebrations. The crowd of Thais and *farang* dressed in shorts and T-shirts looked relaxed even though they were sweaty, hot and hungry. Behind this superficial informality were the serious players on the local scene, the lawyers, bankers, doctors, embassy types, merchants, journalists, NGOs, preachers, and Peace Corp workers. This was the crew of America's Starship Enterprise lost in the vastness of Asian space and time.

Then he saw Harry Markle waving at him to come over to his table. Harry Markle, his Thai wife, nicknamed Noi, and their two kids occupied a table. Occupied was the right word. There were few tables with umbrellas and if you left one for a moment some Hell's Angel, Mormon or preacher would pounce on it and you would need a loaded assault rifle to get it back. Noi was a registered pharmacist and had her own shop which stocked New Age herbal remedies. The shop, the only one like it in Bangkok, was listed in a couple of the travel guides to Thailand and she was thinking of opening a second branch at Seacon Shopping Mall. Harry Markle was a telecommunications expert, linking companies and people to the Internet, setting up nodes in places like Hong Kong and Finland. He laid down software so complex and sophisticated that, once it was hooked into various networks of computers, the effect was to grant Harry lifetime job security; he could never be fired from his job because no one could replace him, and all that transmitted data would go over the side of a cliff like a spooked herd of buffalos in a thunderstorm.

Calvino sat down in a plastic chair as Markle pulled the tab on a can of Bud, beer foaming through the hole and down the side of the can.

"Great weather today," said Harry.

One of his daughters, the fourteen-year-old, came to the table with one of her friends, eating a hot dog, the mustard squirting onto her hand.

Dr. Penguin, dressed in a dinner jacket with a toy penguin head shaped as a hat which he wore pulled down over his ears, removed an egg from Harry's two-year-old daughter 's ear. Her eyes got real big.

"You like that, Honey?" asked Harry, picking her up.

She looked at Dr. Penguin with the kind of face that looked like it could go either way: cry or laugh. She started to laugh as Dr. Penguin pulled an egg from Calvino's ear.

"A private eye shouldn't go around with eggs in his head," said Dr. Penguin.

"And a penguin should keep out of the sun," said Noi.

Harry looked at the egg. "At least it's not scrambled," said Harry.

"Just hard-boiled," said Calvino.

Over the loudspeaker system a Midwestern accent read off a list of lottery announcements, mispronouncing most of the Thai names. At the next table, several Soi Cowboy bar girls in shorts and tank-tops were decked out in gold chains and bracelets. They were trying to keep out of the sun. Bar girls hated getting a tan. Most of them were village girls from Isan and were sensitive about the darkness of their skin. Dark skinned wasn't cool. White, white skin was the meaning of beauty, along with lots of gold to set it off, according to the Comfort Zone standard of desirable.

"The bar girls never miss a Fourth of July," said Harry Markle, as Dr. Penguin wandered off.

"They like fireworks," said Noi, who was university educated, and was doing her best to deflect the conversation about the girls at the next table.

"Yeah," said Harry. "They are like Willie Sutton. Why do you rob banks, Willie? That's where the money is. Ladies, why do you come to the Fourth of July picnic every year? Because that is where the money is. Inside every bar girl is a little Willie Sutton voice screaming out."

Over at the stands people stood three or four deep gorging on the free popcorn, ice cream, and soda. Eating ears of corn, leaning over with the butter running over their hands, giving them a shiny lacquer, and running off into the grass.

"You have any trouble getting through the airport security at the gate?" Harry asked.

"Pratt showed his badge. No problem," said Calvino.

"It helps to be connected. Some guy with a bar girl set off the alarm at security. That made for fun. Some logger chick arrived with a SWAT team to rub him down. He was clean but his girl had one of those toy gun lighters," he said, drinking from his beer. "The logger chick asked her what it was. But her English wasn't so great. So the guy said, 'Look, my friend is a vice challenged person.' And she squinted and asked, 'Vice, what's that mean?' 'Vice as in vice squad,' he said. 'The toy gun makes her feel safe.' The logger chick nodded, gave her back the toy gun and waved them through."

Logger chick was the current expat-speak for overweight middle-aged white women. Someone in a Washington Square bar once defined a logger chick as a woman with the biceps of an axe swinger and the legs of a mature redwood.

"Trust me, it happened. Ask Noi," said Harry.

"About my sister..." Noi said, sounding sheepish.

Harry had phoned two days earlier and said Calvino just had to meet Meow. She was about eight years younger than Noi, smart, beautiful and available. And Meow would be at the Fourth of July picnic.

"She couldn't make it," said Harry, finishing his wife's sentence.

"One of those Thai things."

That always covered a lot of ground. As it turned out, Noi's sister, Meow, had cancelled the picnic because she had a call from her astrologer saying under no circumstances was she to leave the house. The alignment of the stars had forbidden her from going.

"I didn't say she wasn't superstitious," said Harry.

"No, you are right."

"I hope you aren't too disappointed," said Noi.

Calvino drank his beer. "Maybe we can get together on the next full moon."

"Not to let you completely down, I have some work for you. A personal case."

Calvino came each year with the expectation of getting an assignment. What he hadn't expected was that, instead of getting fixed up with Noi's sister, Harry Markle was going to hire him for a job at the Fourth of July picnic. He wished he could wash off the cologne. Pratt was right, it was not such a good idea. Everyone was keeping their distance. The astrologer had guessed that smell from the movement of the stars and moon and had warned Meow away, he thought. In the heat he could not help feel a sadness as the expectation of meeting Meow fell away, drawing him over the edge into doom and disappointment. Shifting his expectation from the personal into a work mode was hard at first. The idea of possible romance was like a loose piece of string; it could be shaped in any way to fit the imagination until the spell was broken and the realization set in that he had deceived himself, strung himself along. He pulled himself together, smiled, and opened another beer. "A personal case," he heard Harry say again. Case assignments at the Fourth of July picnic had a habit of always being an omen of bad karma. Pratt was right. It had been his primary reason for going year after year. One year he was going to break that string of bad Fourth of July cases. He knew that Harry Markle wouldn't let him down.

The year before last, he had gone after a missing son who had run off with a local girl to Koh Chang. He brought the kid back by the eighth of July and left the girl on the island; she had already found a replacement *farang* with more money... The kid fell on the ferry deck and broke his arm. The parents blamed Calvino for not properly looking after their son. It was a good reason to stiff him for the bill.

Calvino had clients and friends who expected him to be at the picnic. It was bad for business to miss the Fourth of July in Bangkok and it was bad to take an assignment at the Fourth of July picnic. No one ever said it outright, but it was a loyalty thing. In the middle of Bangkok, forgetting the Fourth of July picnic was an act of expat treason. The American Chamber of Commerce, he thought, kept some kind of unofficial blacklist of those who didn't show up. This year an old friend had phoned him. Harry Markle said he had a beautiful present for him.

Now at the picnic he was singing a different tune.

"I've got a problem, Vinee," said Harry.

"Who doesn't?" asked Calvino.

He had known Harry Markle for a half dozen years. In other words enough time to learn the basic catastrophes which had blown through his life, the trail of ghosts left behind.

"It's my little brother in Saigon," said Harry.

"He was there for the twentieth anniversary?" asked Calvino.

"Yeah, he was."

"I didn't know you had a younger brother."

"I left home before he was born. So let's say we aren't all that close. Now he's working as a lawyer in Vietnam," said Harry.

So far it didn't sound like much of a problem. But cases which started soft lipped like this often had steel jaws and sharp teeth. "What's his problem? Other than he's trying to follow in his big brother 's footsteps," said Calvino.

"Drew has the usual paranoid feelings of any American thirty-year-old who has never been out of the States and is trying to make a go of it in Saigon."

"Like what?"

"Someone in the office is up to the usual monkey shines. Drew says there's something unethical going on. He kept using the words professional ethics."

Calvino smiled at the word.

"I know, I know," said Harry. "The American delusion. It's what got us into Vietnam in the first place. Drew hasn't found out yet that American ethics aren't as popular as American junk food and movies. But give him time. He will learn."

Markle was ex-special forces and had done two tours in Vietnam. In Asia, every other guy over forty-five claimed to have served in the special forces, or was a Green Beret, a Navy Seal; someone who was a mean motherfucker in the past and who had lived in the jungles on slugs and slit the throats of Viet Cong until dawn. Harry Markle was the only guy Calvino had ever met that actually had done it and survived, with a sense of humor, his life intact. He had a family and had settled in Thailand.

Noi nudged Harry's arm. His eyes followed her to a dozen Marines dressed in T-shirts and shorts picking up one end of a thick, long rope. Next came a dozen Mormons, looking like they had just flunked the physical for army boot camp. They picked up the other end of the rope. For a moment, Markle's brother in Saigon was just a slice of conversation left hanging in the air.

"Who you betting on?" asked Harry, grinning from ear to ear.

"God or the Marines?"

"If there were a God you wouldn't need the Marines," said Calvino.

There was nothing scientific about this. But American Marines from the US Embassy in Bangkok had standard issue bull-like necks. The average Mormon looked as small as a fridge magnet next to the Marine guard. Belief in God had caused men to believe that miracles could overcome neck size differences. So in most years the Mormons entered the tug-of-war contest in Bangkok, mean-ing they would have to face the Marines and hope God was listening. And each Fourth of July picnic in Bangkok it rained like hell just after the US Marines wiped the playground with a dozen skinny Mormons holding on for dear life as the Marines dragged them through the mud in a tug-of-war that was never a contest. Was it the rain which followed God's wrath? Or was it just the rainy season weather with all those black clouds and claps of thunder in Bangkok that time of year?

Harry Markle said, "The Mormons did it once. It was like carrying an elephant up the side of a hill. It can be done. But it's always difficult and messy."

"Those aren't Mormons," said Noi. "That's AT&T."

She was right. She was Thai but she could still tell the difference between the Mormons and the telephone company. One paid dividends in this life, one promised dividends in the next. Thais were forever crossing the boundary between last, present and next life. It made perfect sense in terms of continuity and prevented the uneasy sense in the Christian West that you only got your ticket punched once; it was either up or down, and never back for a repeat of another tug-of-war.

A crowd gathered and they could hear the side bets being made. A small group of old Asian hands of all nationalities were drinking beer and watching the Marines, all that muscle and short haircuts looking down the rope like it was the barrel of a gun. All those black clouds which had accumulated over the playing field opened up and it started to rain. The Marines didn't blink an eye. The AT&T team was one man short, and no one was volunteering to take on the Marines. A vice president found a consultant hiding behind a table of bar girls and ordered him onto the field. Then the contest began. Everyone at the table was on their feet. And the rain came harder. Harry was right; one year the Mormons actually won the tug-of-war. And it still rained. This year it rained before the contest was decided.

§ § § § §

ABOUT eight in the evening the fireworks display started with the whistle of a rocket shooting high overhead, which was followed by a blinding flash and a shower storm of white feathery bursts of white light lit up the black sky. Calvino glanced to his right and saw how the light from the fireworks illuminated Markle. His face looked different, rigid, immobile but alert. He looked like someone caught in the open as a flare floated down on a tiny parachute and guns opened fire. This was the old mask that Harry Markle and a lot of other vets wore every year at the Fourth of July picnic. Vietnam was a one hour and five minute flight away from Bangkok. For a few minutes they remembered something, thought Calvino.

"It beats me why my little brother who was doing perfectly well in New York City would want to try and play lawyer in a communist regime," said Markle, his head turned toward the sky, his mouth slightly ajar.

"Sometimes a younger brother feels that he has something to live up to. Your two tours in Vietnam and the drawer full of medals is a whole lot to live up to for anyone."

"But as a lawyer?"

Craning his head around, Harry pushed the black, horn-rimmed glasses onto the bridge of his nose.

"Maybe it was the only way he could get himself a way to Vietnam."

Another flash burst lit up the sky in red, blue and white. The colors of the American flag draining down the edges of the night sky in Bangkok.

"I want you to go to Saigon for a few days. Check that he's okay, you know. Give him a talk about ethics and business in this part of the world. Three hundred a day plus expenses, right?"

Calvino thought about karma as he watched another star burst of rockets overhead. "Do I go or stay?" he asked himself.

"I'd go myself, but I have this assignment..." said Harry Markle, breaking off as Noi handed him another beer.

"Okay, three days should be enough time," said Calvino.

"More than ample," said Harry Markle. "Take an extra day and get out in the countryside. Let's call that a bonus."

Pratt had not returned from his meeting with Fred Harris.

Calvino was not the only one who managed to find himself involved in a case he had not asked for and didn't really want. The Fourth of July picnic was the leg trap they both stepped into each year, leaving them two choices: figuring out how to open the trap or gnaw their leg off.

All those families in one confined place was an overpowering experience not repeated anywhere else in Bangkok throughout the year. Calvino lived for the rest of the year somewhere in the Zone. Old haunts, new bars. Places filled with a fresh crop of beautiful women, an endless supply. Nothing survived inside the Zone but the moment of pleasure. Ninety percent of the *farang* took their women, short or long term, from some Zone establishment. The ice never left her, the sub-zero temperature of her past froze all possibility of a future. Ice cut off feelings. But the Zone was so much more: there was the surface ice, stages with naked girls swinging around silver poles; outside, the bright neon lights promised warmth, these places were on the maps, deep in the psyche. Cowboy, Nana, Patpong. The dark ice places where the submerged, vast, floating ice fields shifted and creaked; here no one but the hardest of the hardcore *farang* had ever gone, and there were no maps, guidebooks, only word of mouth passed among a small group of Zone warriors. Once they entered the ice fields, anything was possible.

Neon ice, dark ice...in the end, the same thing happened, a man got himself lost, snowblinded by the towering ice domes; there were men inside who would die rather than leave the ice. Abandon the Zone. Calvino had gone to the picnic hoping he was about to find a way out. But Noi's sister had stayed home. He was disappointed. And he had started to think that Vietnam might be a way out, a tunnel away from the ice fields and ice goddesses. He had left the picnic with some hope. A new assignment. But the old fear gnawed at Calvino: there was a way through fire but there was no way through the ice.

In the Zone, the ice walls and ice fields, thick, high, centuries old, translucent, and forever cold, contained unlimited sexual pleasures...the women, the women, the women. Ice domes built from the bodies of women, a Zone empire making tons and tons of ice honey for those protecting the ice against any attempted thaw.

CHAPTER 2

LEARNING THAI

AS THE CROWD at the Fourth of July picnic started to break up, Harry Markle walked through the parking lot with Calvino, promising to phone him in the morning.

"Tomorrow," said Harry, smiling. "Gotta go now."

"Let's go for a drink," said Calvino.

"Have an appointment. Rain check, ole buddy."

Yeah, rain check.

Harry didn't phone the next morning. Calvino thought about calling him but thought it was better to let things ride. Promises to engage a private eye often happened in the flash of an emotional moment of inspired insight; such insight cooled a few hours later, and what seemed like a good business prospect vanished up the same spout as pillow talk, Comfort Zone commitments. Sure, Harry had been all worked up about his little brother's ethical problem in Vietnam, and then he woke up on the 5th of July and decided his little brother didn't really have much of a problem. Calvino picked up the phone and started to phone Noi, Harry's wife, to ask if the sister was still keeping a low profile until her stars shifted. He put the phone back. Play it the Thai way, passively, waiting, no show of interest. The day after the Fourth of July he had a bad hangover. Calvino wanted to forget about Harry's brother in Saigon and Noi's sister whose social life had come under the control of a local fortune teller. He stayed in his office finishing some paperwork on an old missing person's file and waiting for Nah, his Thai teacher, to arrive for his Thai lesson.

Nah walked into his office about eight in the evening of the 5th of July dressed in a tight black dress, high-heels and black nylons. The dress fit her like a body glove that a rock star might wear in a video. Full lips, intense eyes, and with one of those smiles that could pierce the Comfort Zone ice where Calvino had found sanctuary.

"I was just thinking of Saigon," said Calvino, doing a double take, taking her in from head to toe. "And in comes a Viet Cong."

She blushed. "You don't like?"

Calvino smiled. "What's not to like? Saigon would have fallen ten years earlier if you had walked in dressed like that."

"*Pahk wan*," she said. Sweet mouth.

She sat down in the chair, crossed her legs, and removed two Thai-English books from her briefcase and laid them on Calvino's desk. One was for him and the other was for her. She flipped through the teacher's guidebook, her face still flushed red, her concentration a little off. Calvino closed his file and leaned back in his chair. She was some kind of woman.

Nah was in the twilight of her late twenties, single, university educated and from a conservative Chinese-Thai family who worshipped ancestors and played the stock market. She had always been very careful to dress in a stylish, yet non-suggestive, office outfit for his language lessons.

Pure silk outfits with padded shoulders and imported Italian shoes. For the first month of instruction in Thai, Nah had insisted that Ratana, Calvino's secretary, stay inside the office. Her request was standard operating procedure for a riap roi, or respectable Thai woman who had been taught to avoid being alone in the presence of a man. When the man was a *farang*, the alarm bells didn't just ring, they exploded.

"You okay?" asked Calvino. From the way she set her jaw, she looked distracted, deep inside herself, carried away on some ribbon of thought.

She didn't answer at first, pretending she was looking for the right page in the book. Then she looked up, biting her lower lip. "I forgot where we left off."

"I've always wanted to learn how to say that in Thai," he said. "Give me a minute please."

His mind drifted as she stared at the book. On the other hand, Harry might have thought he had already instructed him to fly to Saigon, thought Calvino. After all, they had discussed a fee and the number of days. Harry had even thrown in a one-day paid vacation. So what did he want? A written contract, Calvino was thinking.

She was playing it a little on the dangerous side but not so much that she couldn't handle it if someone raised a question. Nah knew some of her friends were asking themselves, "Has that private eye ever tried to hit on you? Suck you into the Zone?"

The question never passed between their lips. It got stuck deep inside their minds, but when you are Thai, you can read that dead space between thought, desire, intention and the air space between them crackles with information. But no Thai would ever ask such a direct question.

Nah reported that Vincent Calvino was a well-behaved student with an interest in the Thai language. And the listener danced around that image like someone around a camp fire trying to see what was cooking inside the pot lost in the flames.

"Your minute's up," said Calvino. "After all, I am paying by the hour."

"I think we stay to the book."

"How to go to the post office, how to go to the train station stuff," said Calvino.

"It's the way everyone learns Thai," she said.

"We were making progress on what people really want to know," said Calvino.

Her Thai nickname, Nah, translated into English as "face," and sometimes during the first two weeks of lessons she would blush red and Calvino would think how her name had given the right hint of the kind of person that she would grow up to be. Kind, patient, sincere, respectful, and painfully shy at any reference to sex. That was until Ratana no longer was in the office. Gradually she relaxed and let her hair down. Two months into the lessons, Calvino noticed that nothing much bothered her, she taught him some of the raunchy words in Thai. She liked the freedom to say whatever she wanted. There were no witnesses; there were no rules which applied inside Calvino's office during the length of the lesson. Calvino allowed her to rebel, didn't judge her, didn't criticize her. For a few weeks the relationship had started the long march which looked like it might take them beyond the invisible boundary between student and teacher. It was never clear where it was going, but Nah made it crystal clear that she was in control. It was her call to make. So, when this shy product of a Sino-Thai family who had spent her life under virtual house arrest walked into his office dressed to kill, Calvino thought she had reached some kind of decision. Taking a *farang* private eye as a student had been another in a series of small acts of personal rebellion. Nah, on this night, looked like a revolutionary ready to storm the barricades.

"What's the Thai word for train station?"

"I never take trains. Ask me something else."

"For airport."

"Airport," he said. "That's English."

Her dress rode up to her thigh.

"Are you going to a party?" asked Calvino.

"You think I look evil?" she asked.

He smiled, wondering how she had picked that English word.

"What's wrong with a little evil between teacher and student?"

That made three questions in a row. Calvino's law was that three consecutive questions about liking a woman's sexy dress is not about the dress but about who is going to make the first move. Nah was looking for someone to help her break down a family prison wall. But there was something more than this working in her mind. Like romance. Chances were that Nah was a virgin and, the way he saw it, she was offering the one thing she had been taught her whole life was the most valuable thing a woman possessed. This was the first sound of confusion and frustration which would later be amplified into an emotional thunderstorm. But to be warned was to stay dry.

"Tell you what, after the lesson, why don't we go out for dinner to celebrate the transformation of the new Nah?"

That seemed to shut off the steam coming out of his ears. She leaned back in her chair, looked over at his .38 Police Special inside the leather holster looped over the back of his chair. She didn't look all that happy. Like a boxer who had thrown his best punch at the opponent and the guy takes it smack in the middle of the face and doesn't even blink.

"*Dai sia*, say it," she said.

Calvino sat in his office, head back, eyes focused on a small house lizard which hung upside down on the ceiling eating mosquitoes. A small tongue flicked.

"Khun Vincent, if you don't pay attention, then you will never learn to speak Thai," she scolded, her eyes slowly moving up to the spot where he was looking. She let out a heavy sigh and started to get up from her chair.

"Whoah, it's coming to me in a flash, yeah, I've got it. *Dai sia.*"

"The tone's wrong," she said, repeating the phrase with the right tone.

"Tone, tone. It's like taking a music lesson. I can never hear the tone."

"But it's so easy, if only you would try." He tried and failed again.

"Okay, maybe it would help if you told me what *Dai sia* means."

She clapped her hands together. "That was perfect. And you weren't even trying."

It was what *farang* called a tonal accident, like a monkey hitting the middle C note with its tail.

"You think it would help if I thought learning the tones was like love making? Don't think too much. Just let it happen?"

Her eyes looked away and she shook her head.

"*Dai sia, Dai sia, Dai sia.* You know, if you say that more than three times, you could go crazy," said Calvino.

"I think you have said this many times," said Nah. That was an out of character false note; be-cause one of the five rules to be strictly followed in order to survive in Thailand was never under any circumstances, criticize someone to their face. That was what the back was made for.

"Meaning, you think I am crazy?"

"Let me tell you the meaning of *Dai sia.* It means win and lose. Winner and loser. With sex, the man always wins and the woman always loses."

She had said the "S" word without any promp-ting but,

again, in a political rather than erotic context. This time she did not blush.

"*Dai sia*, I like that, Nah."

"And if you turn the word order around then you have *sia dai*. Which means, what a waste, what a sorrow. This is life. A man is always the winner and the woman is, well, sorrowful. I think it is true. Do you, Khun Vincent?"

The phone rang and Calvino reached over to pick it up. His hand hovered over the receiver. He was thinking it was after office hours. Let the phone ring. And he was looking at her breasts under the revealing glove thing she wore.

"So sex will turn a woman into a loser?"

She looked at the phone.

"Aren't you going to answer that?"

He picked up the receiver. "I'm in the middle of a Thai lesson," he said, without waiting to find out who was on the other end.

It was Pratt. "You had better turn on CNN," he told Calvino.

"Pratt, I'm learning Thai."

"Trust me, Vincent."

"My Thai teacher is going to murder me. And because I am a *farang*, your department won't even give her a ticket. There will be insufficient evidence that I'm dead," said Calvino, looking across his desk at Nah.

She liked the word murder. It made her smile. What kind of smile he couldn't quite decide, but the grin probably had something to with the kind of revenge that was packaged in phrases like *Dai sia* and *sia dai*. He pointed a remote control at a television set in the corner. There was a map of Vietnam and, inserted in a box in the left hand corner, was the photograph of a gray-haired reporter with loose skin, wrinkles flaring out from the corner of his eyes and a lipless smile. A high mileage face. In the photograph, the veteran reporter had a tiny microphone clipped to his safari shirt. The reporter was talking by phone to the anchor. The transmission made that crackly noise like the voice was being filtered through a bad line.

"Vietnamese authorities have been seriously embarrassed by a grenade attack about three hours ago in the heart of Saigon. The attack comes three months after the twentieth anniversary of the fall of Saigon. The 30th of April came and went relatively quietly. How the Vietnamese Government will react is difficult to say. We have tried to speak with local authorities but, so far, none have been available. It is all very confused here on the ground, Ted."

Then the screen was filled with the news anchor, a woman in an austere dress and glasses, looking like a sixth grade teacher listening to the report of a fairly dull student.

"Thank you, John," she said in an English accent.

"Please stand by in Ho Chi Minh City. Our latest report is that a young American named Drew Markle from Los Angeles, California, has been killed in a grenade attack. And five Vietnamese civilians were injured. The murder of the American in Saigon has caused an international uproar. His murder has been condemned by two members of congress who have called on the president to cancel the normalization of US relations with Vietnam. Vietnamese authorities have not made any arrests. We have Julia Read at the State Department. Julia, what are officials at the State Department telling you about this tragic death?"

Julia Read smiled into the camera. "One theory is that Markle was not a target but got in the way of a gangland type killing."

The anchor appeared on the screen again.

"John, now that our relationship with Viet-nam has been normalized, is this incident going to set things back between Hanoi and Washington?"

"Not if it is an isolated incident. There have been Germans killed in the state of Florida. No one is seriously suggesting that Bonn and Washington have damaged their relationship as a result. I think it very much depends on who was involved. If it turns out to be that Markle was simply in the wrong place at the wrong time, then I doubt if there will be much political fallout. Some groups and individuals might try to gain some political mileage out of this, but I don't think they will get very far. Domestic crime is an issue in most places and Vietnam is no exception. It is likely they will cite the Oklahoma City bombing to show that Americans have their own home-grown terrorists."

"*Sia dai*," said Calvino into the phone. He pushed the off button on the remote control. And he was thinking, "Harry Markle hasn't called today and he's sitting home feeling pretty bad right now."

He looked up at Nah.

"You have a problem?"

He dialed Harry Markle's number but the line was busy.

"I've got a problem. About dinner..."

"You changed your mind." There was a sadness in her voice, the kind that comes from rejection.

"Something's happened in Saigon, Nah."

"I don't understand, Khun Vincent."

He looked at her sitting across from his desk wearing her designer Viet Cong dress, looking dressed to kill. All he could think about was why someone would have killed Harry Markle's younger brother in Saigon.

"I have to cancel dinner," he said. "I'm sorry about that, Nah. I wish..."

"It's better not to wish," she said. "You got a point."

Her expression didn't change. She simply got up and walked out of his office, slamming the door behind her. She had her kind of hurt, he thought. Harry had another, and the chain of hurt went round and round like bad weather circulating around the globe, touching everyone and everything in a haze of gloom. He tried phoning Harry for another thirty minutes before he decided that Markle had probably taken his phone off the hook.

He dialed Pratt's number. Pratt picked up after the first ring.

"I'm going out to Harry Markle's house," said Calvino.

"Let me know if there is anything I can do," Pratt said.

"By the way, what happened to you at the picnic yesterday?" "Business," said Pratt.

§ § § §

HARRY Markle's family lived in a four-story shophouse on one of the nondescript sois behind the Victory Monument. Noi's New Age pharmacy was on the ground floor. They lived a variation of Chinese shophouse style: family business on the ground floor, family living quarters on the two floors above. On the top floor, Harry had enough computer and telecommunications equipment to rival the nerve centre of a major company. It was his space to jack in, and drop out. Wedged between the high-tech electronics on the top and the high-tech drugs on the bottom, the gravity of family hovered in cyberspace between machines and drugs.

When Calvino arrived at the shophouse he found the metal shutter had been pulled down to the pavement. Nearby, a beggar with stumps for feet sat in the dark; old, bloody rags wrapped around the stumps, the beggar, with no nose and a caved-in face—the withered mask could have housed either a man or a woman— cradled a baby. The child was less than a year old. The baby looked listless, eyes glazed over, a crust of snot around the nostrils. Living in Asia for years, Calvino had learned the trick of looking through, over or under beggars. He had stopped seeing them on some level. They became like abandoned furniture on a Manhattan street, castaways stranded in a walkway, with no use, no value. This time he saw the beggar and thought this person was a marker of suffering, the kind of suffering Calvino knew was going on inside Markle's shophouse. He pulled out his wallet and put a hundred-baht note in the plastic cup near the child. As he got closer, he saw the woman was nursing the baby. She pulled the baby from her breast, laid it on the pavement, raised her hands in a *wai* and fell down at his feet as if to kiss the ground. The odds were three to five that some local gangster would take the money away from her by the end of the night. It didn't matter, thought Calvino. You did what you could and hoped for the best. Otherwise the Zone ice covered your soul, freezing it into a solid block, nothing getting in, nothing getting out and that was the same as being dead.

Calvino took a step forward, turned right and then rang the outside buzzer which had been placed at eye-level on the gate to Markle's shophouse. He waited and, not long after ringing the buzzer, Calvino heard the distant sound of footsteps running down stairs, and the sound of bare feet jogging along the corridor just inside the main door. Then the metal gate came up and Calvino found himself staring at Harry's teenage daughter who stood in the door with her eyes puffy and red from crying. Her face was twisted with grief and she pulled a wadded tissue from a pocket and blew her nose.

Calvino said, "It's Vincent Calvino."

"Uncle Vincent," she said, adjusting her eyes to the dark.

She waited a moment, then pulled up the metal shutter. With her eyes all swollen and red from crying, she looked much different. Like a small child who had been disciplined.

31

She started to blubber, covered her mouth with one hand, and gestured for him to come inside and up the stairs.

"I know about your uncle. I am sorry."

"It's just. Just I never got to meet him. I never saw him. Only a picture."

They walked up the stairs together. What was he going to say? How do you give comfort to a kid who had lost something she never knew? The answer is that you can't, he thought. Harry Markle was in the living room with a bottle of Kloster beer in his hand and a dozen empty bottles at his feet on the floor.

"Vinee, sit down. You wanna beer? Get him a beer. We are having, shall I say, some family shit going down."

"I saw the television report."

"Fuck TV. Fuck the press. Those bastards came to Vietnam before. They never gave a rat's ass about anything or anyone. All they wanted were close-ups of bodies. They called that news then. TV people invented body counts. That's a fact. Distort, make up, fuck up, whatever makes you and the reviewers happy. It all comes out the same. All fucked up."

"That's why you took your phone off the hook," said Calvino.

"You know how many of those lowlifes phoned me?"

Calvino shook his head.

"Many. And I said to each one, 'Sir, kindly go and fuck yourself.'"

"It's not your fault, Harry."

"Of course it's not my fucking fault. But I might have stopped it." Markle reached over and used an opener on another bottle of Kloster. He handed it to Calvino and then opened another one for himself. "You think that I'm drunk?"

On the coffee table were color photographs. There was a youngish looking version of Harry Markle holding an M16.

"You're drunk, Harry. But so what?"

"Of course, so what?" he smiled, the beer suds squeezing out of the corner of his mouth.

Noi came into the room with her hair down, her eyes wild with fear.

"It's so bad for him," she said, as if Harry Markle weren't in the room. "Harry was out when I heard..."

Harry cut her off in mid-sentence.

"I had a job. I finish the job and then I find out Drew's dead. You see, my little brother phoned me and said he had a problem. And what did I say? I said, 'You are going through some adjustments. Vietnam's a new culture. Keep cool. Saigon is safer than New York City.'"

"It's very terrible," said Noi. She stood behind him, her hands massaging the back of his neck, tears running down her cheeks.

When people are feeling the kind of pain that the Markles were going through there was absolutely nothing to say or do. Calvino sipped the beer, sat back in his chair, and wondered when Harry's guilt was going to transform itself into a kind of hate- filled rage. Then what? The guy had a life, a family, a career. The last thing he needed was for his young brother to get himself killed in the streets of Saigon.

"You know how long it's been since an American has been killed by hostile fire in Saigon? I will tell you. It happened late April 28th or early morning April 29th, 1975. The last 122 round fell short at Tan Son Nhut and killed two American marines. Sergeant Darwin Judge and Sergeant William McMahon. That's a long time ago, Vinee. I did two tours. I saw a lot of men die. But that is ancient history. How is it, after all that, my kid brother gets a grenade thrown at him?"

"You want me to go and find out?"

"Yeah, that's exactly what I want. I'm going in-country to pick up the body. After I get Drew's body out, I want you go find the cocksucker who did it. Give it a week or so. Let things calm down. Then go, Vinee. Find this sonofabitch."

"Can I take this?" asked Calvino, picking up the photograph of the younger brother holding the M16. Drew was standing next to a stunning looking Vietnamese woman, strong nose, beautiful teeth, and haunted, sad eyes; she wore a bamboo hat and the barrel of the AK47 she held touched the barrel of Drew's M16. They were smiling at each other like lovebirds.

"Her name's Jackie Ky. Drew's girlfriend. I met her once and I liked her. Nice kid. Viet Khieu looking for her roots. They are at Cu Chi Tunnels in the picture. The communists have turned them into a tourist attraction. You crawl through the tunnels where Charlie crawled, and then for one dollar a bullet, you can fire an M16 or an AK47. Drew chose the M16. Jackie an AK47. Why? Because he thought I would be proud of him. Holding an M16 in Vietnam. How can a guy get through law school, graduate second in his class at Columbia and be such a dumbshit? The last thing I ever wanted for him was to touch a gun."

"When are you going in?" asked Calvino.

"I am on the 10.40 flight out of Don Muang tomorrow. When you go in, look up a Viet Khieu named Marcus Nguyen. He a good shit. Ex-RVN Marine Colonel who's gone back into business after eighteen years in the wilderness."

"In America."

"That's what I said, in the wilderness. Marcus will finish the job."

"Meaning?"

"You find who killed my brother and Marcus will take care of the rest."

Calvino was shaking his head and looking at his beer.

"It's right, Vinee. You know it's right."

"I am not a middle man for contract murders," said Calvino. "Who said anything about a con-tract? And the only murder anyone has talked about is that of my brother. So, what's the problem?"

Calvino was thinking how did a Vietnamese Marine Colonel ever come to be called by the name Marcus.

Comfort Zone

CHAPTER 3

FIVE STAR SUITE

A FLARE FILLED the sky with a streak of blood-red light, a fissure of brightness illuminating the ground and throwing a web of shadows over power lines, houses, shops and cars. In every direction, the sky was on fire. The power of the light blinded him. Calvino rubbed his eyes, looked away, and then at the sky again. Another flare had exploded, floating to earth on a tiny parachute. No more than a hundred meters ahead of his position, the United States Marines had dropped their end of rope, scooped up automatic rifles, and begun firing towards a two-story concrete building which stood like a bunker at the end of the school grounds. The other team members, eyes wide with panic, stood as if their hands were frozen to the end of the rope, mouths open, faces upturned toward the flare scorched sky. One ran away. Two others dropped with swells of red stains on their chests and backs. Muzzle flash came from the south. Someone returned the Marines' fire and, a moment later, other people who had been watching were hit and made that strange gurgling noise as they clutched at their bodies and tumbled headlong into the grass. Women started screaming, picking up their kids, tables fell over in the scramble to get out of the line of fire.

"Who are they?" he found himself asking Harry Markle.

"Religious zealots? Terrorists? Or maybe they are nothing more than your home-grown garden variety crazies. The Fourth of July in Bangkok. Great news story. Attack. And one billion people will watch you do your thing."

"You going to do something?" asked Calvino. A Viet Khieu came out of the darkness.

"Marcus, long time no see," said Markle.

"They are holding the perimeter, Captain."

Marcus Nyugen, a middle-aged Vietnamese with short hair, bloodshot eyes and sweat-soaked face, smoked a cigarette and rested his M60 over one shoulder. He looked like a man who hadn't slept for days. Over his chest he wore two ammo belts. His face was painted black and, in the light of the flare, Calvino could see his white teeth as Marcus smiled, looking in the direction of the bunker.

"We got a job to do, Colonel," Markle said to Marcus. "And you are the ranking officer. So, the way I see it, it's your call."

"We take them out, Captain," said Marcus.

Calvino crouched down on one knee, shelter-ing beside the table. Jets of fire whizzed overhead. There were explosions and more screams. Markle knelt down on his haunches next to Calvino, put an arm around his shoulder.

"And you didn't pack," said Harry Markle, shaking his head, a flicker of a smile crossing his lips. But he was calm as if all of this was just a normal Fourth of July picnic and some assholes had stopped praying and started shooting in the grand tradition of cult members gone to the edge and crossed over to the other side.

"Can you handle this?" Marcus asked Calvino.

"He can handle the weapon, Colonel," said Markle.

Marcus tossed Calvino an M16 rifle which hung like a Tune gun in the air.

Calvino caught the rifle as a man next to him went down with the front of his face shot away, leaking brain and bone.

"So they want to have some fun, Colonel?" asked Markle.

"Follow me. I have an idea," said Marcus.

Markle and Calvino fell in behind the ex-Marine.

"An old dog like the Colonel doesn't forget his training. Trust me," Markle said to Calvino. He dropped back and found his wife beside a pushed over table.

"Noi, take the kids home. We will be along after the Colonel and me finish up with the assholes across the field."

Calvino's heart pounded hard inside his chest as he ran a few feet behind Harry Markle. Marcus was ahead, laying down fire with the M60. A heavy thunder of angry rounds flying overhead. Then they ran a zig-zag pattern on the outer edge of the flare light, circling behind the ferris wheel. In the distance, someone was on the loudspeaker asking people to stay calm, not to run, not to panic.

"Lay on the ground. Do not move. The situation is under control."

Harry Markle stopped, knelt, gestured for Calvino to get down. He whispered, "Whenever you hear from a civilian that the situation is under control, you know you've gotta real problem."

Marcus crawled on the ground, lifted up his head and spoke to them. "Now, what we are going to do is hit that hooch about fifty meters to the right. I want you to go behind. I will take the front. Anything that moves, shoot it. Don't think. Just kill what's inside. That was our job last time out. We didn't get it done. This time let's move it. Let's do it right this time." Marcus reached under his shirt and pulled two hand grenades.

"Be prepared," said Markle, taking one of the grenades.

"It's the boy scout's motto." Marcus handed the other one to Calvino.

"Move out."

Calvino's legs felt rubbery, his breathing was uneven and his throat dry. He shifted around the hooch, waited until Harry Markle dropped his arm, then he pulled the pin from the grenade, arched his arm and aimed for a back window. Harry's grenade struck a fraction of a second first. There was a loud explosion then a bright flash. Calvino's grenade blew out the back of the wall and, as men came pouring out, he opened up with the M16. The rifle made no noise. The men fell one upon another until the ground was covered in bleeding, dying bodies. Then he saw Harry emerge from the haze of smoke.

"Behind you, Harry."

Calvino's M16 jammed. He squeezed the trigger and nothing happened. He tried to clear the chamber, failed, and threw the rifle on the ground.

A man dressed in a black robe emerged from the shadows, stepping forward with a huge sword held in his right hand and Marcus Nyugen's severed head in his left. He advanced with the blade of the sword starting its descent onto Harry Markle's neck.

He tried to shout but no words would come out. He wanted to shout, "The Colonel is dead, Markle. He's dead." Calvino recognized the face inside the hooded robe. He had seen it in a photograph at Cu Chi Tunnels, he had been smiling into the camera with a beautiful girl, the two of them touching rifles. Inside the hood was Harry's younger brother. Drew Markle.

"This is Judgement Day," the voice roared.

Drew started screaming and the blade was a fraction of an inch from connecting with Harry's flesh. Then the words started coming back, and Calvino shouted, "Harry, look the fuck out. It's your brother. He's gonna kill you..."

As the tip of the sword drew a bead of blood on Harry's neck, someone was pounding and shouting Calvino's name. The sword melted into a fist and the blood into sweat as he bolted up in his bed and opened his eyes. He rubbed his eyes. His bedroom was totally dark. He found a light switch and then looked at his watch. It was three in the morning. His pillow and sheet were drenched in sweat. Someone was leaning hard on his front door buzzer, and shouting, "Khun Vincent, wake up."

Only the voice was shouting in Thai and not in English. He opened the door and outside were three uniformed police officers who came inside without asking for an invitation.

Calvino stood barefoot in jogging shorts and a T-shirt, his hair wet with sweat and a black-blue stubble of beard. He looked bleary-eyed at the officers.

"Colonel Pratt has asked for you to accompany us," said a sergeant.

Calvino shook his head, trying to figure out if this was a new dream.

"He asked that you go with us now."

"Go where?"

"To hotel."

"Which hotel?"

The police officer ran out of English words. After a command was given, answering questions was not their style. He let them into his apartment, thinking, why does Pratt send around real cooperative, friendly cops like these? It had to be his revenge for the cologne smell still circulating inside his new BMW. The cops walked around Calvino, picking up dishes, ashtrays, opening the fridge, basically making themselves at home, staring and not smiling.

"We go now," said an officer.

"I guess I should get dressed then." He turned and walked off to the bedroom. It was as hot as hell in his living room. An ancient air-conditioner gathered cobwebs in the window. The officers eyed the layout of Calvino's rundown apartment, the floor broken in places, kitchen walls pockmarked, and green curtains, that looked like they had been dry cleaned in bus exhaust fumes, hanging at each of the windows with their gnarled, dusty screens. There were half a dozen plants in various stages of death, starved for lack of water, and an empty fish tank with green slime growing inside the glass. It was suitable for either a bachelor with an uncertain income or an impoverished family with no other choice in a place like Bosnia.

Calvino, an ex-Brooklyn native, lacked a green thumb and never had a definite timetable on fish feeding, a combination guaranteed to cause household ecological damage, if not a bore hole in the ozone above Soi 27.

"How much rent you pay?" asked one of the officers.

Asking a man's rent, salary, or the amount he had in the bank, was a Thai custom. The worth of a man was in fixed assets. Doing a balance sheet on net worth helped everyone decide how much power, authority and respect were required.

"Let's say my rent pays for a medium night inside the Zone, all-in."

They stared at him. How did such a man have a friend like Pratt? They could not figure out the connection. A couple of minutes later, Calvino came out of his bedroom. He wore his .38 calibre police revolver in a leather holster under his left arm.

"You guys spoiled a great firefight," he said in English.

$$\S \, \S \, \S \, \S$$

THE police, with red light flashing, cut from one lane to another, sometimes driving in the wrong lane. Calvino sat in the back seat looking at the fear in the faces of those who saw the oncoming squad car weaving in the traffic. The squad car passed Erawan Shrine and gunned down the ramp to the parking lot in the basement of the five-star hotel. Calvino towered over the two Thai police officers on either side of him as they stood inside the elevator to the fifth floor. No one spoke during the ride. When the elevator door opened, Calvino was the first to step into the corridor which was a beehive of uniformed Thai police. Several of the cops stared hard at the *farang* who had appeared without warning. What was he doing on the floor? Calvino walked ahead a few steps when he was finally stopped as a policeman stepped in front of him.

"You, you, where you go?" snapped one of the Thai cops. There was a bull whip snap to the word "you". The police officer concentrated hard, then stepped forward. Calvino stood very still, kept his hands in front and showing. The officer glared at him as if Calvino was something foul and evil on the bottom of his shoe. Calvino didn't blink, he kept smiling, that smile that moves across the lips of the feeble minded, hovers for no apparent reason but renders them a harmless, non-threatening shadow against the face of the night. Calvino followed the second rule for surviving long term in Thailand—don't flap around in public, no sudden moves, no gesturing with hands, arms, head or body.

One of the Thai police officers who had come to his apartment on Lt.Col. Pratt's order grunted a few words in Thai, and the other cop blocking his path backed off; he turned his back on Calvino as if he no longer existed. Calvino had satisfied the third rule for surviving the duration in Thailand—he was connected to a powerful and influential person. In this case a police colonel. In fact, he probably could have gotten away with a little flapping around once Lt.Col. Pratt's big name registered on the spectrum of power, authority and fear. Ten was a perfect score. Let's say, it was an eight and a half in a town where a five was good enough to keep you alive.

"Room 509," said the officer.

Calvino nodded, found the door already open with people coming in and out with the grim, tired look of having been witness to something bad. He had slipped into his New York Yankees T- shirt and rumpled trousers, which gave him the distinct look of a tourist. If he had put on a shirt and tie, his presentation would have guaranteed at least minimal respect from the police officers. He did do one thing right—out of respect for Pratt—he had avoided putting on the rest of the cologne.

"It's almost four in the morning. Mekhong and Coke, and murder time."

Pratt looked up from a chair as Calvino walked into the suite.

"At least you are fifty percent right," said Pratt. "Come here. I've got something to show you."

Calvino followed him into the bedroom where three or four officers circulated gathering evidence and photographing the room. On the king-size bed, which was still made up, was one slightly plump Asian male body wearing gold-rimmed glasses, the eyes staring lifelessly at the ceiling, arms sprawled out on the bed.

"Mr. Mark Wang," said Pratt, nodding toward the body.

"Taiwanese?" asked Calvino.

Pratt shook his head. "Hong Kong."

Calvino walked over to the bed and looked down at the body. A police photographer was still taking pictures.

Two bullets had ripped through Mr. Wang's chest, rupturing the heart and lungs. Calvino could tell the lungs had exploded from the bullet causing a thin layer of foam around the dead man's lips. The bullets had passed through the dead man's expensive, tailored white shirt with gold cufflinks bearing the initials: MW. He was found dead wearing red suspenders, tailored trousers and a pair of Italian loafers that looked like they cost five hundred dollars. On the ring finger of his right hand was a gold ring with diamonds which looked like it must have cost a few grand wholesale. Robbery was not the motive, he thought. The knot in his tie was slightly pulled down, otherwise, Mr. Wang looked like someone who had just come out of a board of directors' meeting. That was the thing about Bangkok: you were in the middle of one nightmare, then the cops woke you up and transported you into the middle of another one.

"Good dresser," said Calvino. "Nice ring."

Pratt walked over to the dresser and held up two passports.

"He had a Hong Kong passport and a Canadian passport," he said.

Calvino turned and glanced at the two passports.

"There is an old Chinese saying that a smart rabbit always keeps three holes for his escape," said Pratt.

"I only see two holes, and this guy has both of them in his chest."

"You have a point, Vincent."

He walked back to the door and looked at the sitting room of the suite. The dead man was definitely not a backpacker. Wang had booked into a five-star hotel, executive suite. There were vases of orchids and bowls of fruit, sofa and chairs in a sitting room, and thick, plush carpet, a large bedroom. A TV with an enormous screen was tuned to CNN. The sound was off, leaving only a flow of pictures cut as fast as a professional gambler shuffling a new deck of cards.

"Pricey room," said Calvino, looking back into the bedroom. "The rack rate on the suite is ten thousand baht a night," said Pratt.

"That's double my monthly rent," said Calvino.

"There is a cost difference between poverty and luxury," said Pratt.

"Between being dead and alive," said Calvino. "How is Harry Markle?"

The question came out of the blue. He's looking at a dead guy on the bed and suddenly Pratt's asking him about Harry Markle. "He's going to Saigon to make arrangements for his brother.

As soon as I get a visa from the Vietnamese Embassy, I'll go in and have a look around," said Calvino.

Pratt smiled, figuring that Calvino was holding back.

"It's because of the cologne. Right? You sent the boys to pull me out of bed at three because I fouled up the new car?"

Calvino turned and started for the door, shaking his head. He hated looking at murder victims at four in the morning. Going back to sleep after such a visitation was never quite the same as a good night of uninterrupted sleep. He was thinking how he would stop at the Thermae and order steak and eggs, drink a beer, and then go back to bed. He was almost out the door when Pratt cleared his throat.

"The cologne was bad. But this is worse, Vincent. Mr. Wang arrived from Saigon on the afternoon of the 4th of July," said Pratt.

"You've got my attention," said Calvino, spinning around. Pratt pulled a name card out of his pocket.

"Have a look at this."

Calvino walked back and took the name card and read the name first. "Drew Markle, Esq." and underneath "Attorney-at-Law." And below the name and title was the name of the law firm, Winchell & Holly. It was a name that took Calvino back in time, he remembered Winchell & Holly as a highly specialized, powerful New York law firm.

"Harry's little brother," said Calvino, slowly sitting down in a stuffed chair.

"His little brother has something in common with Mr. Wang," said Pratt.

"Yeah, they are both dead," said Calvino. "And maybe the same killer," said Pratt.

"Sorry about the crack about the cologne."

"Forget it."

Calvino already had as he continued to stare at the name card. In the days when Vincent Calvino had an "Esquire" following his name on name cards and stationery, he had a couple of small-time cases with Winchell & Holly on the other side. One had been a divorce case and the other a broken apartment lease. Each time, Winchell & Holly were doing the legal work as a favor to keep some senior executive of a large company happy. Partners did what was necessary to service an important corporate client, to keep them satisfied, to make certain they stayed within the fold. The actual grunt legal work was given to the most junior associate who was made responsible for throwaway personal cases once he had finished his real legal work for the day. Such work was beneath the partners in such a law firm, and any lawyer who appeared on the other side of such cases was treated like an intelligent primate at the Central Park Zoo. Calvino kept staring at the card, thinking about such a case, the offices of Winchell & Holly, and how he was as cut off from those years as he was from a past life. He recalled the part of his dream where Drew had cut off the head of the ex-Vietnamese Marine Colonel. The image of Mr. Marcus Nguyen's head falling under the weight of the sharp sword had seemed so real that when he had sat up in bed and found the Thai police at his door, he thought they had come through the fog of the same battle, straight from his own nightmare.

"Mr. Wang had the card in his possession," Pratt finally said.

"He looks like a Winchell & Holly client."

"One of the officers found it behind the desk in the sitting room. It had fallen off. There were no other business cards in the room. Just this one, Vincent. And that is rather strange, don't you think?"

A fully loaded top end Compaq notebook was open on a desk. On the color screen a screensaver was a mermaid with bare breasts who was swimming across the length of the screen. The only witness to the murder was a cartoon character trying to save the screen.

"You check the computer?"

"The hard disk has been wiped clean of all files. We'll take it into the lab, run tests, and try to recover what was lost, but our computer guy says it has a virus and we probably will come up with nothing but the mermaid."

"Did you find any floppy diskettes?"

"Zero floppies," said Pratt.

"And no one saw or heard anything," said Calvino.

"That's right. Mr. Wang let someone into his room. We make the time of his death between nine and ten. We'll know more after the forensic people open the body."

"And about the same time in Saigon Drew Markle is killed by a grenade."

"I was thinking the same thing," said Pratt. Calvino handed back the name card.

"So what happened to you at the picnic? One moment you are eating a hot dog and the next moment you disappear into the corner with Harris," said Calvino.

Pratt gestured for the removal of the body. He took in a long breath and held it for a moment, watching as Wang's body was moved onto a stretcher and then covered. The corridor and elevator would have been secured. No one wanted foreigners watching gunshot victims being carried out of hotels at four in the morning.

"Harris, yes. The American Embassy man. Next week in Phuket, a conference is scheduled. Influential investors from America and Asia will be in Thailand. Harris was worried about security. Seems Mark Wang was on the list of people to attend the conference. I had told Harris this wasn't America. Of course, we would provide security, but these investors were far safer in Bangkok than in New York City. Famous last words."

"You ever been to Saigon?" asked Calvino.

"No, but I will be booking a trip to Ho Chi Minh City."

The battle over the name of the city in Vietnam had started.

§ § § §

THE next morning Harry Markle came around to Calvino's office. His face was the color of a peeled onion, white and lined with rings that looked as if they coiled in layers all the way to his skull. The previous twenty-four hours of grief, guilt, and alcohol had rubbed away the shell which had taken twenty-five years to build over that experience called "Vietnam" and now it had broken and he was trying to deal with all the stuff that was spilling out. He had aged about ten years since the Fourth of July picnic. And this was a guy who had seen enough combat in Vietnam to have been beyond grief or guilt. Ratana, Calvino's secretary, had given him a mug of black coffee but his hands were so shaky that the coffee spilled on the floor.

"You burn yourself, Mr. Markle?" she asked.

He sipped the coffee, spilling some more which settled in the crease lines of his knuckles.

"Tastes great."

She backed away and went around to her desk. Calvino was late. And by the time he had arrived in the office, Harry

Markle had some of the color back in his face. He sat there reading the Bangkok Post.

"Sorry to keep you waiting, but I didn't get to bed until six. I stopped at the Thermae for steak and eggs. It's closing soon, making way for a condo."

Harry Markle glanced at his watch—it was a quarter to ten.

"The end of an era. So are you gonna tell me who she was?" asked Harry Markle, lighting a cigarette.

"There wasn't a she," said Calvino.

"You must be the only *farang* in Bangkok who goes to HQ for the food."

"Come in the office and we'll talk about it."

Ratana came in a moment later with Calvino's coffee and newspaper and a couple of messages. Calvino sat back in his chair, thinking that, in the old days, three and a half hours sleep was enough. He had gone through law school on that amount of sleep.

He sipped his coffee, thinking to himself that he was starting to feel old. On the top of the messages and newspapers was a birthday card. Fifth of July. That was his birthday and, as far as he could see, all he had to justify rolling over another year—and this birthday, what was his present? Steak and eggs at the Thermae and two murders. A lawyer named Drew Markle in Saigon and his Hong Kong client Mark Wang in Bangkok with a one-week layover until going down to Phuket for a big shots' conference on Southeast Asia investment opportunities. What separated the two men? One hour and five minutes flight time and one name card, two countries, two cities.

He looked up from the birthday card and stared hard at Harry. "Is there something else Drew might have told you? Maybe about a client. A Chinese client? I need to know if there's something you're not telling me about your brother."

"What's this about, Vinee?"

"He say anything about a client named Mark Wang? A Chinese guy from Hong Kong and Vancouver?"

"No."

"You sure, Harry? Because it's real important that I know what's going on."

Seeing someone you've known for years, drunk with, hung out with, told stories to inside their office, can create an awkward silence, especially when you have hammered them with questions and drawn into contention their veracity. It is as if some big idea comes rushing home. Markle understood something he had known but had not really felt before. This man Calvino had a real job. This was what he did. This was where he went every day to make money. He was a professional in a nonprofessional occupation and he was going to come straight at you if he thought for a single instant you were pulling the Bangkok bullshit number. They drank their coffee and looked at each other like a couple of boxers between rounds sitting on stools, waiting for the bell to ring. Calvino made no effort to make Harry feel comfortable sitting in the chair just opposite his desk. After all, it was Harry Markle and his dead brother that had brought him a dual nightmare and robbed him of a night's sleep on the day of his birthday. Had robbed him of a dinner with his Thai teacher who had come to the lesson dressed for all five tones.

"I am flying in for the body tomorrow. The Vietnamese Embassy in Bangkok has got its shit together. I pick up the visa this afternoon," said Harry.

"I was surprised. I thought it was going to be a bigger problem," he said.

Calvino looked at him. The blood was drained from his face, and his fingers, all discolored that ghoulish yellow from chain smoking, were moving like butterfly wings. Markle's

51

eyes were moist and then some tears spurted out and he wiped them away.

"The sonofabitch got himself dead, Vinee," said Harry.

"So did one of his clients last night in Bangkok," said Calvino. "Do what you think is right. Don't forget to look up Marcus Nguyen."

"I had a dream about him last night."

"Yeah?"

"Actually it was a nightmare."

"He's a tough motherfucker," said Harry.

"Then why do you need me?" asked Calvino, sipping his coffee. "Marcus is too emotional. He gets too close to things sometimes. Everything is very personal for him. I need someone more objective."

"He's fucked up. That's what you're saying," said Calvino.

"Basically, yes."

Harry Markle pulled out a stack of greenbacks and laid them on Calvino's desk. He licked his thumb as he counted them out, his lips moving as the hundreds fanned out.

"I make that one thousand five hundred," Harry Markle said. "Enough for expenses and fees for a week."

Calvino looked at the hundred-dollar bills. This was as close as he was going to come to a birthday present this year. It was up to him. If he had any sense, he would tell Harry Markle to find someone else, deal with the police in Saigon, deal with just about anyone but him. Markle could feel the apprehension. Calvino was having some second thoughts about going to Saigon and Markle decided to play it straight with him, give him a way out.

"I'm not your commanding officer, Vinee. This isn't an order or a command. If you don't want to take the job, then just say, 'fuck it.' This is strictly for volunteers. Some shit is going down in Saigon. What it is, I don' t know. Fifteen hundred bucks is likely not sufficient compensation if you decide to go. And if you throw my ass out, I won't hold it against you." Then he paused, his lips on the coffee mug. He swallowed hard.

"I never got a chance to know him. You know what I mean? The Thais are real tight with family. We have lost something along the way, Vinee. Something called family." There couldn't have been a better speech about the sacred idea of family for one expat to give another, people who lived a life devoid of original family members. Each in their own fashion had lost the frequency on which people in a family communicated until, one day, all that came out was some distant static and a stranger 's voice. Markle was right in saying that was something that the Thais found difficult to do. Not taking Harry Markle's case was saying that family didn't matter, and to say that was to admit you had become a Zone-head, lost, absorbed, beyond redemption and Calvino wasn't prepared to believe that about himself. Calvino had just had his birthday and he wasn't about to turn Harry Markle out of his office and say his brother 's life hadn't meant anything. He couldn't do that. So he scooped up the money and folded it in half.

"I can't promise anything, Harry."

"Just do what you can."

"When will you come back from the States?" asked Calvino. "We airlift the body out in forty-eight hours." His eyes rolled up into his head. "I will be back in Bangkok in ten days."

He got up from his chair and walked out of Calvino's office. Ratana came in and sat down.

"Well, who was she?" she asked.

"It wasn't Nah." He knew she was dying to know if he had stayed up all night with his Thai teacher, and she looked disappointed.

"Then who?"

"Colonel Pratt invited me to visit him in a hotel."

She pursed her lips and cocked her head to one side.

"You go to hotel?"

Calvino nodded.

"He's not cheating on his wife?"

Calvino shook his head.

"Nothing that serious. It was just the murder of a foreigner."

CHAPTER 4

THE HANOI GIRL

THE THAI POLICE were warlords of the Comfort Zone, their kingdom, their domain and all that ice honey spread over a very large piece of toast. Calvino's law of warlords said there was never enough evidence in the universe to convict the powerful who lived on a mountain overlooking the valley where physical evidence never broke through the cloud level, protecting those who lived for generations on the mountain. Weather report: All is sunny and bright from one end of the ice flow to the other, nothing but honey and milk. They might be killed but they would never be convicted of murder. He thought about Mark Wang in the first few hours as the body cooled down and how his family had set the warlord forces of power in motion, a wave of influence washing over Bangkok. A Hong Kong to Bangkok fifty-foot breaker waiting to crash onto someone's head and everyone was scrambling to get out of the way.

Each local warlord had been raised on a steady diet of suspicion and jealousy served by his rivals and neighbors, those who coveted his women, money, power and connections. In Southeast Asia, a lot of time and energy was spent plotting how to get the sonofabitch before he whacked you, and across international boundaries the distrust and tension geared up into overdrive because more was at stake, the odds were higher. Hatred lay just below the surface like in a bad marriage ready to ignite at the first crooked smile. Why was Calvino thinking of warlords? Because Wang's family were Hong Kong warlords. The British colony had been built, run, managed, and finally sold out by warlords. Wang's clan controlled an Asian media empire ranging from magazines, newspapers, to TV and radio stations. Mark Wang's primo godfather quietly let an influential Thai minister, with Chinese blood running in his veins, know that unless the Thais delivered a suspect within a week, the Hong Kong Chinese would assume that some rogue faction in the Thai police had killed him. They would send correspondents deep into the Zone, expose and deliver newspaper articles and TV footage on the kingdom of ice, reveal places, names, money arrangements. They would retaliate with massive, in-your-face coverage.

These threats would never make the TV news or the newspapers. But those who mattered knew and those were the only people who counted. Such coverage would inflict great damage. The minister who had received the phone call from Hong Kong contacted the Ministry of Interior and from there the ball of fear and rage bounced down the edges of the chain of command until Lt.Col. Pratt received a call. He got the ball.

After that meeting at police headquarters, Lt.Col. Pratt looked pale. When he told Calvino the story as they sat in the garden at Pratt's house, he had turned pale again. A long silence filled the evening and was broken when Lt. Col. Pratt quoted Shakespeare, " 'I know not why I am so sad: It wearies me; you say it wearies you; but I caught it, found it, or came by it, what stuff 'tis made of, whereof it is born, I am to learn.' "

"Learn who killed Wang? Yeah, as easy as calling a Chinese take-out in Manhattan," thought Calvino. Asia was a learning experience where the lesson kept shifting and the only goal post was power which, like an oasis against the noonday sky, shimmered, dissolved and reappeared in the middle of the night as something with fangs an inch from the neck.

Pratt could muster a Shakespeare quote at the drop of a foreign body. This time Pratt's inspiration came from the sight of a Chinese man who had two bullet holes in his chest.

Mark Wang's murder could not have come at a worse time. The local English language dailies were running reports about a police gang working out of the airport, kidnapping and murdering weal-thy businessmen. These guys had made a business out of murder, privatized the killing and made a handsome profit. More cops had been caught killing fake cops deep in the Comfort Zone. Chaos, violence, and death. That was the view from Hong Kong. What did they know about the nature of ice? Not that it mattered. The Chinese in Hong Kong drove straight to the conclusion that Mark Wang had been killed by the cops and the higher-ups were going to protect their own. Not to mention that Thais were implicated in a coup in Cambodia. In this land of strange alliances and secret pacts, anything was possible. The Wang family wanted satisfaction. It was no different than the Mafia in Brooklyn where Calvino had grown up. The code was the same: you held your turf and revenged your own. The godfather in Hong Kong was unimpressed that the contents of Mark Wang's wallet were untouched, and that his personal jewelry and other valuables remained intact.

The Thai police neglected to mention that Wang's laptop computer had been tampered with; whatever Mark had stored on the hard disk inside the computer had been worth enough to have him whacked. Comfort Zone forces didn't whack people for data stored on a hard disk. It was cultural factor difficult for a Thai to translate to non-Thai Chinese. The Hong Kong family demanded revenge, fair enough, it was their right under the circumstances, and no one was going to stand in their way, but the only problem was serving up the killer. They didn't want to hear that the Thai police didn't know. They knew how to squeeze hard and before they were finished, they called in chits until half the police had blue balls from all the squeezing that was going on. Blue balls for the Department, yeah. But the police were only part of the overall picture. These Hong Kong guys were powerful enough to cause a black eye and a bloody nose to the image of the Land of Smiles. One rule above all rules was not to tarnish the image.

"I didn't ask for the job," said Pratt.

"But you didn't tell them that," said Calvino.

A mosquito hit the blue electric light and made a zap sound, a little flash, the instant where life passed into death.

He looked over at Calvino.

"You're Thai and can't say no even though you know in your gut that what they want is something you will be lucky as hell to deliver and live to tell your wife and kids," said Calvino.

"They said that it is up to me," said Pratt.

"How is it that, when push comes to shove, it is always a 'they' who push you around with the Thai expression: it's up to you?"

"In Thailand you can always push someone much more with an eyebrow than with a gun," said Pratt.

"I didn't see any eyebrow burns on Wang's body."

"He was a foreigner. Eyebrows never work with *farang*."

"Or Hong Kong Chinese."

That was how an order was issued to servants in Thailand: an indirect, sideways half-command filled with ancient Zenlike open-ended inter-pretations, casting out the possibility of more than one right answer, of more than one right way to save face. Sometimes there was no answer at all. To act or not to act would have had equal value. Yet that old world was nearly dead in Bangkok and in the one which took its place the servant had no choice but to act and to find the one answer. Pratt was forced to choose his path and the sadness came from knowing that no U-turn was permitted.

Before leaving for Vietnam they spent a final night at Pratt's house in Bangkok with long Zen silences filling the garden, broken when Pratt played a Hollis Gentry piece on the sax, something like The Glass Man. The sound of the sax carried through the garden and into the house. When Pratt no longer had any words he used the sax and found a pathway into the Zen, where language was insufficient to express a deeper level of feeling. His superiors in the Crime Suppression Division had given him one week to find Mark Wang's killer. Asia contained a lot of ground to cover in a week, and to find the killer in a region occupied by a billion plus people, harboring its fair share of possible suspects, presented a logistics problem.

How he did his job was up to him. In the Department, they didn't care, they didn't ask questions, they didn't set limits; they only wanted results which showed that someone killed Mark Wang and the murderer was not a Thai cop. Someone who would take the heat off the ice honey business and the eyes away from the workings of the Comfort Zone. When Pratt said he wanted to team with a *farang* private eye named Vincent Calvino, again, they said, they didn't want to know. All they wanted was results. How Pratt got to the result was his business. He played the sax with real feeling for about thirty minutes. His wife, Manee, came out to the garden.

"You have a phone call," she said to her husband.

Pratt got up and went into the house and Manee sat back in his chair, her fingers touching the sax.

"You'll look after him, Vinee?"

"You worried, Manee?"

She forced a smile. "It's not fair they send him to Vietnam. You know the Vietnamese don't like Thai people. It's not good. I don't like that they make him feel sad, you know, real bad."

"Pratt can take care of himself."

Manee leaned forward. "I tell you a secret, Vinee."

"I like secrets."

"I said he should resign. Why should he do this? I asked him. And you know what he said? Kluun may khaw khaay my awk. Can't swallow it, can't spit it out."

Pratt had come up behind his wife. Putting his hands on her shoulders he leaned forward and gently kissed her head.

"…'go, return unto my wife; bid her not fear the separated councils; her honour and myself are at the one, and at the other is my good friend Calvino; where nothing can proceed that toucheth us whereof I shall not have intelligence,' " he said.

Shakespeare in the garden recited with perfec-tion by the sax player. Richard III. It didn't matter which play. All that mattered was that moment when Manee tilted her head upward, finding her lips touching Pratt. Calvino had never seen two people who had been married for so many years and who were so completely devoted, who cared and looked after each other. Outside the Zone, not every relationship was a dance on the razor's edge where every man and woman were destined to stumble, fall face forward, draw blood. He envied them. What they had was beyond money, beyond pleasure, they had collected a cache of hope which sustained them.

"Go to Vietnam. But don't think that I like this," she said, tears in her eyes. She looked over at Calvino. "And Vinee, remember what I asked."

He remembered already. "Bring Pratt back," she had said. His body, his soul, his heart.

"Who was on the phone?" asked Manee.

"Someone from Apex Steel confirming my title at the company," he said.

"You are going into business," she said.

"In a manner of speaking," he said, picking up his sax. It was a great way to end a conversation. She listened to her husband playing, looked over at Calvino, thinking that the two of them knew far more than they were letting on. But what more could she do? But wait, and hope, and think that somehow the one week Pratt would be in Vietnam would flash across the screen of her life like a couple of jumpy frames in a film and, one day, even the memory of that ache and fear would be lost.

§ § § § §

CALVINO had gone into Vietnam first, working undercover for about twenty-four hours before Pratt arrived. His first attempts to contact Marcus Nguyen didn't work because Marcus was in Singapore on business. Harry had said that Marcus was "emotional." That was another way of saying a "loose cannon" which, if you could pin down and point in the right direction, would blow a really big hole in the enemy. But don't expect him to find the enemy in a land which was governed by his former enemy. Twenty-four hours after Calvino had checked into his hotel, Pratt had arrived alone on a flight out of Don Muang Airport. As he passed through immigration and then cleared customs counters at Ton Son Nhat Airport, he knew that he was on his own. No communication was allowed between him and the Royal

Thai Police Department in Bangkok. The assumption was that the security and intelligence people listened to every conversation and read every fax between Saigon and Bangkok. If he failed, then he failed on his own. If he succeeded, then there would be those in the Department who would claim the success as their own.

Pratt wore a business suit and carried a leather briefcase as he sat in the back of the taxi. Playing the sax and quoting Shakespeare were ruled out; businessmen knew nothing about music or art. Pratt glanced at his watch, as the taxi driver laid on his horn, cutting through a sea of bicycles and motorcycles on the way into District One. Calvino would be at the law firm, Pratt thought.

His name card pegged Pratt as Sales and Marketing Department Vice President of Apex Steel (Thailand) Co. Ltd., a real company with offices on Silom Road run by people close to the Hong Kong operation. They were willing to cover for him when someone from Vietnam began checking out why a Vice President of Marketing had gone to Saigon.

It had taken a week for them to put their cover story together and get their visas approved for Vietnam. Calvino was a businessman looking to open a bar with a suitcase of cash and Pratt was a respectable businessman from an established company located in Bangkok. Why shouldn't they strike up a conversation on the rooftop of the Rex? Have a few drinks at a restaurant? After Pratt made several follow-up calls to Mark Wang's relatives in Hong Kong, it turned out that one of the companies in the family's empire had a branch in Bangkok. Apex Steel (Thailand) Co. Ltd. The business was reinforced steel rods used in high-rise building construction, and the Hong Kong parent company had opened a representative office in Saigon. The rep office had been set up by the law firm of Winchell & Holly. The Apex Steel CEO in Hong Kong phoned a senior partner in the New York office and instructed him that their Thai counterpart would arrive in Saigon in connection with the death of Mark Wang. He said they expected that full and complete cooperation would be given to a Thai named Mr. Prachai Chongwatana. No mention was made of Mr. Vincent Calvino, who did not exist in Pratt's universe of high- level business contacts. Apex's annual retainer paid to the law firm, plus all the other legal work from affiliated Hong Kong companies, guaranteed that the request would be honored by the New York office. Money bought access and Apex had paid a lot of money on legal fees.

"What about the jerk-offs in Saigon?" Calvino had asked Pratt that evening in the garden.

He smiled. "That's where you come in, Vincent."

"If they are dirty, they will stonewall."

"Every wall has a small hole. And it is the wise man who can find the entrance the size of a pinhole and climb through as if it were a door to the universe," said Pratt.

"Did Shakespeare write that?"

Pratt smiled. "In his next life he might have."

That night in Bangkok was a lifetime ago. The Saigon morning was this life, a now, a here, promising a pinhole.

From his room in the Saigon Concert Hotel, Calvino watched some Vietnamese messing around in the parking lot. The more he observed them the clearer it became the idleness was a cover for street level activities. Pratt had briefed him that Vietnamese security would likely follow him, tap his phone and room, and he had to assume that his every movement was being recorded. If Bangkok was the big sabai, the big easy, a field of ice in an enormous zone of comfort, then Saigon was the big misfortune, the big hardship, as if the echo of wartime suspicion resounded off every street corner. Saigon was the opposite of Bangkok. Here there was no comfort, only many no-go zones. A nervous, edgy tension. The loose-lips-sink-ships mentality was like one large driftnet that pulled in every kind of fish that got in the way. Everyone was a suspect. Foreigners were assumed to be dangerous.

§ § § § §

CALVINO pulled a can of 333 beer off the fridge shelf, and settled back into his Saigon hotel room. On top of the fridge was his fake American passport which he had bought from one of the Zone's more specialized operations on Patpong Road Number Two. He pulled the tab on the can and opened his passport; it was a good fake. Under his photograph was the name of Vincent Demato. Shirt and tie, hair combed, smiling into the camera. He tossed the passport on the bed and walked to the French doors, opened them and stepped out onto a small balcony. He sat on a small stool, drank his beer, and looked down at a parking lot wedged between two streets. Four Vietnamese men, dressed in what could have passed for pre-1975 clothes, lounged in the parking lot. He watched them, then studied their movements; the casual attitude, the bouts of smoking, eating noodles and, by the time they had gone to sleep, he went back inside his room.

Two days in Saigon was long enough to get the picture that a lot of locals had lots of time and few chances to work. Calvino nursed the 333 beer from the can, thinking this was a necessary piece of stagecraft. There were those who drank too much to drown their sorrows and then there were those who drank too much because they saw too clearly, those who knew too much and could not pretend that the reality did not exist. This morning it was neither sorrow nor knowledge which caused Calvino to raid the fridge in his room. Sometimes having beer on the breath made a point. Like a period, or a full stop as the British liked to say. The end of a sentence with that tiny bullet-like dot said: this man could be taken advantage of and he had a weakness. Maybe Drew Markle had a weakness. It might not have been drink. There were non-chemical cocktails just as dangerous for a certain kind of man. Take the belief in professional legal ethics: consumed in sufficient quantity, ethics caused intoxication. In places like Vietnam they might prove toxic, like a fatal overdose.

Vincent Demato, Brooklyn businessman, had an appointment at Winchell & Holly at eleven o'clock and he was killing time, drinking, thinking and glancing at his watch. On the tape recorder in his hotel room at the Saigon Concert Hotel, Miles Davis was playing. Mellow and dreamy, as if the world of music was one of those escape hatches from the world of Vietnam, or of the world of three-sentence paragraphs where only action mutated along the lines of imaginary reality. But this was Saigon. It was real. The beer had its own taste and the mean streets, like New York City, had a buzz among the assembled legions of beggars, vendors, cripples, spooks, conmen, dropouts, businessmen, police, war vets and common criminals, who fought a hand-to-hand urban combat for their piece of pavement, a piece of dignity, a share of the pie. You have seen it in any big city. The only difference is this city, Saigon, had a history of war and violence which it couldn't shake loose. Calvino liked drinking beer before an appointment and wondering about history. Saigon. The city with two names; two identities; two peoples living side by side, the winners and the losers. The winners lived in Ho Chi Minh City, the losers scrounged along the margins of Saigon. It was good for the city to have two names, he thought. One name would not have been large enough to encompass the full horizon worth of pain, suffering, brutality, disruption, hate, disillusionment. Within twenty hours of entering the city, he felt the divide. In Saigon and Ho Chi Minh City there was an ache, a concealed wound that flared up at three in the morning, survivers hearing helicopters and gunfire, not remembering whether they had won or lost, whether they were alive or dead, whether they were dreaming or had warped back through time and were still trying to find cover, sanctuary. Where did Winchell & Holly practice law? Saigon or Ho Chi Minh City? He guessed they practiced in both cities, for winner and loser, whoever could hire them.

Cut me into that pain, he thought. He tipped the beer can back until it was empty then opened another and drank until the beer came back up his throat and into his nose. You didn't have to be in Vietnam long before you either hated or loved one city or the other. Calvino hated having to choose. It was one of those things which could have gone either way like any relationship; the way you start out is the way you generally end up.

He had to wait until evening to meet with Pratt who had booked into the Rex Hotel. Pratt had come a day later on a separate flight. It was safer to keep a safe distance, their separate identities. They had drawn straws. Calvino got to go in first, to meet the members of Drew Markle's law firm. The Drew Markle who had been sent back to the States in a coffin draped with the American flag. The American Consulate, which had been set up only months before in Hanoi, had sent two representatives in business suits and Marine haircuts.

Calvino lied, and said, "I am looking to set up a business in Saigon. I need to talk to a lawyer."

He got his appointment just like that. And why not? Law firms were in the business of giving advice for bags of money.

He left out some details. For instance, the connection between Drew Markle and Mark Wang. He sipped his beer, wondering what those two had said to each other. What fly on the wall had recorded that conversation? What secrets had been so large as to kill both of them? Here, little fly, come to daddy, thought Calvino.

Whoever killed Mark Wang had a connection in Saigon and/ or Ho Chi Minh City with that firm. So he had the morning with time on his hands. He was thinking that Asia was a funny place where oligarchs and mafiosi had carved up the markets, monopolies, the geography, and the state enterprises, leaving everyone to get by as best they could, putting together whatever patchwork of relations and rank was necessary to stay alive, to stay in business. All Calvino needed was to think about an appointment with a law firm with blood on its hands and the lesson of Asia; one alone was a good enough reason to drink Vietnamese beer for breakfast. Both together were enough reason to get drunk before noon. Fortunately, his appointment was at eleven. He kept telling himself the drink was for the job and not to forget the job. Not thinking about the job let the mind wander and, in Asia, a wandering mind could be a dangerous thing. For instance, he might start thinking about warlords and, if he were listening to Miles Davis and drinking 333 beer, then he might discover a warlord had landed on his shoulder and was whispering in his ear. Warlords don't whisper sweet nothings, not in Asia, not anywhere.

Below his hotel window, one of the Vietnamese swung gently in a hammock; another, a couple of feet away sitting back in a chair, and a third guy straddling the back of a motorcycle, were talking to a cyclo driver. On the far left two *farang* couples walked hand in hand from the general direction of the Continental Hotel. A Vietnamese male came up to one of the *farang* men. He could see them talking. The Vietnamese had a handful of Vietnamese currency, the dong. The *farang* was shaking his head at the offer for the black market currency exchange. Calvino looked over at the parking lot where the guy on the motorcycle casually took out a small camera and began photographing them. He quickly tossed the camera to the guy in the hammock, whose hand came up and caught it like a softball slow-pitched. A few minutes later, one of the men was speaking into a mobile phone. He motioned to the guy on the motorcycle who started the bike and took off. He crumpled up the last 333 beer can and went back to his room. It was show time. Time to talk to a lawyer about a deal, to figure out who was running the show and make that Southeast Asia social connection, invite the man for a drink. Draw him out, draw him out, as if he is one of the boys waiting to score another Mark Wang. Calvino thought about Harry Markle back in America with his Thai wife and his kids, burying the young brother. Harry would get real drunk. What the hell made any sense?

§ § § §

WINCHELL & Holly. Then she appeared as if she had materialized from another dimension in time and space. He could not take his eyes off her. She glided across the carpeted reception area with a firm determination, her course set straight on him, her white ao dai tight around her breasts and the translucent material exposing her bra and underpants.

"Mr. Demato?" she asked.

"Who?" He asked in a momentary lapse.

She stood a few inches away. The edge of the ao dai brushed against his hand. Her nose wrinkled and a purposeful smile edged across her lips.

"Sometimes drinking beer in the morning makes you forget who you are," she said.

The 333 beer had lingered on his breath, giving him a refuge against the kind of lapse that could cause a number of problems with solutions he was in no mood to think about with this goddess towering above him.

"What's your name?" he asked. "Mai."

"That means 'no' in Thai."

"Oh, you speak Thai?"

He started to understand how undercover agents unravelled like a cheap suit when confronted with a beautiful woman.

"I read it in an airline magazine. They have a little section with twenty words you need to know in every country."

"'No', is a good word to learn."

"What about 'yes'?"

"Your English is perfect," he said.

"No, it is not. But thank you for the compli-ment."

It was a touch of madness that made him think her English was perfect. Attraction defeated more men than repulsion. If pain were your friend, then the name of the other city was called pleasure. Pleasure was an expensive commodity. He tried to control his breathing, telling himself that he was on a case. Someone had been murdered. Two men had been murdered. At first it didn't work. The fact that he was alive and they were dead and she was standing there like a vision of heaven turned him into a teenager, irresponsible, stupid, clumsy; basically in a tail dive and, if he didn't pull up, he was about to hit nose first into the ground.

"I have an appointment with Mr. Webb," he said.

"Mr. Webb is in a meeting. Maybe you would like another beer?" she asked.

"Coffee would be better, but I'm okay. No coffee. No beer," he said, and she left with one of those smiles you could never capture in a single word. He felt like he was in a steep descent, breaking a sound barrier, and not wanting to pull up on the controls. He closed his eyes, he didn't want to watch her walk away. He understood how people could be turned to pillars of salt in the bible. Women were the only religious experience worth having and the only altar worth falling on one's knees to pray before.

He slowly opened his eyes, he was still on the ground and she was gone. Stepping forward, he looked around the reception area which had a high-gloss New York feel, polished chrome, antiques, glass and art. The large pieces of art which hung on the walls were local. Vietnamese in bamboo hats planting rice, girls in ao dai on a village path, and one abstract piece which looked like a fish was driving a large hook through the upper lip of a man. Perfect for a law office, he thought. Winchell & Holly occupied one of the old French villas which had been renovated at great expense. The missionaries had come in the great gold rush for souls one hundred and fifty years ago when souls had some value worth killing for, and now the lawyers had arrived promising delivery from poverty and the cycle of misery.

He had made an appointment with Douglas Webb, a senior expat lawyer, who kept him cooling his heels in the reception area. A lawyer showed his power by how long he could decently keep a client waiting and still keep the client.

Dressed in a tailored suit and power red silk tie a *farang* appeared from around the corner. His black, gray-streaked hair was long enough to push the limits of conventionality but stopped short of slamming into the void of rebellion. Calvino guessed that Webb was about forty years old.

"Vincent, I am Douglas Webb," he said, holding out his hand. Calvino rose from the sofa and shook Webb's hand. The guy starts on first-name basis, thought Calvino.

Webb brushed a strand of black hair gone gray which had fallen over his right temple. Calvino could see him doing that same movement in school as a kid. Other kids teasing him, making him feel small and helpless. It was one of those nervous tics which he had probably become a lawyer to overcome, to reclaim some power, knowing that no matter how far he went, he would still be pushing back his hair, twitching his eye until he took his last breath. There was crinkling around the blue eyes, and dark mustache with some red in it. Webb looked fit like a jogger, someone who worked at it, his handshake was strong and he didn't wear a wedding ring. He looked Calvino straight in the eye, taking him in the way a boxer takes in someone at a weigh- in. The look of a lawyer trying to figure out the quality and bank account of his client, and what particular crimes he had in mind.

"Sorry, I'm running late."

Webb showed him into a conference room which was cold enough to keep chilled wine and dead bodies from decaying. Easing himself into a captain's chair at the conference table, he waited until Calvino picked a lesser seat and sat himself down. Webb looked like Captain Kirk on the deck of the Starship Enterprise, thought Calvino, as he handed him a name card which had his name as Vincent Demato and an address in Brooklyn, New York. Mission: going where no other man has gone.

"Your card doesn't list any company."

"Let's say that I am unaffiliated."

Webb smiled. "A free agent? Like in professional sports."

"I'll come straight to the point. My people want to open a bar in Saigon and we need to know the rules of the bar game. We figure this isn't Brooklyn. So, to tell you the truth, we don't know who we have to pay for a license. How much do we pay the police to leave me alone? And how difficult is it to get money in and out of the country? Finally, I would like to know how much you charge an hour."

"I'll start with your last question first. My hourly rate is US$300 an hour. But we have Vietnamese lawyers who can assist you. Their rate is US$100. Now, as to payoffs, since you are an American citizen, making payoffs to government officials is against the law. Those laws, in theory, apply to you in Vietnam."

"In Brooklyn we are more interested in practice than theory," said Calvino.

"Let me ask you another question. What's your background in law?"

Webb played with the name card, looking a little lost in thought.

"Six years with Winchell & Holly in New York, then three years in Tokyo, five in Bangkok and now two years in Vietnam."

So he had been passed over for partnership in New York, thought Calvino, and hit the road, finding a place on the Japanese caravan just as it was hitting the road. Five years in Bangkok and he had never heard of Douglas Webb.

"You practiced in Bangkok?"

"I was in-house with one of the Japanese banks," he said.

"Your old firm brought you to Saigon," said Calvino, with a grin.

"Experience finally carries the day, Mr. Demato."

Experience of having travelled the route from the land of the Sumo to the land of the kick-boxer and landing a partnership in the land of the jungle fighter. Webb was bound to have accumulated some scars and enemies along the way. Drew Markle could have been one of them, a young American who was being groomed by New York to take Webb's position. There was a deep-seated distrust of "local hires" in the large companies; the fear was that an American who was already on the ground couldn't be trusted, going ahead of being sent was a corrupting event, making someone at the home office think that there wasn't something quite right about someone who just up and moved on his own to a foreign place.

"With all that experience, what is your advice?"

"To start with, you will need a Vietnamese partner," Webb said.

"Isn't that where you come in? Can't you make a recommendation?"

"We could give you some leads."

"You don't sound like you're from New York," said Calvino. Webb shook his head. "Wisconsin."

"I guess that makes you an international lawyer," said Calvino. He paused, and then followed up, "You speak the language?"

"Speak, yes, fluent, well, that's another issue. But, yes, I get by in Vietnamese."

"And Japanese?"

Webb nodded.

Calvino stared at him. "What about Thai?"

"*Poot Thai dai, khrap,*" he answered. "I can speak Thai."

Calvino disliked him already. The guy got the tones right in Thai. He couldn't be human or, if he was, then he was a genius, either way, he was glad that the firm had passed him over for partnership ten years earlier.

Webb didn't say anything, leaning back in his chair. Calvino had this feeling that Douglas Webb liked being called an international lawyer and showing off his Thai. It made him feel important. Calvino's law was once you got the other guy filled to the top with his own self-importance he was bound to underestimate you. Because that kind of guy suffered from low self-esteem and would reduce the value of any man that saw value in him.

"How many other American lawyers you got working in the office?"

"We are down to one. Me."

"Yeah, that's too bad. I read about that guy who got blown up in the papers. A hell'va of a thing to happen to an American."

"He was in the wrong place at the wrong time. It was more or less an accident."

"What kind of clients you handle?"

"From large Japanese construction companies to the Forrest Gumps of the *farang* community," said Webb.

Webb was looking at him real close now, wondering how much to say and how much to hold back, thinking this unaffiliated guy who wanted to run a bar in Saigon was asking some unusual questions. Calvino dropped his pen on the conference table, one of those planned accidents to break another man's concentration. "I think you're the right man to handle my case," said Calvino, flashing a Forrest Gump grin.

"We will require a deposit. At least five thousand dollars."

Webb had pulled the figure out of the air. He had no idea what the work would be but made the upfront amount large enough that he was sure that Calvino would say, "Yeah, I'll think about it, call you tomorrow." And then do what most walk-ins did, never showed up or called again.

"No problem. Douglas, do you ever go out on the town in Saigon? Assuming there is any place to go."

This caught Webb a little off guard, the upper left-hook which a first name brought in a formal setting like a law office conference room with the partner sitting in the captain's chair, from a man who didn't look like he had cab fare.

"What do you mean?"

"You know, after work, hit a few bars, have a friendly drink, wind down from the day? If I am going to be doing business with this firm, I don't want a lawyer who never takes a drink or never goes into a bar."

This explanation had the intended effect; it relaxed Douglas Webb.

"You have a point."

"Somebody told me about a place called the Q-Bar. Why don't we meet for a drink about ten tonight?" said Calvino.

"What size investment are you looking to make?"

Calvino smiled. "Around two hundred grand."

"You can get a bar for much less than that in Ho Chi Minh City."

"I know, but I want a bar in Saigon. And you asked me about the size of my potential investment. Not how much was going into the bar."

"How do you plan to bring in the money?"

"In cash," said Calvino. "You have any problem with that, counsellor?"

"Mr. Demato, why don't we have a drink tonight."

So far it appeared to Calvino that Douglas Webb had a divided life: he practiced in Ho Chi Minh City and, after work, he drank in Saigon.

"You mind sending in one of your hundred dollar an hour Vietnamese lawyers? I figure I can get the three hundred an hour advice over a drink tonight."

Douglas Webb had begun to like this Vincent Demato.

"You never said who your partners are in Brook-lyn."

"You're right, I didn't."

Calvino was on his feet and out the conference door, when he turned, and caught a glimpse of the woman in the white ao dai.

"You mind if I ask Mai out?" asked Calvino.

Douglas Webb looked like he had a fishbone lodged deep in this throat, or the fish in the abstract art had hooked his upper lip.

"She's a Hanoi girl."

"What's that supposed to mean?"

"That she won't go out with a foreigner," said Webb.

"Wanna bet?" asked Calvino.

Webb shrugged his shoulders, avoiding the direct challenge to his opinion on Mai's taste in men. There was something about Calvino that made placing a bet as they stood in the reception area seem like dropping into a very deep hole. Every quasi-grifter client hit on Mai. She had that sensual but untouchable look: pure femininity and grace, natural and remarkably unaware of the effect she had on men.

"I'll pass on the bet."

"But not on the Q-Bar?"

"Ten," said Webb.

Calvino pushed through the door which swung shut behind him and a moment later as he waited at the elevator, Mai appeared carrying two file folders. Webb watched them talking. Calvino had his hands calmly resting at his sides, his head tilted to one side. It seemed odd, thought Webb. A wiseguy from Brooklyn not using his hands to talk with a woman...not using his hands to talk with anyone. This Mr. Vincent Demato was an unusual character, he thought. Mai made no effort to walk away. She waited until Calvino had walked inside the elevator and the door closed. When she turned away, her face had a red blush and she was smiling like a girl who suddenly had a thought about a man that she could never otherwise betray.

CHAPTER 5

THE MARCUS MESSAGE

PRATT LOWERED HIS reading glasses and sat back in a bamboo chair. Raising the glass to his lips, he took a small sip of his white wine. Enjoying the taste, he noticed a hedge-like tree in a huge black planter that had been cut to resemble an elephant. The fashion was for businessmen to drink wine on a terrace garden decorated with tropical plants, flowers and birds. He had ordered a glass of 1987 La Tour, a Sauterne, a little on the sweet side, he thought, but not too bad. No doubt the waiters had taken note that he had asked for a glass out of two hundred bottles of wine. What was the English word for trimming trees into the shape of animals and birds? he asked himself. He studied the leafy elephant trunk, taking in some bare spots in the leaves and he could see the branches underneath. The word, what was the word? asked Pratt. All around the outer edge of the rooftop bar were plants cut into a zoo of green animals looking out at Le Loi Boulevard on one side and the square, with a large statue of Ho Chi Minh with a child under each arm, across the street from the entrance to the Rex. The bartenders wore the same uniform: black trousers, white shirts with bow ties, and vests. One of the waiters came to Pratt's table and set down another glass of wine.

"Topiary," Pratt said.

"Excuse me. What language do you speak?" asked the waiter.

"Topiary is Latin for trees trimmed into animal shapes," he said.

The bartender blinked, followed Pratt's eyes over to the elephant trimmed plant. He shrugged and walked away without another word.

Pratt ignored the bartender, making a note of the conversation as he returned to the bar. He reached into his briefcase and pulled out a copy of the Asian Wall St reet Journal and turned to the editorial page. Markets in emerging Asia were bullish. Hedge bulls cut from potted financial derivative plants. Stockbrokers had taken the ancient craft of topiary and adapted it to a new stage of ornamental art, he thought. He already missed Manee and remembered that anguished look as he left the house.

"Go well, come back well," she had said in Thai. "*Pai dii, maa dii.*"

She had had a bad feeling about this trip to Vietnam. She had pleaded for him not to go but once she saw that he had made up his mind, she lapsed into resignation, as if to say, okay, go. But look at my face, this is my widow's face. The face that you will leave behind to confront the world which no longer includes you.

§ § § §

WITHIN the span of three hours, Calvino had been to the law firm twice. After his meeting with Douglas Webb, he had gone back to his room, stuffed five grand into a plastic bag, then waited a couple of hours before returning. This time he had asked to see a Vietnamese lawyer. Webb had sat in on the meeting just in case Khanh, the Vietnamese lawyer, needed any translation help. Believe that and you will believe that his billings are accurate, thought Calvino. But it didn't matter. He had the chance to see her again. He was already mixing Saigon with Ho Chi Minh City, and forgetting that Hanoi figured strongly into the equation. She didn't seem all that surprised when he reappeared, as if she halfway expected him to return that day.

He stood in front of the elevator. His hand covered the buttons so that she couldn't call the elevator.

"You make it difficult to get an elevator, Mr. Demato," she said.

"Vincent, please. And I want to make it difficult. Because I want a few more minutes. You know, to talk."

"About what?"

"I want to learn about Vietnam," he blurted out.

"There are many guidebooks," she said.

"I want to learn from you."

"I think that I am a very bad teacher."

"Let me be the judge. How about dinner."

"That is difficult."

"Lunch, breakfast,... a snack."

"You make me laugh."

"You stop me from breathing."

She looked at him, her mind doing that woman thing.

"Lunch," she said.

"Tomorrow."

"Yes, I can."

Calvino couldn't remember stepping into the elevator or the journey down. All he felt was a floating sensation. How can a guy be in Southeast Asia and fall in love like this? he said to himself as the door of the elevator opened on the ground floor. And how to keep this from getting in the way of the job? It was Pratt's fault, he told himself. Seeing him in the garden with Manee, just watching how happy two people could be. The image had stuck in his mind. Then he found the woman he wanted in his garden telling him not to go, not to leave. Just stay by her side.

§ § § § §

GETTING off the elevator on the top floor—the fifth floor—of the Rex, Calvino still had the Hanoi girl on his mind, distracting him. He walked into the carpeted foyer, turned to his right, and found himself in front of a small newsstand with foreign newspapers and guidebooks. He stopped and looked for a Bangkok newspaper. There was nothing like going out of town to give an expat an addiction to his hometown newspaper. It was late afternoon by the time that Calvino looked through the papers at the newsstand; all the copies of Bangkok Post and The Nation were a day old. As he glanced around he saw a young Vietnamese woman sitting behind a school desk. She was about eighteen or nineteen. Like Mai at Winchell & Holly, she wore an ao dai—a blue top with sheer white pants—and she wore her black hair back over her shoulders. She had not noticed him, lost inside her own world.

She had the innocence of a child; her mouth slightly parted, her eyes vulnerable and concentrated. She sat erect behind a small desk, reading a thin, worn book. He could see from his angle that it was a book in English. He took a step and glanced over her shoulder, and watched for a moment, as she read lyrics to herself from a song book. She ran her finger down the words to "Lost in Love" and then continued tracing the words on the next page to the song titled "Love is Blue."

"You are learning English from a song book?" Calvino asked. His voice startled her, she blushed, looked at him, and then over at the newspaper rack.

"It is a good book," she said, shutting the book as she folded a bookmarker between the pages.

"When do you get today's Bangkok Post?"

"After six, Sir," she said.

"You like to learn English?"

"Yes, I like so much."

"And you study love songs in English?"

"Sometimes after university," she said. "I want to know everything about English."

Learning the English language of love from a song book made about as much sense as learning the Thai language of love from a bar.

"What's your favourite song?"

She smiled and stared hard at the book and pointed at the title which was "Lost in Love." There were romantics in the ruins of Saigon, young girls who dreamt of love in the English language. He watched her reading the lyrics, her lips moving as she read. He pulled a day-old copy of the Bangkok Post off a rack and stuck it under this arm.

"One dollar, Sir," she said.

"A dollar. Everywhere in the world are people lost in love with the American dollar. And here I am paying money for day-old news."

"I think you are wrong. That's not the kind of love the song's about," she said.

"Is there a Vietnamese love song book?" he asked.

"Yes, there are many."

"Maybe that's how I can learn Vietnamese," he said. "It is a good place to begin."

They looked at each other for a moment, then he walked away from the newsstand, leaving her to read her song book.

She would remember him coming to disturb her in the middle of her English lesson. And that's what he wanted: a girl to see him coming in alone, having all the time in the world before going to the bar. Whoever was watching and whoever would question the girl later would come to the conclusion that when Vincent Demato wandered out onto the rooftop, he had already started to read the newspaper. His mind wasn't on the newspaper, but on Mai, as she stood beside him before the elevator arrived.

§ § § §

MOST of the tables on the Rex rooftop garden were occupied with tourists, expat businessmen, and some people who fell between the cracks of tourism and commerce. Nursing drinks, reading papers, talking—nothing out of the ordinary, thought Calvino. Half of the crowd looked like those at the Fourth of July picnic: large, awkward, out of place. Tropical caged birds were hung around the bar area. A large Macaw beak opened, releasing a loud scream, and it flapped its wings as a French tourist, tiny chin beard, dressed in a gray silk shirt and jeans, teased it with a peanut. Calvino kept on walking, wishing that Macaw had the chance of throwing the French asshole over the side of the Rex. He wanted to shove the peanut up the guy's beaklike nose. But he was playing the role of a Brooklyn businessman and that meant he had to forget about the bird abuse, better yet, he should find a way to sell the bird to the guy, to turn a profit. That was business. Taking the advantage faster than the next guy. He had to tell himself that he was on stage and people in the audience might be taking notes. As he passed several tables, he wondered why he had bought the Bangkok Post. It was a small detail, but it amounted to a stupid mistake. A businessman from

Brooklyn wouldn't buy a day-old Bangkok newspaper; only a resident lamenting his time away from Bangkok would bother. It was too late. The paper was tucked under his arm.

Calvino looked around before sitting in the chair opposite Pratt.

"Birds, don't you love 'em," Calvino said. "They make a hell'va a racket."

A waiter came over to the table and stood a foot to the left and behind Calvino.

"Bring me a 333," said Calvino, taking out the business section. "And make it real cold." Pratt sat opposite with his nose in the newspaper.

"Do you speak English?" asked Calvino, bending forward and taking a handful of peanuts from a small bowl.

Pratt lowered his newspaper. "Do you?"

Calvino cocked his head, narrowed his eyebrows.

"Does it sound like I'm speaking French?"

"Topiary French," said Pratt.

He had scored a direct hit, he thought. Calvino didn't know what topiary meant and wasn't even sure whether it was Thai, English or French. And he was dying to ask but knew that it was something he should leave alone. Already Calvino was thinking this idea of pretending not to know each other was not going to work. You might be able to get away with that act, say, with a wife, but with a friend you have known for a lifetime in two countries, that was asking a great deal.

"I'd like to have a look at the Asian Wall Street Journal when you're finished. I bought this Bangkok newspaper by mistake. I thought it was the Journal. Funny, when you're jet-lagged how all the newspapers look the same."

Calvino was behaving himself, thought Pratt. "Like all Asians look the same," said Pratt.

Conflict. Pratt was provoking one and putting on a good show.

"My mistake," said Calvino, starting to rise.

"Stay, it's okay. I have finished the paper," said Pratt.

"The Bangkok Post is one day old. I don't want you to think I am trying to cheat you. But I paid a dollar for it."

In the exchange of newspapers, they nearly knocked over Calvino's can of 333 beer. The can wobbled on the table but Calvino caught it before it could fall.

He held up the can and shouted at the bar for another beer. Calvino opened the newspaper, put the can of beer to his lips and finished it off. He set the empty down and, without looking at Pratt, began to talk as if he were lip-reading the newspaper.

"The *farang* lawyer at Winchell & Holly is a guy named Douglas Webb, I can handle him. You should start with a Vietnamese lawyer named Khanh. He's their guy from Hanoi. We had a little boc phet."

Pratt flinched. "What's boc phet?"

"Vietnamese for bullshit session. Now we're even for topiary," said Calvino.

"He tell you anything useful?"

Calvino shrugged. "Not really. Not so far anyway. He asked if I was an American and I told him, 'Yeah. But I didn't kill anyone. I gave the war a miss.' And he said he was a kid during the war. His father was a colonel or something. He's got relatives in one ministry and school friends in another so he's got all the right connections in the government. The firm uses him to grease the wheels. My guess is the entire office is full of Hanoi lawyers and staff. They did win the war. Whoever would have thought law offices were part of the spoils of war?"

"Did he bring up Mark Wang?"

"No way. But I did throw in the fact that I didn't think

much of how the Chinese did business, and that seemed to please him. I asked him about the Chinese. Whether they would give me a problem. Or who was running the business side of things. The Chinese or the Vietnamese."

"And?"

"He said that he hated the Chinese. The Vietnamese would never let them run the show like in Thailand. That's what he said."

"He sounds like a sweetheart."

"You're gonna love him. His rap on Thailand is that it is the land of crooks and pollution."

"Unlike Vietnam where, so far, they have only crooks," said Pratt.

"He said corruption was an Asian disease. That observation could earn him sixty days of in-house hospitality in Singapore," Calvino said, smiling.

Calvino took out some American dollars and put them on the table.

"Thanks for the Wall Street Journal," said Calvino.

"Thanks for the day old news," replied Pratt.

"Careful you don't get hurt," said Calvino.

As Pratt watched him disappear from the roof garden, he thought about how much pressure the force was under to solve the murder of Mark Wang. If they hated the Chinese so much, then why didn't they have the common decency to murder them in Saigon? Instead, they had a dead American in Saigon and a dead Hong Kong executive in Bangkok linked in death by a common thread—the billable hour at the same law firm.

§ § § § §

THE streets were congested with traffic outside the Rex. The moment Calvino walked down the steps from the front entrance on Nguyen Hue Boulevard, a heavy wall of street people threatened to collapse on top of him. Some vendors waved toy helicopters crafted from empty 333 beer cans, others sold the usual street food—fruit, soup, fried pork, and still others carted fans, books, maps, and postcards; some wanted to change money, others offered to sell themselves. As a group they were on the move and they homed in on Calvino. One hundred meters away from the Rex, he crossed Le Loi Boulevard and Calvino found himself heading a parade of beggars, children in rags, then as he kept walking, a wall of shoe shine boys joined the black market money changers, cripples, and amputees. H e turned a corner and nearly tripped over the twisted fragment of a human form stretched out stomach down on a flat cart with wooden wheels. Calvino caught his balance and saw this face staring up at him with a smile. How could this guy smile? His skinny, naked legs and bare feet were knotted behind his ass. On his hands he wore dirty pads to propel himself along the pavement, looking for a parade to join. Here was the world at ankle level. All one had to do was to keep the eyes above knee level to miss the last link of the food chain on the streets of Saigon. Calvino recovered himself and dug out some money. He knelt down on one knee as the rest of the crowd gathered around him and stuck a five-dollar bill inside one of the guy's ragged hand pads.

"Thanks a lot, Mister Vincent," said the man in a perfect American accent.

"You not only speak English. But you know my name. How is that?" Calvino couldn't believe his ears.

"I picked up some free English lessons during the war. You a vet?" Calvino shook his head.

"Who told you my name?"

"Marcus, who else? Are you an American?"

Calvino nodded, thinking, what had happened to this

guy? What marriage of incomprehensible evil and madness had torn his body apart?

"Marcus Nguyen?"

"Colonel Marcus. Me. I stepped on a landmine two months before April 30, 1975. That's what the communists call Liberation Day," said the man, reading Calvino's mind. It wasn't difficult to do. Most foreigners thought the same thing first time they laid eyes on him.

"What's your name?"

"My friends call me Tan. Marcus wants you to meet him for dinner at the Saigon Central Mosque on Dong Du Street. He's waiting for you now. I didn't think you were ever coming down from the Rex. You got a whore up there or what?"

"How did he know I would come this way?" asked Calvino.

"Marcus knows because you don't exactly make yourself invisible. You could use some friends like Marcus and me."

"I could use a friend," said Calvino. "Someone who knows what happens on the street. Listens. Watches. Can remember what happened."

Tan smiled at the fiver. "I'm your man. But Marcus is the dude in the know. Believe it. Tomorrow, if you are interested, I'll be at the noodle stand just before the Central Market on Phan Bol Chau. See you around, buddy."

He whipped around Calvino's right-hand side and disappeared into the crowds on the sidewalk. It was the way Tan said Liberation Day that made him think this wasn't exactly the word he would have chosen to describe the NVA entry into Saigon. And the guy spoke English better than the Vietnamese staff at Winchell & Holly. Marcus Nguyen's messenger had been the message: Marcus could have used a dozen ways to send a dinner invitation but instead he chose Tan, a street freak, with perfect English. Why would Marcus do that? Harry had said that he was emotional, a bit of a loose cannon. In this case, Marcus was showing that he had a presence on the street, the lowest level was often the most reliable level to plug into and listen for the advance of the enemy. Marcus was plugged in. Tan was his eyes and ears on the street and he had delivered Calvino to him. Marcus had made his point. And Tan had made his, no one was going around Saigon saying that he should be referred to as physically challenged. The challenge was never physical, it was always mental and Marcus had sent the perfect messenger to deliver that message.

§ § § § §

THE bronze plaque on the side of the Mosque on Dong Du Street said that it had been built in 1935. This would have been during the time of French rule. What the mosque needed was another plaque saying it had survived the intervening sixty years in one piece. Calvino walked down a passage and into a courtyard with outside brick ovens and a few tables. Cooking smells of curried goat, beef and chicken were in the air. He saw a middle-aged Vietnamese man stand framed in the doorway of a room in the back. The man was smiling and waving to Calvino. This was Marcus Nguyen, ex-Marine Colonel, thought Calvino, trying to reconcile the image formed in his mind at the Fourth of July picnic in Bangkok with the reality inside a mosque in Saigon. Of course, there had been the nightmare Marcus Nguyen whose severed head had been held high by Drew Markle. Neither Calvino's conscious nor unconscious imagination had been sufficient. In real life, Marcus had black, gray-flecked hair which was cut short. He looked perfectly ordinary, dressed in a white shirt, dark trousers, and wore gold-rimmed glasses. Marcus would have blended into any group of people; he might have been a government official or a school teacher.

What he didn't have was the look of a jungle fighter. Then what did such a person really look like? Not the guys in a Hollywood film, he thought.

"Vincent," said Marcus, extending his hand as Calvino entered the small, private room off the main courtyard. "I have been waiting for you. A friend of Harry Markle is a friend of mine. I saw Harry last week. Not in the most pleasant of circumstances, but then, Harry and I never seem to find circumstances pleasant whenever we get together. It has something to do with our karma, as the Buddhists say."

"Then you know why I've come to Vietnam."

"To find who killed his little brother. Not that Saigon is any more Vietnam than Bangkok is Thailand."

Calvino looked hard at him.

"Nothing personal, Mr. Nguyen, but next time you want to arrange a meeting, you should make a phone call." He glanced at Marcus's mobile phone on the table.

"The phones in your hotel are bugged," he said. "Is that a fact?"

"It's a fact."

"I'm curious about facts."

"Such as?"

"Where were you the night Drew was killed?" asked Calvino. Marcus's mobile phone rang. He answered it and spoke in rapid Vietnamese.

"Harry said you were a man who came straight to the point. And so am I. I was sitting right here on that night. That's a fact," said Marcus, switching off the mobile phone.

"You can ask the waiter...any of the staff. We heard the explosion."

Smooth, planned, flawless, thought Calvino. Marcus Nguyen had brought him to his alibi, a courtyard inside a mosque. If you wanted a back-up story for a murder then a mosque had to be an inspired piece of forward planning.

Several bowls of steaming rice and curry had been placed on their table. Marcus helped himself to the rice, spooning it on his plate.

"Do you like curry?" asked Marcus. "This mosque is famous for its curry. Pre-1975, I came here often with friends. The old grandfather knew me and he brought me beer in a brown bag. Beer in a mosque. Another fact. But we Vietnamese are pragmatic people. And the Indians who have been living and working more than four generations have picked up on this small adaptation which has allowed for all of us to find a way to survive. For every rule there must be an exception."

"And for every murder there should be a revenge," said Calvino. "Yes, you are right in theory. But, in practice, when there is so much murder, you have to be selective in your revenge or you wouldn't have time to clean the blood off your hands before meals."

"The Chinese have a saying, if you set out to get your revenge against another man, dig two graves," said Calvino.

"But Harry's not Chinese. Besides, as Harry knows, in Vietnam, we would dump Chinese bodies in both holes."

Calvino had, despite himself, started to like Marcus. Committed, self-assured and guarded, he thought, as he faced the window looking out onto the courtyard. It had metal bars like a prison, and a cob-webbed screen covered the bars. A cover on a cover on a cover, he thought. The room was small, protected. It was a perfect meeting place. The possibility of the government having an agent or listening device inside seemed remote. Beside the window was an old mirror with a red plastic comb wedged onto a rusty nail. How many faces had looked into that mirror over the past sixty years, how many men had combed their hair, walked out and died? After Marcus spooned more curry onto his rice, he turned his attention back to Calvino.

"Harry asked that I help you in any way that I can. And I said that will be up to your friend. Some people want help. Some ask for help. Others prefer to do things on their own. So I said to Harry, 'I'm here. I will contact him, and let him know that, if he wants help, then all he has to do is ask.' You phoned while I was Singapore and I took that to mean that you wanted to ask me something."

Marcus spoke with an American accent.

"How long were you in the States?" asked Calvino.

"Eighteen years."

"Why did you come back?"

Marcus smiled. "To help my country."

Bullshit, thought Calvino.

"Who do you think killed Drew?"

"The communists killed him. Of course."

"How do you know that?"

"When you are Vietnamese you know things."

"They arrested an ex-RVN sergeant for the murder," said Calvino.

Marcus nodded, then sighed. "A crippled vet who bore the scars of violence, the helplessness of being on the losing side. He was a soft target. Nothing can save him from losing this war again and again. Sometimes I look at the cadres from the North. The winners. And I ask myself, how could such people have defeated us? Curled in the mud, the rain on their necks, they knew they had a larger capacity to absorb damage, to accept injury and pain. It's given them a hangman's conscience. After a while you no longer notice who is dropping through the hole in the scaffold. An ex-RVN sergeant was no more involved in the killing than you or me."

"Did you become an American citizen?" asked Calvino.

Marcus nodded. "But inside," he pointed at his chest, "the heart is Vietnamese. You know what I am saying?"

Harry was right about Marcus being emotional. He had an emotional stake in the communists being the bad guys, the collective fall guy for every misery, death, and fucked up thing. He had fought against them with all that he had and they had won. That he had come back to help his country was a good line, but Calvino wasn't buying it.

"You know anything about overseas investors and a fund being launched this week in Saigon?"

"It's not a state secret. It's called the Vietnam Emerging Market Fund. Their timing has been perfect. This is the twentieth anniversary of the communists marching into Saigon. Confiscation and re-education camps. That's how they celebrated their victory," said Marcus, sounding, for the first time, a little bitter. He polished off the rest of the beef curry.

"No beer in a brown bag?" asked Calvino.

Marcus looked up. "In the old days, I knew the old man who ran the restaurant. He knew how to turn a blind eye. He was their grandfather. He died a long time ago. The new generation, well, let's say they are different. Not so pragmatic."

"You think that Douglas Webb had a reason to kill Drew?" asked Calvino, nursing his drink. One of those compact, crude questions flying out of the blue.

Marcus shifted his head from shoulder to shoulder, weighing the possibility.

"He's not the murdering type."

This was spoken casually by someone who appeared confident in his judgement on who was capable of murder. Again, Calvino asked himself what emotional agenda was Marcus playing out. If he was going to rely on this ex-Marine's assessment of an American lawyer practicing law in Saigon, then he wouldn't be doing the job Harry Markle had sent him to do. Harry could have left the job to Marcus but didn't do that. He had his reasons and Calvino had to trust his gut feeling that Harry had enough experience of Marcus to back his decision.

"You and Harry go way back," said Calvino.

Marcus's eyes narrowed. "Yeah, you can say all the way to hell. Let me tell you something about Harry Markle. He never called me a gook or a slope. He never called any Vietnamese those kind of names. Even when we were in the shit. We were human beings to him. I thought all Americans were like Harry Markle. But after eighteen years in America, I didn't find many like him. People who saw me as one of them. This acceptance, tolerance, whatever you want to call it, I think it was what kept Harry from ever fitting back in the States."

"What were you doing in Singapore?"

Marcus cracked a smile.

"Making money."

§ § § § §

CALVINO returned to his hotel after leaving the mosque. He was asking himself how he was going to play the case. This was an abstract question and the image of Mai flooded back into his mind, getting in the way of an answer and making him feel frustrated and foolish. How many *farang* had arrived in Bangkok and, twenty-four hours later, were sucked into some ice castle inside the Zone, and had fallen "in love" with a local girl over a lady's drink? Many (he answered his own question) and the failure rate pushed the hundred percent marker. She wasn't a bar girl, he told himself. Forget about Ho Chi Minh City, but not even Saigon had anything approaching the Zone. He was starting to sound to himself like Marcus Nguyen justifying his world view according to who were communists and who were not. He decided to leave it alone, took the elevator down to the reception, pushed through the hotel entrance and walked twenty meters to the Q-Bar.

Like his hotel, the Q-Bar was part of the Municipal Theater Complex which under the old regime—the term the communists used—became the National Assembly. Cyclos and motorcycles were parked on the walkway between the bar and a concrete fountain. Across the street was the Caravelle Hotel and floodlights illuminated a giant construction crane driving piles. The earth shook each time the pile driver hit the top of the pile. On the wall of the theater complex he came to a large, bronze Q, and pushed the door.

The Q-Bar might have been downtown New York City on a rainy night. On one side a couple of Vietnamese women floated in and out of the shadows like a couple of cobras protecting their nests, as if warning you never to take your eyes off the eyes around you, the position of the next person's head, you kept alert waiting for a strike. There were Aztec copper light fixtures keeping the lights dim, murals on the walls, jazz playing and a crowd at the bar. The clientele was overwhelmingly *farang* with a few Vietnamese women in cocktail dresses, high-heels and heavy make-up standing around the bar, others seated at some of the tables. He was running half an hour early because he wanted to check out the place. He heard his name called.

Douglas Webb got off his stool and walked over to him. They shook hands. Caravaggio figures had been painted on the wall. To choose the images from this Northern Italian painter was like an inside New York joke. Caravaggio was an alcoholic, gay and a fucking genius; a high Renaissance painter, in the early baroque style. He was a painter who loved street people and used them as models for saints, immortalizing the most flawed as the most sacred. There were Caravaggio's street men, young, brooding, sullen men embedded in dark reds and greens, their flesh illuminated by overhead lights. Their doomed eyes, staring back at people standing two deep inside a Saigon bar. If there were a Caravaggio's law it would be: Look for the face of the saint among the faces living in the back alley, the bars, the gutter. Webb's eyes followed Calvino's to the wall paintings.

"Caravaggio is the painter. Bar owners love his images. And why not? How many painters have the claim to fame of getting themselves killed in a barroom brawl?" asked Webb.

"Caravaggio's an icon."

Calvino had that moment where he almost slipped, and said, "No, people who know nothing about art say Caravaggio was killed in a barroom brawl. Not true, though the record was shrouded in doubt, he died on the 18th July, 1610, sick, feverish, broke. He died at a young age. Some said he was about the same age as Jim Morrison when he died. Others said he was older. Whatever his age, Caravaggio was definitely in the running for the original rebel without a cause."

A wiseguy from Brooklyn would say what Calvino said, "Yeah, killed in a bar fight. When I open a bar, I don't want that kind of trouble."

Calvino was thinking that working undercover was a lesson in humility, you stayed the course by keeping to your role, not showing off. Webb was a guy who turned up late for his appointment but early for a drink.

"What are you drinking?"

"Beer," said Calvino. Behind the bar and below the Caravaggio figures was a glass shelf with the premium bottles lined up: Glenlivet, McAllans, Cardhu, Black Label. Better stick to beer, thought Calvino.

"If you want to run a bar, you have to set a good example for the customers by drinking premium whisky. Then you get the right crowd. A beer crowd isn't where the money is. They vomit on themselves, get drunk, fight, spill beer. That kind of thing."

Calvino wondered how long after he had left the offices of Winchell & Holly, Douglas Webb had waited to phone the New York phone number listed on his card to check him out. Did he phone after the first time or after Calvino had returned a second time with the five grand deposit? Would he do it himself or go through his New York office? That was the fork in the road. You either made a left into light or a right into darkness.

"Glenlivet. So long as it doesn't come out of my deposit," said Calvino.

"This is on the firm," he said, smiling. "Why the generosity?"

"Getting a lunch date with Mai. Impressive. A Hanoi girl, too." He had obviously reassessed placing Calvino in the Forrest Gump category of clients.

"She's attractive," said Calvino, wondering whether Mai had volunteered the information or if Webb had asked her. "You've got a point about attracting the right crowd. I have something to learn about Saigon and the bar trade. But that's why I have hired your firm."

A bartender with a scarf tied around his neck and a large white Q on his black T-shirt set down before Calvino on the bar a neat shot of Glenlivet. Douglas Webb raised his glass for a toast and as Calvino followed, their glasses touched. "Here's to success, Vincent. In the bar business. You appear to be a lucky man. With women and with money. Hopefully your luck will rub off on your Saigon bar."

"How do you know that I'm lucky?" asked Calvino, sipping the Glenlivet.

"I'd say winning two hundred and fifty grand in a lotto is running with luck blowing in your sails," said Webb.

"How'd you know about that?"

"I made a discreet inquiry. I'll be honest with you. When you practice law in Southeast Asia you have the reputation of the firm to consider. Today, when you came into the office and started talking about moving large sums of cash, well, it was only natural," and Webb let his sentence trail off into silence as he drank from his glass.

"Like running drugs," said Calvino, flashing an innocent smile. Webb exploded into a cough, some expensive whisky spilling down the side of his face which was turning red at the same time. On his business card, Calvino had used his brother-in-law's address and phone number. Frank Demato had been briefed to expect some overseas phone calls, and that Vincent was his brother and the two of them had won two hundred and fifty grand in the New York State lotto but Vincent, the asshole, had split for Asia with the entire amount of money, and that Frank was going to personally kill the sonofabitch and anyone who withheld information about where Vincent was hiding out.

Webb drank from a glass of water the bartender brought. He took a deep breath, then took a handkerchief from his pocket and wiped his face. Calvino stopped himself from making a crack about how beer drinkers throw up while whisky drinkers just coughed themselves to death. Fortunately Webb had recovered before Calvino said anything.

"I spoke with Frank. He's pretty upset with you."

"You didn't tell him where I am?"

Webb shook his head, coughed into his hand.

"Attorney-client privilege. I couldn't do that without your prior written permission."

This fell out of his mouth like one of those tape-recorded messages heard inside a high-rise elevator.

Webb had made a right at the fork in the road. He hadn't gone to his New York office but had phoned directly, keeping things private. It didn't necessarily mean anything. He might have done both. Faxed New York and phoned

Frank Demato directly to double check that New York had done the required due diligence. What mattered was Webb was satisfied that Calvino's story checked out.

"Thanks, counsellor, I guess I owe you one."

"That's what I'm here for. To help in any way that I can. And, of course, we must stay within the law." Webb ordered another round of drinks as one of the Vietnamese girls with long hair and in a red cocktail dress came over and planted a kiss on his cheek. He spoke to her in Vietnamese, she giggled and slipped away.

"Your girl?" asked Calvino.

"No, she's a working girl. Nice, but expensive. A Saigon girl."

Calvino watched the hooker go and sit at a table with two other girls.

"You speak the language well."

Webb gave a crooked smile. "I try to practice every chance that I get." He paused for a second, rolled the ice around the inside of his glass.

"I am concerned about your funds, Vincent."

"The lotto money?"

"That's a lot to be carrying around Saigon. Where is it?"

"In my hotel room," said Calvino.

"Bad idea. You should deposit the money in a bank."

"I heard the banks here are a risky place to keep US dollars. I might not ever get the money out of the country."

"So the conventional wisdom goes," said Webb. "I can arrange to keep your money in our office safe. We do this for some of our clients. You put it in the hands of a local partner, and you might as well not have bought the lotto ticket."

"I'm starting to feel better already," said Calvino.

He was thinking about the bag of counterfeit hundred-dollar bills that Pratt had arranged to borrow from the evidence deposit room of the Crime Suppression Division of the Department. It was only a loan, Pratt had told them. Sometimes they used the notes to pay ransom demands. Sometimes they used it to trap drug dealers. Sometimes they tried to trap bad actors who had gone too deep inside the honey ice. The money had many uses, many lives; died and was reborn over and over again and had found its way to Saigon. Stashed in a plastic bag in Vincent Calvino's room at the Saigon Concert Hotel and soon it would be in the possession of Winchell & Holly. A Vietnamese girl, mid-twenties, came in without warning on his blind side and wrapped an arm around his waist.

"You like me?" she asked.

Webb was watching him closely.

"How would you like to work in a classy bar for me?" he asked her.

Before she could answer, another Vietnamese stepped between Webb and Calvino. The other girl melted away into the crowd. Her replacement was dressed to kill in black ao dai with gold sequins fashioned in flower petals. This was no ordinary bar girl. She carried herself like a boardwalk model, with confidence, elegance, and the way she made a small half-smile suggested she had some inner strength to deal with Saigon and a whole lot of other places just as ugly.

"How's my little toc dai?" asked Webb. Toc dai, long-haired women Viet Cong soldiers, was not a term this woman liked.

"Toc dai means a woman Viet Cong," she said to Calvino. "Webb likes showing off his three or four words of Vietnamese." She sounded agitated, hostile.

"Unlike most Viet Khieu who can speak five or six words of Vietnamese," said Webb, not letting the slight go past without a rebuttal.

"So who is your new friend, Webb?" asked the Vietnamese woman, who looked to be late twenties.

"A new client," said Douglas Webb, looking nervously away at the bartender.

She turned to face Calvino. "Webb doesn't like me that much. Ever since Drew was killed, Webb hasn't missed a night at the Q-Bar. He did come to Drew's funeral but he didn't stay around long, did you, Webb?"

"Jackie, give it a rest," Douglas Webb said under his breath.

"Vincent Demato's my name. I am from New York. I'm staying just around the corner at the Saigon Concert."

"A fellow American," she said. "My name is Jackie Ky."

It was dark in the bar but he remembered that oval face. She was in the snapshot with Drew Markle. He was holding an M16 in one hand and had his arm around Jackie Ky with the other and the barrel of her AK47 was touching the barrel of his rifle. If ever there was a look of contentment it was on Drew's face. Every man should experience that feeling once before he died. Drew Markle had his one shot and this was the woman who had shared the moment with him.

Douglas Webb got off his stool. He grabbed Jackie by the arm and started to move her away from the bar.

"I'm trying to have a private conversation with a client, if you don't mind. Phone me tomorrow. We can talk."

"I want to talk now, Webb." But she didn't stop him from leading her across the room and then outside. Calvino watched through the door as they argued outside. She burst into tears and Webb came back into the bar, sliding back onto his stool.

"Sorry about that. She's Viet Khieu and, like most of them, she's a nut case," said Webb.

"She hung around poor Drew like a bad smell. He certainly had better taste than to go for a Viet Khieu like Jackie Ky. None of the Vietnamese trust the Viet Khieu. They cause trouble. They make problems for themselves.

Misfits. They don't fit in the States. They don't fit here."

"What's she do?" asked Calvino. He wondered if Douglas Webb knew about the photograph at the Cu Chi Tunnels with the dead lawyer and his girl.

"Some kind of bullshit interior design business."

"A bar needs interior design. Otherwise, you get all those damn vomiting beer drinkers," said Calvino, peeling off a twenty and then a ten from his wad of notes and putting them on the bar.

"See you later, counsellor."

By the time he was out the door, Jackie Ky had vanished into the night. Street people were sleeping on the lip of the concrete fountain. Other figures leaned against motorbikes. People of the night on their patch of turf. On the short walk back to his hotel he heard a distant sound closing in on him. The sound of bamboo sticks keeping a jazzy beat.

"That sound, it has a meaning," said Jackie Ky.

"Meaning what?"

"Meaning, soup's ready," said Jackie Ky, stepping out of the shadows.

"Basic, isn't it? You're hungry. You can eat. You hear the sound and your stomach moves. You can't help yourself because this sound is so deep in your blood."

Comfort Zone

CHAPTER 6

SLAUGHTERHOUSE SONGS

THE HOTEL RULES included a strict no-guest rule, meaning no women were allowed in the room of a male guest. The hotel was government owned so the rules had the force of law and the doormen acted like civil servants. Jackie Ky explained to Calvino the hotel would not allow her to go up to his room. Calvino put on his best Zone face and walked to the front desk and asked for his room key. The Vietnamese counter guy eyed Jackie and, keeping both hands flat on the counter, he leaned forward and spoke in broken English.

"Cannot have Vietnam girl go to room," he said. "Cannot." The switch from cannot to can has no mystery; it lurks deep inside the inner folds of a wallet. Calvino turned around and saw Jackie Ky fumbling with an American passport.

"I'm American," she said, slapping the passport down.

"Vietnam girl," the clerk said, ignoring the Amercan passport.

Calvino laid a fifty-dollar bill on the counter next to Jackie's passport. The clerk looked at the passport, then at the $50 bill. There was little doubt which carried more authority. Fifty bucks was a month's salary for a university professor. Fifty dollars would buy a bowl of pho for six months with change left over for beer. The bamboo sticks were keeping a beat outside. In the beginning, there was only sound and no listeners, rules, no cannots. And later, the sound found an audience, and in Saigon, the sound of "soup is ready" never ceased.

"Give me the key, close your eyes and think about Liberation Day."

There was a tense moment as the counter guy looked at the note. His hand edged forward, pushing the room key toward Calvino. He touched the money and lowered his eyes. Jackie Ky snatched back her passport. "Bastard," she whispered under her breath.

In the elevator a Russian air-conditioner blasted a Siberian wind. As the doors closed, Jackie Ky collapsed against the railing, throwing her head back under the cold airvents.

"How did you know I would come looking for you?" asked Calvino.

She didn't say anything, the run-in with the counter clerk was eating at her, he thought.

"In America, I got discriminated against because I was Vietnamese, and in Vietnam they discriminate against me because I am an Ameri-can. What's left? Where is it that I belong?"

It wasn't the kind of question which required any answer. Maybe she didn't know where she belonged, or who would come looking after her, maybe she just guessed, taking a step at a time. Maybe she was hoping that Webb would follow so she could stick a knife in his guts. The toc dai comment suggested the threat of violence. The beautiful long-haired girl with a market basket full of explosives flung into the belly of a helicopter on an LZ. Calvino had witnessed her behavior in the Q-Bar: she had one of those out-of-control rages, whirling threads of hate with despair, a tsunami of violence erupting into a brawl like the legendary one that had killed Caravaggio. Reaching the third floor, the elevator doors opened and Calvino walked out, unlocked the door, stood back, and let her go in first. He switched on the lights. It was a large room with green, musty carpets, two double beds and heavy curtains. Nothing quite matched, like a different bureaucrat had been in charge of each item ordered two years in advance from a state-run factory. He went over to a small fridge, took out a cold 333 beer, and popped the tab.

"You wanna beer, Jackie?"

"You got anything stronger?"

"Let's start with beer."

She sat on the edge of the bed near the balcony doors. She put a finger over her lips, then opened her handbag, took out a piece of paper and pen, and wrote for a moment before holding up the paper. He looked at her open handbag on the bed. A package of condoms had fallen halfway out, along with a pack of cigarettes and a tube of lipstick. The woman was prepared for a Saigon night. Was this chance meeting at the Q-Bar the same way that Drew Markle had found her, or had she shifted into the bar scene after his death? wondered Calvino.

She had written, "Your room's bugged. They can hear everything you say."

Calvino gave her a thumbs-up. She handed him the piece of paper and pen.

"Do you know who I am?" he wrote.

"Of course, I know who you are. Harry said you would come," she said without sound, letting him read her lips.

"Let's have a drink," he said.

"I shouldn't have come up here with you," she said. "You will get the wrong idea about me."

"It's not a state crime to talk business in a hotel room, is it?"

"You have no idea what prudes people are here. It's like living in the middle of the Bible Belt."

Her torso was twisted in a provocative way on the bed.

"Only the locals wear a lot less polyester," said Calvino.

She laughed, the kind of laugh that relaxed her, made the tension go out of her face. Tear streaks still stained her cheeks, cutting rivulets through the make-up, but she was okay now.

"You get used to the rules after a while," she said.

He opened a second can of beer and handed it to her.

"I am thinking of opening a bar in Saigon. I will need an interior designer. Webb said you had a business. I pay cash. No problem about that. But I want it real classy. Not for beer drinkers. I want the single-malt guys in red suspenders and Italian shoes."

"I think I can help you," she said.

"I mean really help."

"I was hoping you might."

She looked at her watch as he opened the balcony doors. He could see how Drew Markle might have fallen head-over-heels in love with this girl. She had the cultural thinking pad of an American woman but she was packaged in a slim, tall perfect body. A woman like Jackie Ky could have just about any man she wanted, he thought. She chose a young American lawyer from Winchell & Holly, and the man she picked won the grenade lotto. A small, hand-thrown bomb had arched skyward like a Fourth of July rocket, and when it burst, a pinkish mist of flesh, muscles and bone rained down on the lawn and street. Drew Markle's life had ended that fast. The time it took sound to travel is the distance between life and death. The bamboo sticks echoed somewhere beyond the parking lot below.

"Soup's ready," said Calvino.

"Twenty-four hours a day you hear that sound," said Jackie Ky.

The young children were sent out like African bush beaters to draw the game out into the open. "Yeah?" he asked, turning away from the balcony.

"After a while you hear them in your sleep. You dream of soup," she giggled. "You know that you aren't in America."

She picked up her pen and started to write again. He watched her, thinking about his friend, a Catholic cleric, Father Jim, who lived in the Klong Toey slums of Bangkok, talking about the sounds of night; one neighbor, an old woman, wanted to exact revenge on the neighborhood; she used parrots. These parrots created an overpowering dread. She had raised these two parrots for years. The parrots had grown old and cranky like their owner. They had acquired their sound track of parrot calls from the slaughterhouse. When the old woman was angry she left the cage uncovered, and the pair of old slaughterhouse birds cried out all night in the high-pitched screams of pigs being slaughtered. The parrots would shriek and follow this with a sharp intake of breath and finally, the gurgling noise of a throat being slit. On those nights, Father Jim never dreamed of pork chops. Instead, he dreamed of terror and pain, and the void that followed.

She handed him a name card. On the back she had written:

"Meet me at Giac Lam Pagoda tomorrow at 3.45 pm. I will be in the main sanctuary. Don't be late."

"You ever designed a bar before?" asked Calvino. "No, but like sex, there is always a first time."

"A bar takes skill not innocence."

"But a great bar draws the best of both."

She was a shrewd lady, he thought. Quick, bright, and too smooth not to understand that fine sensibilities and correct manners bought you nothing. It was like an American passport, it got you in the door but not into the right meeting.

§ § § §

MARCUS Nguyen's messenger, Tan, lay on his cart, a bowl of pho in front of his face, spooning in noodles when Calvino came up from behind. But he had a rear-view mirror on his cart and saw Calvino before Calvino had seen him.

"Pull up a chair. Take the weight off your feet," said Tan. "And then ignore me."

Calvino pulled back a wobbly chair and sat down at a table. He ordered a bowl of pho from the waiter.

"The owner says I am bad for business," chuckled Tan.

"So he gives me a bowl of pho every day and I promise to stay away."

"Business is business," said Calvino.

Marcus Nguyen, carrying his mobile phone and wearing sunglasses, appeared from a crowd and sat down at the table.

"Business is friends, connections, money," said Marcus, as if he had been following the conversation.

"That's the way I see it at street level," replied Tan, looking up at Marcus. "How does it look up there?"

"The American who got himself killed a week ago…" Calvino started to say to Tan.

His bowl of pho, with strange pieces of meat and green vegetables in watery noodles, arrived. The waiter gave him the soup and left.

"Markle," said Tan, slurping his noodles and inter-rupting Calvino.

Calvino was impressed. "Yeah, Drew Markle. What's the buzz on the street?"

Tan looked up at Marcus, as if to ask for permission. Marcus nodded.

Calvino leaned down and pushed a twenty-dollar bill under the bowl of pho Tan burped and kept on eating. "Someone didn't like him. You know how it is with lawyers. You either love or hate them."

"Who didn't like him?"

"Twenty bucks buys a lot but not that much."

Calvino found another wad of twenties in his coat pocket. He unfolded them and stuck one between his fingers and lowered them until they touched Tan's hand. Tan stuffed the crumpled bill under his belly. He picked up the bowl and drank the soup.

"Who didn't like him and who killed him could be different."

"The newspapers say he got killed in a dispute between security guards and beggars in a turf war near the river. And an ex-RVN sergeant threw the grenade," said Calvino. "The government says Markle just got in the way."

"Got in the way of whom?" asked Marcus. "Surely not some river beggars. These people know how to survive. They are clever. I spent time in a refugee camp with a lot of other boat people. Authorities came to the camp one day and offered to pay ten cents for every rat, dead or alive. It didn't take long for a half dozen RVN soldiers to figure out how to breed rats. Soon they were in business, raising rat colonies, cages hidden throughout the camp. It took months before the authorities found out that huge sums were being spent on the rat eradication program and every week there were more rats to pay for. So, when the government says an ex-RVN sergeant threw a grenade, I don't believe them. We know how to survive. Killing a foreigner is throwing yourself headfirst down the rat hole. Where's the profit in that?"

Tan shook his head, raising it as high as he could.

"The guys following you are talking into their walkie-talkie," said Tan, checking his rear-view mirror.

"How many of them?," Calvino asked.

"Two," said Marcus. "Another across the street."

Calvino was starting to understand why Marcus had used Tan to send a message the first time. And why he made a point of coming separately from Tan this time. Marcus had been right.

"Life on a skateboard puts your face in more shit than you would ever believe possible," said Tan.

Marcus peeled off some dong notes, put them on the table, rose and walked away. He didn't say goodbye. He didn't say anything, because once again, he had found a location which did all the speaking for him, saying "Marcus was here."

Calvino pushed the half-eaten bowl of noodles away. Here was a ruin of a man with a healthy first-class brain living at a rat's-eye level in Saigon. Bangkok had its share of street beggars and cripples hanging around hotels and on concrete pedestrian overpasses. But if you pooled all their brains, they would have fallen short of Tan whose broken body hugged the meat cart he called a skateboard.

"You don't think Markle's death was an accident?" asked Calvino, looking out at the traffic, like a man talking to himself.

"Like Marcus is always saying, the universe is the only accident. Everything else has a reason, a cause, a purpose. Meaning, Markle was capped by a pro. Someone brought down from Hanoi. That's all I know. See you around."

Calvino called for the bill and counted out some thousand dong notes. He pulled back his chair, as Tan rolled off, chasing after a couple of tourists wearing cameras over their "Lift the Embargo"T-shirts.The embargo had been lifted but the stock of T-shirts remained.The American law firms were among the first to hit the new beachhead. Drew Markle, the first new casualty in the ranks of the new American army. That was the way it was. Peace or war, people getting in the way of someone with power and discovering that, in the real world, power and influence were always backed by guns and bombs and the will to use them.

§ § § § §

MAI wore a Western-style jacket, a white blouse underneath and black slacks. She sat alone at a small table, reading an old, tattered Penguin edition of Chekhov Plays. A set of earphones were plugged into her ears and a Walkman lay on the table. As Calvino walked into the restaurant, he spotted her immediately. Sweat ran down his neck, the collar of his shirt was wet and stuck to his neck. He had finally lost his minders behind a huge stack of chicken thighs in the back stalls of Ben Thanh Market.

"I'm sorry that I'm late," he said.

She didn't hear him. With two fingers he slowly pushed down the book, and as she looked up and saw Calvino, she smiled, then pulled off her earphones.

"I love Chekhov's The Seagull," she said.

He was trying to remember the last time he had heard a woman say that on a first date after he had arrived forty minutes late. He sat down at the table and ordered a beer.

"This part, here, listen, 'What a wonderful world you live in! How I envy you—if only you knew! ... How different people's destinies are! Some just drag out their obscure, tedious existences, all very much like one another, and all unhappy. And there are others—like you for instance, one in a million—who are given an interesting life, a life that

111

is radiant and full of significance. You are fortunate.' "
She closed the book, her eyes half-closed, as if she were
remembering another time and place.

"In Hanoi, everyone learns to love literature from a very
young age," she said, as the waiter brought Calvino's beer.
"It becomes part of our lives."

"In Brooklyn, we learned to read comic books at an early
age," he said. "And we try to grow out of the habit, you
know, move on to TV."

"To miss Chekhov is a great tragedy."

"Tragedy we had," said Calvino. "And some comedy."

"Then America must be very much like Vietnam."

She reached for his can of 333 beer, refilled his glass,
and then gently set the can back precisely from where it
had been removed. There wasn't a wasted movement. He
had started to cool down in the air-conditioning. He was
thinking to himself as he looked at her across the table
that this extraordinary woman worked as a secretary in a
law office. She read Chekhov in her spare time. They had
only met briefly at the offices of Winchell & Holly, and
yet she agreed to meet him socially. Webb was willing to
bet money she would turn him down. What fragment of
memory had he stirred? What turn of mind caused her to
reach out to him?

"Douglas Webb was surprised you would go out for
lunch with me," he said.

"My social life is not any business of his," she said. There
was nothing hard or stern in her tone; just a matter-of-fact,
assured sense of her right to draw such a line.

He sipped the beer, feeling awkward for a moment.
What was the main story line of The Seagull? Why couldn't
Pratt have gone around quoting Chekhov rather than
Shakespeare? At least, he would have something clever
to say. She sat across the table, patiently waiting for him,

reading her Chekhov, and at the end, he sat like a lump, drinking cheap Vietnamese beer from a chipped glass. All he could think of was Father Jim's slaughterhouse bird stories. That the birds weren't seagulls but parrots was all he could come up with on the spot. Mai laughed, brushing back her hair, tilting her head back, exposing some emotion in her eyes that baffled Calvino.

"You're joking," she said.

He shook his head. "And then one neighbor decided he had had enough of the squeaking pigs. So he bought a bird, left it in a friend's motorcycle shop until it could make the sound of someone working the throttle of a two-stroke motorcycle. They would have these bird wars. The slaughterhouse bird against the motorcycle bird. About a week into the war, a neighbor who was a hitman murdered both birds. Wrung their necks. He slipped in real quietly and killed them. No sound. No evidence, but everyone knew he was the murderer."

Calvino could see how happy she was listening to every word. "I love the story very much. But I'm confused. Was this Bangkok or Brooklyn?"

There he was looking at the Caravaggio painting and not telling Douglas Webb that the painter had not died in a barroom brawl, only to forget who he was and where he was. Chekhov, beer and a beautiful Hanoi girl had had their impact on him.

"A guy on the plane told me the story."

"Still, it's a wonderful story," she said.

"When I open my club, I am going to buy a bird. I'll call him Chekhov. You can help me choose it. Not one bird but many beautiful birds. We will buy them cages. But there'll be only one Chekhov. We will keep it our secret. From today, the first time we had lunch."

"So far I haven't seen any food," she said.

They both laughed. She ordered without looking at

the menu. For a moment, Calvino was thinking, why not open a club? What was really holding him in Bangkok? The easy reasons like dirty air, the traffic jams, the swell of people fighting each other to make a dollar at any and every cost never moved him; but when the old gang had begun to disperse, then, that was different: some had gone upcountry, others back home, and others were dead. The sense of belonging had begun to chip away. People needed to belong. He lived alone in a Bangkok slum and, as far as he could see, he had no more chance of buying himself out of that hole than the noodle vendor on Sukhumvit Road had of becoming Prime Minister. Vietnam might be a fresh start and with a woman like Mai, what had started as a murder case, was slowly shifting into something else he couldn't quite name. Maybe it was a new way of belonging, the way he saw that Pratt and Manee belonged in the garden that night in Bangkok. Then the food came and they ate French bread, crab soup, a cheese omelette, mixed vegetables, and chicken. Whenever his plate started to run low she spooned more food onto it.

"When can I see you again?" he asked, looking at his watch.

"You have to go?"

"I have an appointment," he said, paying the bill. He pushed back the change on the small wooden tray and as the waiter left, he said, "Did you know Drew Markle very well?"

The question was out of the blue, as he counted out a stack of dong notes on the table.

"Why do you ask?"

"A young American guy. I just thought that you and him..."

"He was very nice. I am sorry he died. I don't know what else to say."

Calvino watched her eyes. There was a thing that

happened with most people's eyes when they lied. Lying was an unnatural activity—except for his brother-in-law in Brooklyn, who had fielded the call from Douglas Webb about the lotto winning, he lied much better than he told the truth. There was a slight movement, less than a twitch. Certain professionals in the security, intelligence and policing business learned to control this eye movement, they mastered the art of breaking down false material into small segments so that each bit was true but the overall piece of information was a lie. Mai was still looking at the world with her clear, straight, romantic Chekhov eyes, and there was no hint of a lie. She was either telling the truth or she had been well trained. Outside the restaurant, a cyclo driver stopped in front of them.

"You, where you go?" asked the driver.

Mai turned and said, "You must be very careful. Many of these drivers are mafia, and their cyclos are stolen. I think it would be better if you had a car or a motorbike."

"A motorcycle," said Calvino. "I like that idea."

Mai's new Honda Dream was parked outside. "You go in a cyclo. I will meet you there," she said. She arranged his fare and told the driver the location, then disappeared on her motorcycle.

She was waiting for him at the rental stand opposite the Rex Hotel when his cyclo driver pulled up to the curb. It would be easier to shake his minders who had been following him if he had a motorcycle, he thought. They went up to the rental stand and a rat the size of a cat ran over Calvino's foot. He thought of Marcus's story about the refugee camps and how they had raised rats for ten cents a head. That rat had to be worth about a dollar, he thought.

"I'm sorry I couldn't take you on my motorbike," she said.

"A Hanoi girl cannot," he said.

She smiled. "You know a lot for someone from Brooklyn."

"I know that Saigon and Paris both have a Notre Dame Cathedral," he said. He had passed the Cathedral which was like an island fortress squeezed between Chau Van Liem Boulevard and Phung Hung Street.

"Not everything you know is in a guidebook," she said.

They walked along a row of rental motorcycles, Mai leaning down to check the tires, working the brakes, starting the engine of a couple.

"I think this one is okay," she said, turning to the Vietnamese man with a pointy black beard at the end of his chin. They had a brief discussion, then she turned to Calvino.

"Five dollars a day."

Calvino stuffed fifty dollars cash in an old man's pocket, took the keys out of his hands and walked over to an old green Honda 50cc selected by Mai. The bike looked like it had been in some Japanese museum a hundred years. But it worked. It was transportation and was slow enough to make it a challenge to lose those who were following him. Because Mai had been along he hadn't exchanged a word with the old man who just looked at the cash, then he walked away and stood near Mai.

"Tonight for dinner?" he asked her.

"I cannot," she said, straddling her Honda Dream and starting the engine.

"Because you are a Hanoi girl."

She laughed.

"Because I have plans. Tomorrow for dinner, yes. But you haven't asked me."

She pulled into the street.

"Dinner, tomorrow, then," he shouted after her.

She looked around, waved, and was swallowed up in traffic. And she never asked why I was late, he thought.

§ § § §

HE immediately regretted having made an appoint-ment to meet Jackie Ky. All day he had been running late and his appointment with Jackie was no exception. Being on the back of his rental Honda motorbike reminded him of the time he had been in Phnom Penh, on the back of a Honda 50cc with a bar girl named Thu. It had been after midnight, there had been gunfire from a checkpoint, the driver had made a wrong turn, and twenty minutes later the driver was dead in the mud and someone had tried to kill them. An UNTAC patrol showed up in time. Saigon was thick with bicycles, motorcycles and vehicles made from spare parts and boat engines held together with bailing wire.

A thousand years in the future they would refer to Southeast Asia of the 90s as the Honda 50cc era, he thought. The era when the peasants hit the streets on cheap second-hand motorcycles imported from Japan. The Honda 50cc would become the metaphor for the state of mental, social, and political development only a small engine away from our ancestors swinging through the jungle canopy.

Every street swarmed with peasants, workers, office girls—hundreds of people riding in twos, threes, some-times fours, on motorcycles and each intersection was a chaotic dance, street lights counting for nothing, as everyone looked for a small opening to escape. Five minutes later, he had seen two accidents and blood. A pedestrian hit by a jeep and a girl on a bicycle mowed down by a speeding biker. Blood in the streets. Calvino got the hang of the method, just drive, forget stop signs, lights, pretend you are in a dream, and nothing can harm you. He drove in the direction of Cholon—Chinatown. The pagoda was a few kilometers beyond Cholon.

Jackie Ky had chosen a Buddhist pagoda which had been

around two hundred and fifty years. Giac Lam Pagoda had been around since 1744; before there had been a United States of America. He managed to get lost. He asked one, then another person where the pagoda was. Everyone shrugged and shuffled away. He asked three cyclo drivers, figuring he was far enough away from home base that they were probably exactly what they appeared to be: cyclo drivers and not security people pretending to be cyclo drivers. He guessed that he was right. The drivers knew nothing. If the communists had done anything, they had re- educated the cyclo drivers of Saigon to forget the location of what was probably the most famous pagoda in Saigon.

By the time he entered the grounds of Giac Lam Pagoda, he was running an hour late and by the time he arrived at the pagoda, had taken off his shoes, and walked into the dark interior, passing rows and rows of dusty framed photographs of men, women and children, he could hear the bronze gongs and chanting from the main sanctuary. The smell of incense stung his nose and eyes. Thick clouds of it hung in the corridor. Jackie Ky spotted him and, half-crouched, came up to him as he entered the sanctuary. She held several sticks of burning incense. By being late, he had interrupted her prayer time, he thought. She had wanted to avoid that, but what was done was done. She walked over through the reception hall and stopped, looking up at the funeral tablets. Calvino walked over and stood beside her. She was looking at a photograph half-hidden in the back row. It was Drew Markle.

"You're late," she said. "Drew was never late. He was very exact. If he said 7.30 pm, you better believe that he would be there no matter what."

"Being precise you can sometimes get yourself killed,"

said Calvino.

"Meaning?"

"It's easier to kill someone who is predictable."

"Drew liked this pagoda," she said, changing the subject.

"Any reason why you wanted to meet here?" he asked.

"Harry liked this place. He came here to collect Drew's body. It was a special place for Drew and then for Harry. I thought it would be a good place to talk about them. I would feel more comfortable since I really don't know you," she said.

"You were comfortable to come to my room last night," he said.

"I wanted you to know that you were in danger."

"And the pagoda is safe?"

"No, but it's not bugged."

She had the incense sticks pressed between her cupped fingers, the tips of her thumbs touching her nose, her eyes closed, her lips moving. She stayed like that for what seemed like a long time.

Then she said, "We loved each other. Drew was a decent man. He didn't deserve to die."

Calvino looked at the photograph which had Drew's name, date of birth and death. He was smiling into the camera when the shot was snapped. Like someone behind the shutter had squinted with one eye and looked through the lens with the other, and said, "Drew, say cheese."

"The night Drew was killed he was coming to see me. We were going to have dinner. I arrived early because I wanted to watch the light on the river before the sun set. It's a nice time to watch the boats, the people, the light, the water. I heard the explosion from inside the restaurant. He was close enough to have seen me sitting at the table," she said. Tears were rolling down her cheeks and she started to sob.

"I want to think he saw me that one last time, you know, before..."

Watching her performance, listening to the words, he could understand how she had inspired trust in Harry Markle. And Harry was someone who had lived in Southeast Asia long enough to know the danger of trusting anyone other than yourself, and then to look at yourself real hard in the mirror before telling yourself a secret.

"Harry said something about Drew having an ethical problem at work. You know what that might have been about?" asked Calvino, after she had dried her tears.

"As I told Harry, I don't know for sure. Drew tried not to bring his problems home. Just for us to be together was a problem. You don't know how it is here. The authorities see you with a foreigner and they call you a whore. They don't want any Vietnamese women to even look at a foreigner. But, if you love someone enough then you don't let it get to you."

"Did you get to know the people he worked with?"

"A little. You know, at a dinner, or I would come and meet him at the office and we would go to lunch."

"So you know Douglas Webb."

"He's a shit," she said. "Forgive me, Lord Buddha. But he is."

"Khanh?"

"A politician who wants to be a lawyer. Like most people from Hanoi, he's very small minded about foreigners. Not to mention how he feels about Viet Khieu."

"Which is?"

"Let's say that he always glared at me any time Drew would take my hand. And he would say things in Vietnamese like, 'Hanoi girl would never let a foreigner do that in public. Saigon girl, Viet Khieu, okay, they are different.' Meaning,

Christopher G. Moore

we are whores."

"Jackie, I want you to try and remember," said Calvino.

"It is real important. Did Drew ever say anything about a Hong Kong client named Mark Wang? What did Mark Wang want from the firm?"

The sound of chanting monks in the sanctuary filled the silent space between them. She turned and was looking at Drew Markle's photograph.

"I can't remember," she said.

"You tell me how much you loved this guy. If you can't remember, no one will ever solve his murder," said Calvino, in a loud whisper.

She waited until two visitors walked past and into the sanctuary.

"Okay, I do remember something Drew said. About how the Chinese avoided banks. One guy had deposited huge amounts at the law office. He thought this was not something a law firm should be doing. That's it. He didn't say anything else. It didn't seem important. There are millions of dollars of gold in the shophouses in Cholon. It's normal here. People keep money out of the banks. I don't see what it has to do with Drew dying."

Now she was crying again.

They walked out of the pagoda and sat down together on a bench under a large bohdi tree. Some Vietnamese were eating, others squatting down, watching.

"Last night at the Q-Bar, you were spoiling for a fight with Webb. Why?"

"That crack about being toc dai as if I threw the bomb at Drew. And because he showed disrespect. He came late to Drew's funeral and left early."

"Webb and Drew did not get along at the office, am I right?"

"I think Webb was jealous of Drew," she said.

"Why?"

"He had made a play for me before Drew came to Saigon. I wasn't interested. Even after Drew and I were together, he would try and hit on me. He got tickets for one of those Vietnamese-Thai concerts and gave two to Drew. He showed up with this hooker from Bangkok named Darla."

"Darla's not a Thai name," said Calvino.

"She's an ex-nurse from Seattle. Webb flies her in for a screw once or twice a month. Otherwise he would never get laid."

"When was she here last?"

"I told you, at the concert."

"How long was that before Drew..."

"Was killed? I can't remember. I think about four or five days."

"And there were Thai singers?"

"The usual rock 'n roll stuff. No one famous enough to remember. At least, I can't remember their names."

Calvino got up from the bench, looked up at the roof of the pagoda which was covered with porcelain plates. In Bangkok, the Temple of Dawn was decorated with millions of broken pieces of porcelain. He had taken his daughter Melody to that place once and they released balloons one at a time, and he told her how this was a Buddhist lesson in letting go. Some people could let go easier than others. Some never released their grip on something they wanted and Douglas Webb seemed to be that kind of guy.

As he turned to leave, Calvino felt the hard pull of his conscience and arrived at a decision.

He whispered, "I am here to find who killed him."

She nodded. "I don't think..." She stopped in mid-thought.

"Think what?"

"Drew ever knew how dangerous it was here."

"I think you're one hundred percent right."

They walked out into the courtyard to where he had parked his motorcycle, and he turned to Jackie Ky, as he inserted the key.

"You know anything about a fund? An investment thing?"

"You mean the Vietnam Emerging Market Fund?"

"Yeah, that's it."

"Drew was assigned to work on the Fund. I am even investing some money in it. The timing is right. With all the business activity happening here, how can I possibly lose?"

As Calvino rode away, he thought about Father Jim's story, about the slaughterhouse birds kept in cages in Klong Toey. They had heard the sound of losing so long that they could mimic the final shriek of a death rattle with blood curdling accuracy. He had started to wonder if Drew Markle had repeated something he should not have heard. He might have been a slaughterhouse bird who made the right sound in the wrong place and found himself on the wrong end of a grenade. Jackie Ky was putting money in the Fund. Drew Markle had been assigned to do legal work connected with the Fund. Some connections were sexual, others were financial, and yet others, perhaps the majority, were a mixed connection of money and pleasure. He picked up speed, getting the feel of the machine. If there was anyone following him, they would have their work cut out. He was riding a crest, a wave in his mind, he could almost see the beach where it would crash.

Halfway back, he passed a second-hand bookstore on the ground floor of a shophouse. He doubled back, parked the Honda and spent nearly an hour going through shelves and boxes of old books. A flotsam of stories, ideas, hopes, and dreams abandoned in Saigon, yellowing, curling and falling apart in the tropics, as if being reclaimed by the heat and humidity. Soon they would be pulp. He twisted around a stack of magazines, then found what he was looking for in the bottom of a box and paid without bargaining for a copy of Chekhov's collected plays. The Russians had been in Vietnam for years. Chekhov had been one of the few good things left behind. He stuffed the book inside his shirt and entered the traffic again, Chekhov riding high against his belly. His spirits sailed like someone who had found a neglected masterpiece overlooked by the shop owner. Chekhov had a new dimension: He offered to show Calvino an emotional course with a woman who had nothing to do with the Zone. Someone who didn't know that the Zone existed. He was riding high and he was happy to be in Saigon.

CHAPTER 7

BACK STAGE

PRATT HAD CIRCLED around the old Opera House a number of times and each time there was something disturbing him about the structure. The one hundred years of French rule in Vietnam left its mark in the buildings and boulevards of Saigon. Dropping an opera hall onto an island like setting a perfect pearl into a gold necklace was something only the French would have thought to do in the tropics. While the French had come and gone, the buildings and streets remained. The *farang* had not marked Bangkok in this way. He wondered, how does a country take pride in the sense of beauty that other people impose on them? What is to be done with the legacy after the *farang* have left? Tear it down? That would violate the unspoken rule that one destroyed only that which was no longer practical. The old Opera House could be made practical, so it survived; the classical scalloped front entrance looked faded, worn, like a once beautiful woman after years of an abusive relationship.

On the corner of Dong Khoi Street and Le Loi Boulevard stood another French building directly opposite the old Opera House. On the ground floor was the Givral Patisserie & Cafe. The entire building was the mixed symbol of old Saigon and modern Ho Chi Minh City—a three-story J&B bottle designed as a bright green neon sign stuck onto the side of classical French architecture. The J&B bottle cap half obscured the window to the room where Marcus Nguyen kept a mistress, a vantage point that provided him with a Lee Harvey Oswald view of the old Opera House. He stood in the window with a pair of binoculars, watching Pratt stopping before the steps of the Opera House. What thoughts would be inside the mind of this Thai policeman? Marcus thought. What eyes was he using to look at the street? To turn the old Opera House into a shopping mall, or club? Thai police had a knack for business. Harry had told him that this Pratt had an appreciation for the arts, in particular, for Shakespeare. Perhaps the Thai policeman viewed the old building as a piece of history which had survived all kinds of dramas—tragedy and comedy.

Before the fall of Saigon, the government had used the Opera House as the National Assembly. Then the government not only fell, many of the politicians had fled before April 30th, 1975, leaving the communists to turn the main hall, where the National Assembly had met, into a people's theater. In the rear of the building, there was a small hotel. Next door was the Q-Bar. On the Continental Hotel side was another bar. People's Theater, People's Hotel, and a New York City bar with Caravaggio murals on the wall. Change was in the Saigon air the twentieth year of the liberation of the city.

Pratt, as he walked alone, had wondered if some communist committee, filled with people who had spent half their life fighting the jungles, had been given the job of making practical use of the old Opera House without compromising the principles of the new regime. Who had served on the committee? A collection of fighting men, ex-soldiers and cadres whose reward for winning was a chance to take revenge on the building where the old regime had resided. This might have explained why a number of rooms had no windows. The architecture of war predominated and the Saigon Concert Hotel—its name evidence of the schizophrenic character of the city—was like a blueprint of underground tunnels and chambers. Calvino had come up with the idea that Pratt should move into a room within the vast complex of the old Opera House. He would have music, he would have privacy, and more importantly, there was a place they could meet in secrecy. Calvino had discovered that the cheapest room in the hotel was also the largest. There were special rooms located at opposite ends of the fifth floor, each with a private staircase and landing; the giant space which was left over had been converted into three rooms.

"Why so cheap?" Calvino had asked the assistant manager behind the front counter. After he asked the question, he knew that he had automatically lapsed into expat-speak. He had made a literal translation into English from the Thai *tum my took?*

The assistant manager flashed an official smile, as if she had been asked that question many times by *farang* new to Saigon. The smile a mother bestows on a child who asks why there is a sky, why are there clouds, what happens when I die?

"Some people think too much noise. But if you like music, then you should take. I think room very cheap for Saigon," she said thoughtfully.

The rough corridor between cheap and expensive had squeezed out just about anything in the middle. Calvino nodded that the room would do fine for the right person after an inspection. It was perfect, in fact, for the purpose he had in mind. On the left of the small entrance leading to the fifth floor room was a door, one of those Alice in Wonderland, tiny doors. All that was missing was the rabbit. Calvino played the role of Alice as well as was to be expected, he hunched down beside the door and discovered that a piece of copper wire had been used to fasten the door. One end of the wire disappeared inside the room. He needed less than a minute to pick the lock and open the door. Inside was a narrow walkway about forty meters above the main stage and large backstage area. On the scaffolding it was dark and below some musicians were practicing. From the look of the wooden walkway no one had been up there in years. No guest was going to complain and the performers and musicians below could not have cared less. It may have been one of the few unbugged areas in the entire building.

Pratt checked into the room sight unseen; he had based his move solely on Calvino's recommendation. He stood in the doorway and looked around a reception room. On one wall was an eight foot by fifteen foot painting of Mount Fuji capped with snow. He looked over his shoulder at the bellboy.

"Beautiful," said the bellboy in a soiled shirt with a Mao collar, grinning at the painting.

"Splendid," said Pratt, thinking the decor was the ultimate revenge on the French sensibility, on the old regime, on everything an educated, cultured *farang* would have held in high esteem.

The final destruction of the Western sense of artistic beauty, the desecration of the high temple left by French culture. In the bellboy's eyes, he was gazing upon a masterpiece. This bellboy spoke the language of the modern Saigon, a place which had sealed its fate twenty years earlier when the tanks rolled into Saigon and the National Assembly was no more. Only the building was left behind once again, like it had been left by the French, as it had been left after the Americans had gone.

§ § § § §

AROUND two in the morning, Pratt slipped out of his room, quickly entered the small side door, edged his way along the scaffolding toward a figure in the shadows. Calvino squatted in the dark like an Isan laborer, staring into the dark and drinking a 333 beer. Pratt pointed his flashlight and Calvino lifted his beer as a kind of salute.

"It's not exactly front row at the Met," said Calvino.

"But then Saigon isn't exactly New York City," said Pratt.

"New York is five floors down in the Q-Bar," he said.

Pratt looked around the vast space below, the empty stage, curtains and rows of seats.

"It would be difficult to bug this area. Not impossible. But what would be the point?"

"Exactly. No point. So how's your new room?"

He had worked out the math in his head. The cost of two glasses of the 1987 La Tour Sauterne at the Rex was roughly two nights in the Mount Fuji room on the fifth floor. When it came to the division between investors, there were those who drank the cost of a hotel room before dinner, and there were those who drank 333 beer and dreamed of one day affording the corkage charge on an expensive bottle of wine.

"From the art on the wall, I have the strong feeling that management made a decision to appeal to the Japanese investor," said Pratt.

"I doubt there are any Japanese in this hotel. Too down-scale for them."

"That also crossed my mind," said Pratt. "But there's always hope."

"How did your meeting go with Khanh?"

"Another boc phet session that ran an hour. He spent half an hour complaining about wasting days and days with State Department officials and American Consulate officials from Hanoi. They came alone or in twos. They asked the same questions about Drew Markle. They asked him if he had ever had an argument with Markle. This upset him. Who did these Americans think they were? Did they know where they were? State Department people in Saigon treating him like a criminal suspect."

"Sounds like he let his hair down."

"He said that the *farang* didn't understand the Asian mind. It wasn't useful to kill an American lawyer. It wasn't useful to kill any American. They were trying to open up their economy, their country. They wanted American technology. Killing an American was the last thing any Vietnamese would do. Why were the American State Department people so stupid? he asked me."

"Khanh has a point, Pratt."

"In police work you find most criminals have a point."

"You think he's covering up something?"

"What do you think?" asked Pratt.

"The word on the street is that Markle was capped by a Vietnamese. Someone brought down from Hanoi for the job. But I don't know what to make of the theory. The Vietnamese way of thinking, loyalties, fears, are divided between North and South. It's hard to know the direction on the compass to find the truth. Of course, whoever did the job must have followed Markle. Tracked him. That takes some skill. Of course, the fact that Markle was never late made the killer 's job easier. But someone had to give the hitman the information. That Markle was going to the restaurant that night and give him the time."

"Any idea who that might have been?"

"He was meeting someone special for dinner that night."

"A woman," said Pratt.

Calvino nodded, finished his beer and put the can down on the scaffolding.

"A Viet Khieu named Jackie Ky."

"*Kee?*" asked Pratt.

The English word translated into Thai, depending on the tone, as either "shit" or "ride". Pratt waited until Calvino repeated Jackie's last name in a neutral tone, playing the name over in his mind. How would his superiors in the Department in Bangkok react if the killer they had to turn over to Mark Wang's family had such a name? The Hong Kong Chinese would think that the Thais were playing a joke on them. So much rested on family names in Asia, so much more than any *farang* ever knew.

"Yeah, Ky," he said again. "She's as American as they come, and a babe, Pratt."

"What was her relationship with Markle?"

"Close enough. She made a point of letting me see her go through the usual rituals. The lit incense sticks she put in front of his picture at a wat. She shed the right amount of tears. All the time I am looking at this framed photo of Markle in the second row of a hundred photos of other dead people."

"Sounds impressive."

"It was intended to be."

"So she was putting on a good act?" asked Pratt.

Calvino wavered, balancing all he knew about Jackie Ky, which wasn't a great deal, and each time he came down on a different side.

"She's pretty broken up over Markle's murder," he said.

"I don't think it's an act."

He had been on this side of the Jackie Ky equation before. Pratt waited a beat, taking in Calvino's observation.

"Did you ask her about Mark Wang?"

Calvino nodded, pulled another beer from a brown bag, popped the tab, and drank from the beer can.

"She said that she met him once. But she didn't remember Wang's name until I reminded her."

"Maybe he was using another name," said Pratt.

"I thought of that. So I asked her if Markle had mentioned anything about Chinese yuppies from Hong Kong. And she said, yes. There had been a Chinese guy who hated banks and wanted Douglas Webb to hold a lot of cash for him. She said Drew was against taking cash into the office. She said Markle told her that lawyers didn't do that sort of thing. He thought it was unethical for a law firm to keep cash like a Chinese laundry."

"She said Chinese laundry?"

Calvino smiled. "I added that."

"Cute."

"Markle also worried about violating Vietnamese currency regulations."

"How much cash are we talking about?"

"Don't know. But I think we can assume it was enough to get two men killed," replied Calvino.

"Someone in the law firm overruled Markle and told Wang they would keep his money."

"Khanh seems hungry," said Calvino.

Pratt knew that in Vietnam, like in Thailand, there was a vast difference between those with hunger in their belly and the few with the opportunity to fill their rice bowl.

They had worked together for so many years, Calvino could see what was bothering Pratt about this suspect, and he said, "Khanh wouldn't have the connection to get someone like Wang killed in Bangkok. If Wang had been killed in Saigon, I could go with it."

"Then that leaves Webb," said Pratt.

"Webb told me he had been in Bangkok for five years," said Calvino." He speaks Vietnamese. And Thai. And Japanese. That's a good enough reason to hate the bastard. Americans aren't supposed to speak anything but English."

"Five years," said Pratt. "That's more than enough to make the kind of local connection to get someone killed."

"Jackie said they had gone to a Thai-Vietnamese friendship concert a week before Markle was killed. She said that Markle and her went along with Webb and some bimbo who was from Bangkok."

Pratt rolled his eyes, expecting the worst. Calvino let it hang for a moment.

"The bimbo was a *mem-farang*," said Calvino. "Who lives in Bangkok."

Calvino nodded, "So Jackie Ky says."

"I'm thinking out loud now..."

"You're on stage. That's permitted."

"Thanks. But what I was going to say is, sometimes Channel 9 or 7 sends a crew to record a concert. Then they show it on TV. My kids watch them. And sometimes the camera scans the crowd."

"Maybe you should check it out."

"You have a safe phone yet?"

"One hundred percent."

"Nothing is one hundred percent."

"It's a figure of speech." Pratt hunched forward and looked down at the stage below. "If I were at home, I could deal with Webb."

"The distance been Bangkok and Saigon is a short flight given they seem to be a million light years apart," said Calvino.

"I know. We have no back-up in Saigon. It's just you and me. And I have been thinking it's not such a good idea for you to pal around with Webb. Forget about giving him the cash you brought in."

"That's why I brought the cash, remember. You were the guy who said, 'We might need some spending money to get someone out of trouble,' " said Calvino.

"The idea was to bait a trap not feed a rat. That's different. You don't corner a dog and expect him not to come at your throat."

"You're mixing your metaphors. Rats and dogs."

But Pratt was right, thought Calvino. If Webb were a cornered dog he would come out all claws and fangs. What had Webb been doing in Bangkok? He claimed he spent five years working in-house for a large Japanese bank. Maybe. Before that, he had been an associate at Winchell & Holly in New York City. He had gone to the minor leagues, showed that he could hit the ball, and they called him back to the majors. Not an ordinary career path but then Winchell & Holly wasn't exactly an ordinary law firm. The lawyers shared a common specialized tax background. This was a perfect fit for a tax law firm boutique, handling offshore business for extremely wealthy people. Maybe after he signed on in Saigon, Webb was treated like a minor leaguer. By then, Webb would have gotten his nose into some of that wealthy lifestyle and decided he was tired of waiting for real respect out of New York.

Calvino turned around in the half-darkness of the scaffolding and nodded his head. The conversation went into one of those dead-stick dives, neither pilot wanting to try and pull up before the other one. Calvino crumpled up the empty 333 beer can, and looked at it in the palm of his hand. He thought about the little helicopters street vendors had made from the empty beer cans and smiled. And he thought about Marcus's sidewalk buddy, Tan, who had a body like the crumpled beer can flattened out on his skateboard, sailing at rat-shit level through the streets of Saigon, his life bounded by no more than half a kilometer of mean, dirty sidewalks and gutters. Most of all, he thought about the anguish Harry Markle had felt that night when he was told that his kid brother had been killed in Vietnam.

"I am going to make Webb work for it a little bit more. It's no good making it look like I am in a hurry to give him the cash. He would get suspicious. All the government types hanging out in the office. If the guy's dirty, he has to be at max level paranoia right now."

"I asked Khanh about the expat lawyer."

"What did he say?"

"He didn't feel dong chi with Webb."

"Meaning Webb wasn't exactly like a brother or comrade."

"It's hard to think of Webb as a fellow comrade."

"Khanh didn't like the way the *farang* looked at the Hanoi girl who works in the office. Like he was undressing her in his mind."

Calvino accidentally knocked one of the empty 333 cans off the scaffolding and it bounced off the stage. He tried to grab for it and almost fell himself.

"Be careful, Vincent."

He had asked Mai about Drew Markle. It wasn't as if he had overlooked the possibility and she said, well, she implied, in so many words, that there had been nothing outside the working relationship. Why would Khanh have made the crack about Markle undressing her with his eyes?

"What's wrong?" asked Pratt.

Calvino turned in the darkness. "Nothing."

"Every time you say nothing, it's something. What is it?" asked Pratt.

There was pause.

"What did you feel the first time you saw Manee?"

The question caught Pratt by surprise.

"For me, it was love at first sight. But she didn't like me."

"At Winchell & Holly there is a Vietnamese woman. Webb calls her the Hanoi girl. Her name's Mai."

Then he stopped.

"What's this got to do with Manee and me?" Pratt held his breath. He didn't want to hear. "I am in love with this woman."

"You know how crazy that is?"

"Yeah, I know," said Calvino. "She reads Chekhov. Do you know Chekhov?"

"I only remember one piece from The Cherry Orchard."

Calvino raised an eyebrow and he grinned.

"Aren't you gonna tell me?"

"This is no good, Vincent."

"Pratt, I want to know the line."

Pratt saw there was no way, now that he had brought up this piece of knowledge, that Calvino was going to let him off the hook.

"Okay. In The Cherry Orchard there is a failed writer named Yepihodov, who said, 'Personally, I'm a cultured sort of fellow, I read all sorts of extraordinary books, you know, but somehow I can't seem to make out where I'm going, what it is I really want, I mean to say—to live or to shoot myself, so to speak. All the same, I always carry a revolver on me. Here it is.'"

While he had been inside the Q-Bar with Webb, he had had to hide his knowledge of Caravaggio, and that made him feel humble playing the idiot. Only it was worse with Pratt, he hadn't remembered a single line from Chekhov, and here was a Thai, delivering a line that hit belly high, one of those emotionally guided missiles with a tiny camera in the nose straight on target. Life should have been structured fair enough so that the Chekhov offset the Caravaggio, but somehow there was a gaping void, he thought. His feet hanging over the edge of the scaffolding. He had felt superior knowing more than Webb. How was it that both Mai, a Vietnamese, and Pratt, a Thai, with their knowledge about a Russian writer, had made him feel like a high school dropout? He did what he could do to salvage some pride.

"That sounds like something I might have said," said Calvino. "You're right, Vincent. It does. That's why I have never forgotten it. And whoever killed Wang and Markle may try and kill you, Vincent. Don't forget, at the end, Yepihodov shoots himself."

"Russians have no sense of humor, Pratt. You know that. And there is one other difference. I know who I am and what I am capable of doing."

"I don't think you understand what I said before. In Saigon..." Calvino waved his hand. "We are alone. You and me, Douglas Webb and sixty million plus communists."

"Something like that."

"You know that in New York they pulled my ticket to practice law for fraud and violation of ethics," said Calvino.

"That was a set-up."

"There is something in the way this Webb looks at me that reminds me of that time. I was thinking it through earlier. Webb would have been working at Winchell & Holly when I was still practicing in New York. There's something about the guy that's familiar."

Pratt turned the flashlight on his watch. It was time for some sleep.

"Same time, same place, tomorrow," said Pratt.

"I wouldn't miss the second act for the world," said Calvino, looking at Pratt and then down at the stage.

As Pratt got up and started to walk away, Calvino called after him, "I forgot to mention Marcus Nguyen, ex-Marine Colonel. Tough guy. Mobile phone. Chauffeured car and claims to know everyone in the Party. He's a friend of Harry's who told me to look him up."

"Has he given you any help?"

"Too early to tell. But he might before it's over."

"About the Hanoi girl," said Pratt.

"Her name's Mai."

"What if she's..."

"She's not. I know it," Calvino said, feeling a cold chill go up his spine and shatter into icicles behind the sockets of his eyes. God, he hoped that he was right. After Pratt left him alone in the darkness, he remembered the dream in Bangkok, the one with Drew Markle holding Marcus Nguyen's severed head. The eyes half-closed in death. Was this a sign of what happened when you got too close to someone you should doubt? He hoped not.

§ § § § §

UNTIL you have tried it yourself, it is difficult to believe that two hundred thousand dollars, broken down into one-hundred bills, fits perfectly into two Johnny Walker Black Label boxes. The Johnny Walker box appears to have been unintentionally tailored to house exactly one thousand bills. The genius of the design, the genius of the practicality of making a box for either a thirty dollar bottle of whisky or a hundred grand in cash. One thousand individual bills a box. Calvino had bought two Johnny Walker bottles in their boxes at Don Muang Airport and carried the boxes into Vietnam inside a plastic duty-free bag. He had stuffed the bills into the boxes in a toilet cubicle and left the bottles behind. Someone who had gone to take a shit got a two bottle bonus. Bangkok's Don Muang Airport rarely gave such a deal. But someone was a lucky customer, thought Calvino, as he walked down the long corridor to his plane, carrying the plastic bags with Tourist Authority of Thailand printed in big letters on the side.

Calvino got out of the metered taxi in front of Winchell & Holly's villa off Nam Ky Khoi Nghia Street in District One. He paid the driver in dollars. As he approached the front gate, two soldiers dressed in olive green uniforms, carrying AK47s, stopped him.

"What's the problem? Post-Liberation paranoia?" asked Calvino.

The soldiers said nothing, tightening their grip on the AK47s. He had violated one of Calvino's cardinal rules for long-term survival—never, ever challenge an armed soldier who gives an order unless you are carrying two hundred grand and are at the door of the branch of a powerful American law firm.

The taller one with a square jaw waved Calvino over to a table and gestured with the barrel of the rifle at the plastic bag. Calvino opened the bag, the guard looked in, and without any change of expression, waved Calvino through. He was about to open one of the Johnny Walker Black Label boxes when Mai came out the door.

She spoke to the soldiers in rapid-fire Vietnamese. The soldier inspecting his bag handed it back to Calvino. Still he had no smile, no offer of apology, just tiger eyes, watching him as he followed Mai inside the main entrance of the villa. Calvino's law: men with war weapons never apologized for stopping and searching a foreigner.

"What did you tell them?"

"That I knew who you were. That you were an important foreigner."

"And they believed you."

"Of course." She turned and smiled, brushing her hand against his.

His Hanoi girl had vouched for him, turning a red light into a green light. Winchell & Holly was wired to provide an express lane with only green lights for their clients; that was their reputation, how they made their money. Smooth passage in troubled waters. Even power brokers needed military protection. Sometimes.

"How long were you waiting at the door?" "I saw you come in the gate."

She had wanted him to taste the power and fear, he thought.

"Who are the boy scouts? Khanh's private army?"

She laughed. "No, it's not like that. We have always had a guard. It's normal. And since Mr. Markle died, we thought more protection would be good. Since we don't know why it happened, Mr. Khanh wanted to protect the office and, of course, our clients. Like you."

The set-up looked like an idea Khanh would come up with. He wondered if Webb had to restrain Khanh not to park a couple of APCs, flying the red flag, outside the front gate. He followed Mai into the elevator. One of those old-fashioned caged lifts from black and white French movies, the kind with an accordion metal gate pulled closed with a handle. The lift had a fine mesh on the sides and ceiling, exposing the thick wires and cables moving slowly as the lift started to move. Mai stood next to the control lever, pressing it forward. She glanced back at Calvino, giving him a crooked grin.

"Did you say something?" she asked.

He raised an eyebrow as the lift shuddered. Yeah, he was about to say something and she had sensed it before he had opened his mouth and this made him nervous. He had never given a speech in an elevator before. Nor did it help that Mai's ao dai tightly clung to her body, showing each contour, and smelling of perfume.

He had found the speech in his second-hand copy of the Chekhov, the one that Pratt had committed to heart. After an hour, he had memorized it. As the elevator started up, he started, " '*Personally, I'm a cultured sort of fellow, I read all sorts of extraordinary books, you know, but somehow I can't seem to make out where I'm going, what it is I really want, I mean to say—to live or to shoot myself, so to speak. All the same, I always carry a revolver on me.' *"

Mai's eyes beamed, she folded her hand around his. "Chekhov. I so love Chekhov."

"I know." His throat constricted, his knees weak. He felt like he was under an attack of teenage hormones, an overwhelming assault on the mind and body. The way she squeezed his hand, and then what seemed like a miracle happened—though he later found out this was almost a daily occurrence in District One—there was a power failure and the elevator came to a halt between floors. They were close enough to each other that their bodies touched in the total darkness. Calvino took a lighter from his pocket and flicked it, the flame illuminating her face, as he leaned down and kissed her on the lips for the first time.

"We are between floors," she said.

"How long until the power comes back?" he whispered.

"One minute, one hour. It's never the same."

"*Toi muon co*," he said in broken Vietnamese. "I want you."

She laughed and corrected his pronunciation. He repeated after her.

"You say that well," she said.

"It took longer to learn than the Chekhov."

"When did you learn that?"

"Last night."

"And the Chekhov?"

"Last night was a busy night."

"What time did you go to sleep?"

"Four or so."

"I remember looking at the clock at four am. And thinking of you. I'm glad you learned the Chekhov. And the Vietnamese."

"And I'm glad the power cuts off in Saigon."

He extinguished the lighter flame. There was a long pause. Neither could see the other. Out of the darkness, or maybe because of the darkness, he felt her hand touch his face, her fingers trace the groove of a scar which ran three inches from his eyebrow to his forehead. It was an unexpected exploration, an assertiveness that caught him off balance. He was in the Winchell & Holly building on business. All this talk about being a Hanoi girl as if to telegraph that she was beyond any sexual expression.

"How did you get this?" she whispered.

"Someone tried to kill me a long time ago," he said. "It reminds me of someone."

"A boyfriend?"

"No, not a boyfriend. What happened to the person who hurt you?"

"Things came to an inky end."

He heard her laughing gently in the dark.

He left out the detail that he had been working a case in Bangkok when he was jumped by a katoey, a lady-boy, who had been positioned upstairs in a Patpong bar, waiting to stick a knife in him. The katoey ended up with a Reynold's fine ballpoint pen plunged so deep into his eye only an inch of the tip was exposed.

They kissed first with just a brush of the lips. Then with lips parted, and, after that, their mouths opened as if to swallow the other. As they kissed she quietly stepped out of her ao dai pants. Her arms around his neck, he leaned her back against the railing. Her breathing became more irregular, her face against his; as her tongue touched his, she sighed. She pulled her face back for a moment. It was too dark for her to see him. There was some why question in her mind, a fight to ask overcome as her mouth found his again. Her breathing was the only sound as he entered her. Her long fingernails were under his shirt, running up his back. Her legs wrapped around his waist, her back against the side of the elevator, with two hundred grand in fake hundred-dollar bills on the floor, Calvino made love to the Hanoi girl. He was still inside her when the lights came back on, and the power. He reached over and hit the control lever. She quickly slipped into the bottom half of her ao dai, looked at her face in the shiny chrome control panel. Turning around, she rubbed the smudge of lipstick off the side of his face.

"This was an omen," she said. "The power going out." She shook her head.

"No, your coming to Vietnam. I knew you were the one the first time I saw you."

He looked at the eyes for some trace of irony, of a lie. There was none.

"I came to Saigon because I wanted to open a bar."

"You came to Ho Chi Minh City because you were meant to." He had obtained what he had desired, thought about alone in his hotel room, and nanoseconds after he had fulfilled his desire came the terrifying moment of realization he would leave the Zone forever because of one woman. When faced with the solid reality of such a prospect, he found himself asking whether he could ever leave the Zone, or whether the Zone would be carried like a seed inside him, ready to sprout anew sometime down the road and destroy their relationship. He had possessed her, this was what he told himself that he really wanted. Did he believe himself? He touched her hair. He wanted the power to go back off, for time to stop, and for the darkness to surround them again. Then he wanted her to go with him, he saw himself with her in the elevator, as he pushed the control lever and a moment later they reached the ground floor.

Then they were in a taxi on the way to the nearest place which performed civil marriages and he said, "I do." For life and all of the other lives to follow, "I do take this woman." And then there was the personal vow, "I am declaring myself free of the Zone."

The elevator stopped and she opened the door. "We are here," she said.

He reached down and picked up the plastic bag with the two hundred grand. He hesitated for a second inside the elevator. From the way she looked at him with full concentration as if she could read his mind.

"You will be late for your appointment with Mr. Webb," she said.

He had a case to finish. After that, he said to himself, he would be a free agent, then he would ask her.

"After all this business is settled, things will be different," he said.

"After the war things were supposed to be different," she said. "But mostly they have been the same."

"We'll talk about it over dinner," he said.

She thought about this.

"Good idea," she replied.

"And about Chekhov."

"Him, too."

Her English was nearly perfect, and the way she moved walking away from him made his breath snag in the back of his throat. He had just made love to his woman. The Hanoi girl, he thought, the untouchable girl who Webb would have bet the bank would not go to lunch with him. After she led him to the reception area, Mai had turned coldly formal in the presence of the other staff.

She disappeared without saying goodbye. Then, they had made love without really saying hello.

Two gray sofas were on either side of a glass table. A man in his late 40s dressed in a gray suit and green tie sat reading the International Herald Tribune. Calvino sat on the opposite sofa. Fourth of July picnic, Bangkok, Thailand, raced through Calvino's head. He felt a moment of sheer panic. He knew this guy, and more important, this guy knew him and could blow his cover with one word, "Calvino." He waited like someone looking an executioner in the eye. Do it. Let's get the fucking thing over. He was almost happy. I go back for Mai and get out of here, he thought. But then nothing happened.

Calvino then recognized the man as Fred Harris, a Bangkok based US Embassy guy. Harris returned to reading his newspaper as if he had never laid eyes on Calvino before. Harris had worked for a couple of years at the US Embassy in Bangkok. Harris had taken Pratt away at the Fourth of July picnic. He had a problem: Something about providing security to investors who were meeting in Phuket. Harris could not have looked more American in Saigon if he had had the Stars and Stripes tattooed on his forehead. As soon as he started to worry about Harris blowing his cover, he thought, Harris isn't going to blow my cover. And there was one very good reason: Harris was working on special assignment himself. He had caught the sonofabitch red-handed in the middle of some black bag operation, thought Calvino. He watched as Fred lowered the newspaper and stared at Calvino, then looked away.

"Dan Bryant," Fred Harris finally said. "From Akron, Ohio."

Calvino didn't blink. There were clerks and secretaries running back and forth. One brought Harris a mug of cold water.

"Vincent Demato, Brooklyn. I'm opening a bar in Saigon. How about you?"

"I am in the investment business."

"Yeah? The business of America is business. Isn't that what they say? Besides, I'm an investor myself. You got a brochure or card?"

"Sorry, but I'm fresh out," said Fred Harris.

One of the secretaries, who had overhead Calvino's request, left and reappeared a moment later with an impressive brochure.

"Mr. Bryant not have. But we have. You take this," said the secretary, handing it to Calvino.

"Thank you, you are very helpful," he said, as she turned and went back to her desk.

"The Vietnam Emerging Market Fund," said Calvino, reading the front of the brochure.

He opened the brochure. Inside were a list of names, and he found the name of Daniel Bryant, financial consultant.

"Financial consultant for a Vietnamese mutual fund?" asked Calvino.

"Yes," said Fred Harris, lying through his teeth.

Harris was a Vietnam war veteran having served two tours in the army. Harry Markle knew him vaguely and said that Harris had been in that oxymoron called Military Intelligence, if Calvino remembered correctly.

"So you spend a lot of time in Vietnam," said Calvino, enjoying the sight of Harris squirming on the expensively upholstered Winchell & Holly sofa.

"Enough to do my job," he said, curtly.

"We all have a job to do, and what is sufficient time to do a job? I ask myself. And I say to myself, 'That is always a difficult question.' It must be the same in your line of work. A new mutual fund must be complicated to pull off. You spend a lot of time with lawyers, bankers, underwriters, accountants. God, just about everyone who is important in the commercial sector. Being a financial consultant must be just about a full-time job. Or do you have other clients?"

Harris pulled the newspaper up, covering his face, as if he were reading rather than figuring out some way to get Calvino off his case.

At the Fourth of July picnic, Harris had been cheering on the Marines in the tug-of-war contest with AT&T. That was insight into how the government worked, a CIA guy would never doubt that his allegiance was to the Marines first. Companies could be taken over, liquidated, or go broke, but the Marines would always be ready to pick up their end of the rope and pull on command.

Calvino nodded to himself, looking at the brochure and thinking how guys like Fred Harris looked like they were born to work for the government. Anyone in the private sector had an edgy, nervous, pushing aggression, that showed their ass was on the line, they had to perform or else they were in the street. Fred Harris who was balding and sprouting jowls had a civil servant's attitude, I'm in control, I can fuck with you, but you can't fuck with me. I have the power on my side, so I can relax, cross my legs, and calmly read a newspaper in the Saigon law offices of an American law firm which had just lost a lawyer to a grenade attack.

Douglas Webb suddenly appeared.

"Mr. Demato, how are you doing?"

Calvino didn't reply, he reached down for his duty-free bag, got up and followed Webb into the conference room. He pulled back a chair and sat down before Webb had said anything. Mai came in with two cups of coffee. She didn't look at Calvino, and he tried not to look at her. Webb noticed all the non-looking that was going on between the two of them, and made a mental note to ask Mai about why she had become so cool, detached with the new client she had flirted with the day before. He had probably made a pass and she knew that she had made a mistake, thought Webb.

"I'm sorry I am late with the coffee, Mr. Demato. But the maid forgot to boil the water until just a few minutes ago."

She left as quickly as she had arrived, softly closing the door behind her. Calvino exploded, hitting the conference table with his fist.

"What the fuck are you pulling?" he shouted at Webb.

The outburst caught Webb off guard. At first he wasn't sure whether it was a joke or if Calvino was seriously upset. As he lowered himself down into the seat at the head of the table, Douglas Webb saw a flash of anger cross Calvino's face.

"What's the problem, Vincent?"

"That guy sitting out in reception. He smells of government. I come to your office with two hundred grand, and what do I find sitting opposite me? Some guy who looks like he works for the Internal Revenue Service. I don't need this shit. I want to know what that guy is doing here."

Douglas We bb sat back in his chair, his fingertips pressed against the surface of the table. He looked satisfied and a smile broke over his face.

"How do you know he works for the Internal Revenue Service?"

"I'm from Brooklyn, and anyone with that kind of haircut and cheap suit works for the fucking government. And I wanna know if you've done some deal behind my back with that asshole brother of mine in New York. Because if you have, then..."

Webb raised one of his manicured hands from the table.

"No threats, Mr. Demato. I am not working for your brother. I have no relationship with the Internal Revenue Service other than filing an annual return."

"So who is that guy in reception?"

Douglas Webb took a deep breath and then slowly exhaled.

"Mr. Bryant works for an important client. We have had a number of visitors from the US government since Mr. Markle's death. Some have said up front they were from the government. Others have, well, shall we say, some creative stories. But we have known Mr. Bryant for sometime. There's nothing to worry about."

"Of course I'm worried. You phone back to Brooklyn,

checking up on me. You've got an army of Vietnamese thugs in uniform carrying AK47s and CIA types in the reception. All I want is something real simple. A lawyer to do my legal work for a bar. And not only am I worried, I have to pay three hundred bucks an hour to tell you that I'm worried."

"Relax. It's my job to tell you when to be worried. And as your lawyer, I'm telling you to relax," he said, and paused.

"If you aren't happy, then I will see that a secretary brings in the five thousand dollars you left with us yesterday."

"Five grand? All of it?"

"All of it," said Webb, smiling.

"Okay, tell me one thing. What is the law?"

Calvino sometimes had clients who asked stupid questions like that. It was a lawyer's test of patience, and his ability not to start laughing was immediately subjected to the most severe test of all.

"Good question," said Webb.

He was a real pro, thought Calvino.

"Forget about law as you know it in New Yo rk. Here it is Confucian morality. Think of a government made up of wise elders who decide who can do what to whom and when. Who gets to run a bar, a shop, a hotel. Rules would be an insult. Because wise elders should be able to do what they want, what is right. Instead of rules, you have the wise elder's personal virtue to protect you. In the West, we have lost our belief in personal virtue—maybe any kind of virtue—and in its place we plug the gap with thousands of laws. In the East, there is no belief much beyond virtue and when the virtue falls, then there is only a void. Not laws. Just a void which can suck you in, clean you out, and spit you back all the way to New York."

Calvino nodded. "And you get three hundred bucks an hour watching people go into the void?"

"What I'm saying is there is a problem with the law."

"What you're saying is there is a problem because there is no law."

"That's going too far. Think of Vietnam more like Sicily a hundred years ago. Elders, godfathers, whatever you want to call them, call the shots."

"I like you, Douglas. I never heard a lawyer talk straight before." He took the duty-free bag off a chair and put it on the table.

He pulled out the two boxes of Johnny Walker Black Label.

"Premium whisky is the only way to go," said Calvino. He opened the box and pulled out a bundle of one hundred dollar bills.

Webb took out a fountain pen, unscrewed the cap, and began to write out a receipt for the cash. "I am writing a receipt, Mr. Wang," he said.

"You mean, Demato."

Webb stopped writing and looked up with a mixture of fear and dread.

"What did I say?" he asked.

"I don't know. But it wasn't Demato. It sounded like a Chinese name, one of those names they put on computers," said Calvino. "Like Wang."

"Yes, it was Wang. I had him on my mind. He

was one of our Chinese clients. I am sorry. That's the problem when you try to do two things at the same time." He finished writing the receipt, held it up, blew on the ink, then passed it across the table to Calvino. It read: "I, Douglas Webb, have this day received from Mr. Vincent Demato, American citizen, resident of New York, New York, the sum of US$200,000. I shall hold this sum according to the instructions of Mr. Demato and dispose of such sum as he so instructs."

It was signed by Douglas Webb.

"It doesn't say anything about Winchell & Holly," said Calvino, looking up from the receipt.

"Nor can it. I am doing this as a personal favor, Vincent. There is no way that Winchell & Holly could officially do this. It would violate a half dozen laws. But, for a client doing business in a place like Saigon, I can understand this makes business sense. Sometimes laws aren't written by people with business sense or experience."

"Yeah, I know what you mean."

Calvino slid the duty-free bag with the two Johnny Walker Black Label boxes to Webb's end of the table.

"Aren't you gonna count it?"

"I think we can trust each other."

"I was thinking about checking out the Q-Bar tonight. Come around and I'll buy you a drink. What do you say?" asked Calvino.

"Let's say the usual time. About ten. Now I had better attend to Mr. Bryant. He does look government, doesn't he?"

As they stood in the door of the conference room, Webb shook hands with Calvino. The plastic bag was in Webb's other hand.

"There is something familiar about you, Mr. Demato. I am sure I've met you before. Maybe in New York."

"Maybe in Little Italy. I had an uncle who ran a restaurant there. I used to wait tables going through college," said Calvino.

"My ex-wife said that I look like a lot of people in New York. That was another way she had of saying that I was no one special. Once I get this bar, I mean, club, off the ground in Saigon, they won't be saying that Vincent Demato isn't special, will they?"

He stood in front of the elevator, waiting for it to come up from the ground floor. Mai walked toward him, then she caught sight of Webb watching Calvino through the glass window, and kept on walking without saying a word. She had wanted to say that she loved him. But there was no time. Inside the lift alone, he felt a thaw setting in; the ice was melting and he was finding for the first time what was inside a man who loved and lived free of the Zone.

CHAPTER 8

DEAD ZONE

TWO THINGS STRUCK Calvino as he left the offices of Winchell & Holly. The first thing was a long distance kiss. He saw Mai in the window on the third floor, looking down. She was smiling and threw him a kiss. He thought how happy she looked. Pratt had said that Manee hadn't liked him the first time they met. Well, Calvino told himself that he was just that much more lucky than Pratt. Then Mai abruptly left the window and, a moment later, he saw We bb framed where Mai had been standing throwing a kiss. That's when the second thing struck Calvino—a long distance in time, one legal case, years before in New York City.

Webb had been right about his gut instinct—he had met Calvino before in New York. At the time, Webb worked as a first-year associate for Winchell & Holly and had been assigned a divorce case. None of the white-shoe partners at Winchell & Holly would ever stoop to personally handle a divorce case; they might get their hands dirty, but it was a deeper fear of becoming caught in the emotional chaos where people killed each other over who got the TV or blender. Calvino had represented the husband, Gentleman James, they called him, an English conman, who had made a very good living marrying many different women on both sides of the Atlantic. His wives were always rich, well-educated, and a hallmark of a James wife—she was always slightly older, say five to ten years older that James. Like many conmen, James was extremely good-looking, well-spoken, and people thought he had attended a public school like Eton or Harrow which, of course, he had not. About six months into the marriage the problem started. James started to have a minor accident—he pissed in the bed. He apologized to his wife, saying that it had never happened before. Before long, Gentleman James was pissing the bed every night, buckets of warm piss, soaking into the sheets, mattress, smelling. He pissed like a horse. The bedroom smelled like a medieval hospital. He had asked Calvino to represent him in the divorce action launched by his wife. His wife was amicable throughout the proceedings so there had been no shouting or recrimination. She actually adored him and, like Gentleman James's other wives, this one was sorry to see him go. But a lifetime of wet beds, well, that was beyond the rail which fenced in love. Janet, that was Gentleman James's wife, the one Webb had been given the duty of seeing through the bedwetting divorce. Calvino had met Webb once in midtown New York to look over some documents, the meeting couldn't have lasted for more than thirty minutes; just long enough to burn a small impression into the back room of a lawyer 's memory. With Calvino appearing out of context, in another role, with another name, the door of the memory had opened a crack. Webb was smart, thought Calvino, someone who would find time to tease apart a memory puzzle; it would bother him that he couldn't place Calvino's face. And getting into the back of a taxi, Calvino started to think that he didn't have much time to find out who killed Drew Markle.

Fucking Harris, he thought. He filed a mental note to ask Pratt exactly what Harris had said at the Fourth of July picnic. He glanced through the Vietnam Emerging Market Fund brochure, even Calvino recognized the names of two Americans: an ex- general and a high-ranking government official from the Vietnam War era. They were coming back to Saigon as businessmen on the twentieth anniversary of the failure of their earlier venture, he thought. Post-Fourth of July, the Fund was being launched at the Continental Hotel. Perfect timing. One revolution had succeeded; another had failed.

§ § § §

THE metered taxicab cut across District One, honking at every cyclo and bicycle, moving in and out of the traffic without ever slowing down. Like Saigon, the driver was in a hurry. Calvino climbed out at the curb and beyond were a series of riverside restaurants. Behind him was a bronze statue of Tran Hung Dao, an ancient warrior in full battle gear, a lifeless witness from the past who would have been looking down on Drew Markle as he took the last couple of steps from this life and entered the next with Tran Hung Dao. Jackie Ky had been waiting at the same restaurant for Drew Markle the night that he was killed. The restaurant was on a converted ship and a gangplank led up to the main deck. This time she was waiting for Calvino, fingering her watch as he walked in and sat down at the table. She looked worried and started to cry before he could ask her what was wrong.

"I don't know if I can stay here. It's too painful," she said.

Her hands were shaking as she lit a cigarette, she looked pale, listless; someone wanting to break and run.

He looked out at a barge going down the Saigon River. Beyond the barge, in the distance, a ferry loaded with peasants crossed from District One to the slums and shacks barely visible on the opposite side of the river. Calvino waited until a waiter arrived and then ordered a whisky and coke. He took his time before saying anything, whatever emotion was going through her head, he thought, it was better to let it play out before he got down to business. He looked over at Jackie.

"You want a cola or something?"

He looked directly at her, direct, hard, the way he had seen district attorneys look at the accused in the witness box. It fixed them, made them edgy, looking for something or someone to hang onto.

"A Bloody Mary," she said. "A double Bloody Mary."

The waiter took the order and left them alone at their table beside the river. She had started to calm down like someone who was breaking free of a panic attack, floating back to solid ground. She sat with her back toward the spot where Markle had died. He looked at the grass. There was nothing to mark where Markle had fallen. Her slender, long neck turned and followed his eyes, then turned back around quickly. So far he had come up with nothing. Webb might have killed Markle for money. Jackie Ky, his girlfriend, might have had her reasons. And with guys like Fred Harris snooping around Saigon under an assumed name, the list of suspects kept growing. Marcus Nguyen was on the emotional side, that was what Harry had said. Emotions killed people—all you had to do was switch on the TV or read a newspaper to see that; strong emotions were required to squeeze the gun trigger and pull the grenade pin. Unless the job was sub-contracted out to a professional. Had Markle seen the man—or the woman—who killed him? Would he have recognized the person? Reading the mind of the deceased was a waste of time, there was no mind left to read; instead of tapping into the world of the dead, the world of the living was where all the answers were waiting to be discovered. The world was filled with people like Gentleman James, Douglas Webb, Jackie Ky, Fred Harris, and Marcus Nguyen. Living somewhere between the range of a con and decency, not knowing when they had crossed the line from one side to the other. The more he let those faces confront the full run of possibilities inside his mind, the more futile it became. Why not pack in the job? Why not go back to the hotel and phone Harry Markle and tell him that he was taking himself off the case? He had done it before on other assignments. Something held him back, something called the wise elder, a voice which made him pause, listen, and believe there was a through line if only he had the wisdom to see it. What had Webb said about the virtue of the wise elder being the glue that held things together? That was it, he thought. Calvino sat up in his chair, a smile crossing his face. Markle must have committed the ultimate cross-cultural sin in Southeast Asia, he had tried to rein in a wise elder with his faith and belief, a religious-like commitment, in the American notion of law. Not law standing alone but the rule of law. His bred-in-the bone connection to the law was what had got Markle killed. Yes, thought Calvino. Markle had been trained to think like a lawyer in a part of the world where lawyer-thinking was hazardous.

He mentioned in passing to Jackie Ky that he had bumped into Fred Harris before his meeting with Webb at Winchell & Holly. Only he didn't call him Fred Harris, he called him Dan Bryant.

"Yeah, I remember the name. He was one of Drew's clients. I am not surprised you saw him. He has run up a huge legal bill for that new fund. Drew was getting rich on client credit points."

"What did Drew say about Dan?"

She shrugged.

"I don't remember all that well. It's not like we sat around talking about his cases, you know."

"Try and remember."

"I've had Washington, D.C. investigators flashing badges in my face ever since Drew was killed. Asking me to remember, I'm sick of trying to remember. I've had it up to here. I want to start forgetting. Isn't that what it means to get on with your life?"

"I can't blame you, Jackie. All I want to know was if Drew ever said anything about this client."

"He might have said that the guy was a bit of a cowboy. Whatever that means. He said Vietnam was like the badlands in America over a hundred years ago. Indian country. Every man, woman and child walking wounded. That's what I told this guy from the State Department."

He shook his head, thinking she was about to start crying again. The waiter came to their table with a tray of drinks and bucket of ice.

Calvino watched her drain half the glass as he ordered the crab and shrimp salad for two.

"And you've told them everything?" asked Calvino.

"I hate that question. It's a dumb cops question. If it were a movie, I'd walk out. Of course, I told them everything. Why wouldn't I tell them? I want the person who killed him cut up and used as fish bait. Am I making myself clear?"

She was watching a fishing boat pass on the river.

"I am not a cop. And it was a dumb question. Sorry," he said, drinking from the whisky and coke. He looked at her carefully, trying to understand what was in her head, what she had seen, what she had remembered, what she might have forgotten.

He didn't let up.

"You think that the hitman was Vietnamese?" asked Calvino.

"I suppose so. This is Vietnam. Why would a Cambodian or a Thai bother? But anything is possible in Saigon. And it happened so fast. There are a zillion motorcycles on Ton Duc Thang Street the time of day when Drew died. How long does it take to throw a hand grenade? Two, three seconds? By the time it explodes you have no idea where it came from. Who threw it or where he went."

"Are you sure it was one guy, or were there two?"

"It happened so fast."

"In the movies you have one guy riding a motor-cycle and shooting or throwing a grenade. Not so in real life. Once you pull the pin on the grenade, then you hold tight on the spoon. If you have to brake hard to avoid an accident, the next thing that happens is you need two hands, the spoon slips off the grenade because you are reaching for the handle and you are blown up."

"So there were two guys, does it matter?"

"Given the authorities said one man threw the grenade, yeah, you could say it makes a difference."

She was right about one thing: how short the distance was between the act and reaction in the world of bombs hurled from the street. No question about it, Calvino thought, that in real life no one is clocking traffic flows, looking for two guys on the motorbike carried on a sea of motorbikes, except for one difference: this one was armed with a grenade. No one thinks or lives that way. There were certain sections of New York where kids lived this way, thought Calvino.

"I want to know about the concert. The night you went with Drew and Webb and Webb's friend."

"What do you want to know?"

"Like who was sitting where. You know, the seating arrangements."

She took a sip from her Bloody Mary. "That's a funny question."

"Did Drew sit on your right or your left? Who sat next to him? Who sat next to you?"

"Wait, you are going too fast. Okay," she said, closing her eyes. She moved her hand to her left and pointed.

"Drew sat here."

"And next to Drew?"

"I guess it was Webb," she said.

"Take your time. Don't guess."

"No, it was Mai, the secretary from Hanoi."

He felt someone had kicked him in the stomach.

"And where was the bimbo from Bangkok? Next to Webb?"

"Yeah, she was. It's true. I am starting to remember now."

"And next to the bimbo?"

"It was dark in the concert hall. And I spent most of the time talking with Drew. You know how I feel about Webb. I can't even look at him without feeling like a worm attack in the gut coming on."

"So you don't know who was sitting next to the bimbo."

She closed her eyes again. "I think it was a client of the firm."

"American?"

"Asian," she said. "You're sure?"

"There were hardly any whites at the concert. They were mostly Vietnamese and, of course, some Thais. If the client had been white, I would have noticed. Since I didn't, he must have been Asian."

Calvino sipped his drink. Women's powers of deduction were immense, he thought. And it was because women noticed the small detail and then pulled back and looked at the larger picture. Most men just tunnel down the middle, missing the detail and the overall perspective. She probably had come to the right conclusion and for the right reason.

"The client was male."

"I guess so. I would have noticed if the client were a woman."

"You've been very helpful," said Calvino.

"I haven't done anything," she said, finishing her drink. "I am not really hungry. Why don't we go back to my place? I hate it here. Do you mind?"

How could he mind? He paid the bill and they walked together down the gangplank.

Walking out of the restaurant, Calvino headed toward the spot where Markle had died. Jackie Ky tried to pull clear of him, but he had her hand. He wasn't exactly certain where it had happened but he stopped on the grass and faced her.

"Do you know an overseas Vietnamese named Marcus Nguyen?" he asked.

She started to smile, then shook her head.

"You are bizarre. Know him? He's my uncle."

§ § § §

JACKIE Ky paid two thousand dollars a month to rent a villa which was near the Cong Vien Van Hoa Park end of Truong Dinh Street. She told him the full story of how she had put another thirty grand into the renovations. She unlocked the door. Calvino walked inside the entrance and then into the living room. He had the feeling that he had been transported to somewhere in Southern California. Chrome furniture with floral pattern cushions gleamed in the sunlight streaming through sheer curtains with tiny, pink lotus buds. A scruffy looking parrot with feathers missing around one leg squawked as it jumped around a large cage suspended from the ceiling. Potted plants six feet tall and tropical flowers in full bloom shot an aura of blues and reds and greens, a Fourth of July night sky exploding with a hundred fireworks, showering an arc of colors across the sitting room, spraying the ceiling to floor mirrored wall in reds and greens. Opposite was a sliding door that led out to a small garden, with well-manicured lawn and flower beds. She turned on the overhead fan which rotated slowly, and then she walked over to the liquor cabinet, one of those black-lacquered Chinese chests with bronze hinges and inlaid mother of pearl depicting epic scenes of family, war, seduction, weddings, and death. Only this black box stood over six feet high. If one were going to shoot a single object into deep space, this piece of furniture would have been a prime candidate for the mission as an artifact of life on earth.

"You live pretty well," said Calvino, looking out at the garden, before turning back and taking in the room.

"Meaning, I wasn't after Drew for his money," she said. Jackie Ky had the ability to read minds, he thought.

"Pre-1975 my uncle owned this villa."

"Marcus owned this?"

"Twenty years ago, the People's Committee con-fiscated the property. He wasn't alone. A lot of people lost everything. But it is understandable," she said.

"How so?"

"The revisionists say we lost the war. I don't believe that," she said. "But the war is in the past. Now I rent my uncle's old villa from someone who is a Party member."

"When did you leave Saigon?"

"I was seven years old. 1973. My life changed. I still remember being a tomboy. Going around the neighborhood topless at seven, playing football with the boys. I was a roughneck. Big for my age and tough. Next thing I knew, I was in America. I was suddenly small for my age and not so tough. Big change, huh?"

"What else do you remember?"

"My father beat my hands with a rattan stick if I misspelled a word or screwed up playing scales on the piano. I remember the stinging. My face all flushed, and the tears going down my face, but I never cried out. That would be giving in. I held it all here," she said, pointing to her stomach.

"I swallowed the fire."

"What does Marcus do?"

"He's a consultant. Why?"

Calvino loved the word "consultant": it was one of those titles heard from one end of the Comfort Zone to the other. Men with vague titles were drawn to the Zone life. There were others, though, like Fred Harris who used the title of "financial consultant" as his cover. Every grifter in Southeast Asia was some kind of a consultant. Jackie Ky said it so innocently as if her uncle Marcus were a doctor or a professor. This wasn't the time or place to rattle her bones about her uncle's business in Saigon. He was more interested in how she was making ends meet.

"And you have no problem coming up with two grand a month for rent?" asked Calvino, moving around the living room. No expense had been spared. The curtains, the chairs, tables, cabinets, mirrors, plants, all had the touch of first class attached.

"Don't tell me you're a consultant as well."

"It wasn't just curiosity which killed the cat, it was irony too."

"Yeah, is that so?" he said, looking at a photograph of Drew and her. It was the same photograph that Harry had given him of the two together at Cu Chi Tunnels.

"My father did very well in California real estate. We were not poor yellow trash," she said.

"Did Drew live here with you?"

She had taken a cigarette from one of the drawers in the Chinese chest and lit it. "What possible business can that be of yours?"

She exhaled the smoke which the overhead fan blew away.

"Because that's what I do. Ask a lot of questions. Like a man who can't hear trying to figure out how jazz sounds."

"You like jazz? I love jazz." And without waiting for his reply she took three steps over to the stereo and slipped a CD disk into the CD player.

"You know how you get Fusion Jazz?" asked Calvino. She shook her head.

"By putting a CD into a cassette player."

This was the first time that he had heard her laugh, and it surprised him. Then the first track of the CD kicked in. It was the Miles Davis and Marcus Miller Siesta album. Lost in Madrid Part I had the sound of death at a bullfight. As it played she made him a drink. A double Chivas with ice and a tall gin and tonic for herself. She walked across the room and closed the curtain over the sliding door to the garden. The room went from brilliant light to twilight. She stood next to him, touching her glass to his.

"Cheers," she said.

"You didn't answer my question. Did you and Drew live together?"

At first she looked stunned, then her lower lip started to tremble.

"We didn't see other people," she said.

Calvino looked around the room and saw a photo-graph of Drew with an arm wrapped around someone dressed in a yellow, fuzzy big-foot outfit with a monkey-like headgear attached. She followed Calvino's eye line.

"We were in Dalat on holiday. Why don't I just come out and say it? I hate playing stupid games, you know. Drew stayed in the villa often enough to qualify as a live-in."

She suddenly reverted to her state in the restaurant: all pain, raw and open, the kind of pain that feels like it is eating you alive and nothing you throw in its tracks is going to slow it down. Now he understood why she had asked him back to the villa. There was a lot of pain in the room, even more memories, a past that hung in the air, hovering in every plant and flower in the garden. Maybe she was hoping Calvino might have some idea of how to wipe the pain of Drew Markle from her life. Or maybe she just wanted someone else to understand what it was like stranded between the land of the living and the land of the dead. Looking at her standing in the sitting room, fighting back tears, he remembered a time in Bangkok when the wife of an ex-client phoned him one Sunday evening. She was crying and could hardly talk. She needed to see him immediately. She had checked into a short-time hotel not far away. He went around and found her waiting for him, half-undressed. She was crying and half-drunk. Her husband had beaten her, and she had the bruises to prove it. She was scared and angry and confused. She didn't know what she wanted and the only person in all of Bangkok she could think to phone was a private eye named Vincent Calvino. The only one she could trust to come around and find her in that condition. She was going to take her revenge on her husband who had disappeared deep into the Zone one too many times. And, at the same time, she was going to rub that pain out of her life. A woman was no different than a man in looking for the easy solution. In her case, he had been selected as the man who could blot out the memory of the smell and touch of her lost man.

Jackie Ky snuggled up to him, purring, then reaching around his waist, holding her glass against the small of his back. "I want you," she said. Jackie Ky was the person who had taught him that phrase in Vietnamese, he hadn't told Mai about that.

That night at the short-time hotel, the wife of the old client had said the same thing. But what the woman wanted in Bangkok and what the woman in front of him that moment wanted in Saigon was something beyond sex, something he couldn't give her and live with himself. They wanted someone to save some small piece of pride, to make good on a personal promise that by doing this one act the pain would go away and never come back. That there was a man who wanted, desired her. Her tongue was inside his mouth. That time in Bangkok and this time in Saigon. Lost in Madrid was still playing when he pulled her back.

"It's not how to deal with it," he said.

"You think that Douglas Webb would pass up the chance to fuck me?"

"I'm not Douglas Webb," he said.

She was hurt, wounded in her pride which was already on low voltage from batteries worn down by Markle's murder. She slapped him hard on the face.

"Get out," she said.

Calvino sat down on the sofa, stretched his arms out. Now they were getting somewhere. The gloves had come off and, for the first time, she had lost that controlled, balanced, intellectual distance she had been using to put galactic space between herself and the rest of the world.

"Are you going? Or do I have to call the police?"

"Ho Chi Minh City or Saigon branch?"

The question drained away her anger and she started to giggle.

"What was the first word you learned in English?"

She flopped down, blowing her nose into a tissue, wadding it up in her hand.

"Contempt," she said. "I was young at the time. It's the first English word I remember learning. I was at a movie with Uncle Marcus in LA. The movie was Chariots of Fire, and I heard the word. Contempt. I asked my uncle, what does it mean? He said it means how the people in America treated us Vietnamese. And how the communists who had taken away Saigon treated us Vietnamese."

§ § § §

OUTSIDE, in the hot Saigon afternoon, Calvino walked towards the park. She had talked about her childhood as if it were a record still playing over and over again inside her head. Once he left the villa, Calvino needed some fresh air and some time alone to think. He had done the right thing, he thought. Contempt was a good word to learn in any language. It was the kind of word you learned over again as you grew up. He remembered another woman, the wife of an ex-client, who had used that word. She was in Bangkok, a battered woman who had begged him not to leave her that night. Just stay in the room, she said. He sat in the corner of the small, mirrored room all night while she slept on the round bed. At six in the morning he left, took a taxi to the ex-client's house, rang the doorbell and when the door opened he punched the husband in the face, breaking the man's nose and sending an arc of blood over the carpet.

"Don't ever touch her again," Calvino had said. The husband and wife split up a month later. She went back to the States, the husband slipped into some outer reach of the Comfort Zone, and he never saw either of them again. He hated the domestic stuff, it was evil, violent, demeaning, and senseless. He walked into the park, passed lovers sitting on the grass and on benches, wondering whether Douglas Webb was planning to kill him. He had murder in his eyes when he stood in the window of the villa housing Winchell & Holly. Mai had been there a second earlier, then vanished, replaced by a face which wanted him dead. Another grenade. Nah, that would be boring. A knife? Maybe. A single shot in the head. Or two shots in the chest, like Mark Wang. There were so many ways to die in Saigon, he thought. So many lovers in the park, huddling together, as if death never stalked the earth.

§ § § § §

"YOU gave Webb the entire two hundred grand?"

"The whole enchilada," said Calvino. He had a stupid grin on his face.

"And I have this awful gut feeling this is the best news I am going to hear. That there is something else even more insane," said Pratt.

Pratt covered his face with one hand and rubbed his eyes. He was tired, not sleeping well. He had phoned Manee just to hear her voice over the phone, to talk to his kids about school. The conversations had cheered him up at the time but the good cheer had faded within the hour as he had waited for Calvino to arrive at a French restaurant on Dong Khoi Street. He missed them.

"I am going to marry Mai," said Calvino.

So that was it, the reason he was acting crazy, laying all the fake money on Webb.

"You once said you'd never remarry. That you might make it a week, maybe a month, outside the Zone but it would always pull you back. The ice was in your blood."

Calvino nodded. "True. I also once said I'd never take another drink."

"If women are the addiction, marriage isn't the treatment."

"Is that from Shakespeare?" asked Calvino.

"No. And it's not from Chekhov either."

"I want to thank you for that quote."

"I knew it was a mistake to quote Chekhov. The Cherry Orchard just cost the Royal Thai Police Department two hundred grand. And I signed for it."

"The money's counterfeit," said Calvino. "Webb doesn't know that."

"That's the whole point. If he had Drew Markle and

Mark Wang killed over a cash deposit, then we should know pretty soon."

"Maybe that's it."

"That's what?" asked Calvino.

"Since you have a pretty good idea someone will try to kill you in the next seventy-two hours, you can talk about marriage."

"I've been married for seventy hours before," said Calvino.

"The average duration of a Zone marriage."

"And for less than twenty hours as I recall."

The smile dissolved from Calvino's face as Marcus Nguyen stood at their table, holding out his hand. In his other hand was his mobile phone.

"Vincent, I thought that was you."

Calvino introduced Pratt to Marcus, making sure he kept Pratt's cover intact, there was no need to involve Marcus any further than he was already involved. By the time the introduction had finished, Marcus had slid into the booth next to Calvino.

"I saw your old villa this afternoon. Your niece showed me around. She's done wonders with the decoration and the garden. Out of Town and Country," said Calvino, having a reasonably good idea that Marcus already had learned of this from Jackie Ky.

"As I tried to teach Jackie, you have to learn to let go of the past. It is a hard lesson and some people learn quicker than others. Some just turn bitter," said Marcus Nguyen. "For example, take a look out of the window."

Pratt and Calvino looked out and saw a beggar eating a sandwich, squatting in front of a row of carts loaded with bamboo and coconuts. The beggar was looking in the window, his head tilted up. Calvino turned and saw the TV on the wall. A Charlie Chaplin movie was playing on the VCR. Charlie the little tramp being watched by an old Vietnamese tramp.

"See the building across the street? There is a sign that says Hotel Catinat. Before 1975 the entire block was the Hotel Catinat. The street had the same name. And what is left of all this now? It's been chopped up into dozens of shops selling Marilyn Monroe bead curtains, lacquered bowls and chopsticks. The Hotel Catinat no longer exists. The street has a new name. It is all in the past as if it never existed. Only the words carved in that part of the building survive. Not even all the King's men and all the King's horses could put Humpty Dumpty together again."

"Or Drew Markle," said Calvino.

That caught Marcus a little off guard, the sweep from disintegration of property to the destruction of a life. He recovered with a wave of his mobile phone.

"But we can ask for justice in the case of Drew Markle. Or, if we wish, we can do the work of justice."

"And the man who owned the Hotel Catinat, what became of him?"

"He never let the loss of his hotel turn him into a bitter man. He moved on. He was smart. He never asked who the new owners were, where they came from, what right they had to split up his hotel into hundreds of shops and apartments. It didn't matter. Might has always been right. He didn't own it any longer, the title had gone to strangers. It was enough that it had once been his. No one could take that away from him."

"What kind of work did you say you did?" asked Pratt.

"It's there on my name card. Consultant."

"My company sometimes employs consultants."

Pratt had read the name card. It said consultant and he thought about this English word. Southeast Asia was crawling with consultants, a title that meant almost nothing. You consulted fortune tellers, your friends, your old teachers, a wise monk, but the modern Western consultant was like a hired gun from the old West, making connections, wiring networks, using the phone, fax, and computer to move funds, designs and secrets around the world, as if offshore bank accounts, investors, managers, and corporate offices were all intermingled on a vast international grid. Consultants were hired by someone who wanted to break a grid-lock in the system, or break someone who was breakable. Who hired Marcus Nguyen and what had they asked him for his fee?

"What's your speciality, Mr. Nguyen?" asked Pratt, keeping the conversation on a formal level.

"Finance," said Marcus.

"You still think the communists financed the killing of Drew Markle?" asked Calvino.

Marcus stared at the window, his eyes on the old Hotel Catinat. His eyes swung back to Calvino's and he sipped on a gin and tonic which a waiter had brought over from where he had been sitting.

"I think maybe he got in the way of a lot of money," said Marcus. "That gets you killed in Asia no matter who you are."

"That's why there is such a big demand for financial consultants," said Pratt.

After Marcus left the restaurant, Pratt and Calvino watched him get into a car, the driver holding the door for him.

"What do you make of him?" asked Calvino.

Pratt shrugged.

"I don't think too much of his history. Rue Catinat changed names after the French left in 1954. I can't remember, I think the name was Tu Do . And the Catinat Hotel had been divided into shops while the Americans were still in Saigon."

"That's the problem with Vietnam," said Calvino. "Everyone personalizes the history."

"Not unlike America," said Pratt.

"Not unlike Thailand," said Calvino.

§ § § § §

IN the early evening, Calvino sat on his balcony, thinking about what Marcus had said about how Drew Markle had got in the way of a Brink's truck of money and that had been the reason Drew had been killed. Mark Wang had left a lot of money in the offices of Winchell & Holly. Calvino thought about how little money was enough to get in the way of and how quickly the dead were forgotten by those who divided the spoils. Cash, a hotel, a villa. It all got divided, redivided, and the original owners were dead, fled to another country, or fighting the illness of bitterness and plotting their revenge. That much was human nature. Then someone rang the door buzzer to his hotel room. He swung around and looked back through the French doors. Pratt wouldn't be that stupid, he thought. He got up and walked through the French doors, across the room, and opened the door a crack. Jackie Ky was standing outside, holding her handbag with both hands. Calvino's law said a woman who comes to your hotel room unexpected, holding her handbag with both hands does so because it's heavy, either with the stuff she plans to move in with or with the gun she plans to use because she plans to move you out.

"Can I come in?"

"Why don't I step outside?"

They stood in the narrow hallway with the peeling lino.

"You're right. Inside we have your invisible audience plugged in. Even sometimes I forget and act as if this place is really normal."

She opened her handbag and took out a handgun.

"I thought you might need this."

He pulled a Smith & Wesson .40 caliber handgun out of the leather rig. It was loaded with a full fifteen slug clip inside.

"It's a beautiful lady," he said.

"But she has a bad temper. Kind of like me. Hey, I'm sorry for what happened."

He smiled and kissed her on the cheek. "You certainly know how to make up."

This Smith & Wesson was one of those modern guns made out of hard plastic. A killing machine should be made out of steel, he thought, as she dug out two extra clips and handed them over. Killing a man is bad enough, but insulting him with a plastic killing machine is another thing altogether. But Calvino wasn't going to let a bit of plastic stand in the way of accepting a gift in a place where an insult was the least of his worries. He looked up from the gun.

"Why are you really giving me this?"

"Because I acted like a real shit. And you didn't do what Douglas Webb would have done. Try and take advantage of me when I am obviously willing to throw myself at you."

"Was that some kind of test back at your place?"

She smiled. "I'm a testy girl. Gotta run now. Hey, watch yourself with that beautiful lady you've got between your hands."

"Did Uncle Marcus put you up to this?"

"He likes you, Vinee. I like you. He promised Harry to look after you. Harry knows, like Marcus, that this isn't your turf. You have no idea how crazy you are playing private eye in Saigon. Nothing is private here. It's all public. That's what communism stands for. You just don't go around asking all sorts of questions about someone getting killed without attracting attention. Bye." She pushed the button for the elevator and, before he could say anything, the door to one of the other rooms opened and Calvino ducked back inside his doorway. When the door closed, he looked out in the hallway but Jackie Ky had gone. He slipped the leather rig on for size. Perfect fit, he thought, looking at himself in the mirror. Already he was starting to feel better. He leaned his head against the back of the door to his room, and thought about the darkness of the elevator when the power had gone out, and how Mai had sounded and smelled. He remembered everything as if it were the last chance for a memory to occupy his mind.

§ § § §

WHEN Mai said she had to be home by ten, her fingers ran up and down his hand across the table. She lived in a shophouse with an assortment of relatives from Hanoi and Hue—uncles, aunts, cousins—he couldn't keep track of all the connections, as his eyes watched her lips move. What it all meant, in the end, was that a Hanoi girl had strict family orders to be off the streets before it was late.

"After ten, the Saigon girls claim the night," she said.

"And if I am out, then my family feels it sends the wrong message. Foreigners can become easily confused. They don't see the difference. So I have to be careful."

"And pray for blackouts at ten in the morning."

"That's a good idea," she said, squeezing his hand.

"Were you Drew Markle's secretary?" he asked. It was a question that had been bothering him for some time and he had wanted to ask her as they were riding up in the elevator and the power gave out, and the question slipped his mind in the total darkness.

"Yes, I was his secretary."

"Did Drew use a computer for letters, agree-ments, that kind of thing?"

She nodded.

"What happened to all of his computer files?"

"The Intelligence people came to the office after it happened. Khanh said they took the diskettes. He didn't have any choice, you understand. They just took all of them for the investigation."

"No one kept back-ups? For instance, did Webb keep copies?"

"I don't think he had time to make copies of Drew's files. It happened very fast. An hour after Drew was killed, the security people were in our office. They wouldn't let Webb in. It was okay for me and Khanh and the rest of the Vietnamese staff, but no foreigners were allowed."

"Very efficient," said Calvino.

She was stroking his hand and smiling. "Except one thing."

"Which is?"

"I kept a private set of his files. The diskette is at home. It was Drew's idea. And, as it turned out, he was smart to have thought something might happen."

"Did you tell anyone at the office or the police about this?"

She shook her head. "I was too scared. I didn't know what to do. Or who to trust."

"What about Khanh? You don't trust him?"

She shrugged her shoulders, withdrew her hand from across the table and drank her cola.

"It doesn't matter. You trusted me enough to tell me."

"I don't see what Drew's death has to do with you."

"Could you let me have a copy of the diskette?"

She had made love with him as they stood in the dark elevator, he had been holding her hand in public in a restaurant, it was all happening so fast, too fast. She needed time to think. Think about what she wanted, who she was, and who she was with. Everything had seemed clear and certain when they had sat down at dinner together, and now she couldn't find the right word to describe the sudden unease she felt. It was like the night when she heard that Drew Markle had been murdered along the river. She had cried and the next morning her eyes had been bloodshot and people asked her all kinds of questions. She told them her eyes were red because she hadn't slept well. She didn't tell them that she had been crying her eyes out. Calvino didn't push her any further, feeling her withdraw, folding back into herself.

"I'm going to ask you to believe one thing."

"What is that one thing?"

"I will make it work for us," he said. He reached for her hand but she moved away.

He stood beside her as a guard rolled out her Honda Dream. She straddled the saddle, brushing her long black hair away from her face. This was no way to end the night, he thought. He grabbed the handlebars and leaned forward, his lips touching hers. She didn't stop him this time. She gave him a long, passionate kiss and froze a little as she brushed against the Smith & Wesson.

"What's that?" she asked, pulling back.

"A way to communicate with people. Except you only use it as a last resort."

"Like a mobile phone." She smiled.

"Yeah, when you want to deliver a message."

He didn't say anything, having made up his mind that he would not lie to her. If asked, he might be as indirect as possible, but he would not tell an outright lie.

"Be careful," she said.

"Ho Chi Minh City isn't New York."

"New York is much safer," she said, twisting the ignition key in the Honda.

They both started to say something at the same time. They laughed the way lovers laugh, filled with joy and happiness, that's where it starts, but the heart of such a laugh is in the feeling of hope it carries. Like a piece of music that inspires, such a laugh is a song, a duet of shared hope.

"Okay, I will do it. I will get you the diskette. If that's what you really want. If it's important. I won't even ask why it is important to a man who wants to open a nightclub. But you must have your reasons."

"I'll call you tomorrow," he said. He had never felt better or worse in his life. A woman he loved was willing to do what her basic instinct told her not to do, and she would do it simply on the basis of trust, an offering given to a man she loved.

He stood watching her motorcycle until it disappeared into the night and then he took a taxi to the Q-Bar.

§ § § §

RUNNING a cover story about wanting to open a Saigon bar made for a good excuse, but changing the cover story to opening a nightclub gave him a perfect reason to be hanging out in a swank District One bar; it wasn't just drinking, it was studying how the competition made it all come together, the layout, the staff, the furniture and, above all, the way they handled the clientele. Calvino eased onto an empty stool at the first bar, the Caravaggio wing, just inside the front entrance to the Q-Bar, and no sooner had he settled in and ordered a drink, than some guy in his late 20s, blonde hair, red-eyed, his jaw a little slack from drink, leaned over and pressed his shoulder against Calvino.

"I remember you from the other night. You're Doug's friend, right? He said you're gonna open a bar in Saigon. Not an original idea but it seems cool."

"I'm thinking about it real hard," said Calvino.

"Well, you should think real hard about putting your money here," he said, taking a long drink out of the Tiger beer bottle.

"What's your name?" asked Calvino. "Josh."

"Vincent," extending his hand.

The young, well-built American shook it. "If you really want to know what I think, it's that opening a bar in Saigon is a fucked idea."

"Yeah, you got a bar?" Josh shook his head.

"No, but I got an English school. In Saigon, running a bar is easier than operating an English school. Fewer people to pay off. I taught English in Jakarta before coming here. Jakarta is corrupt but it's not a patch on Saigon. One day I'm painting the walls in one of my classrooms and some asshole guy from the government comes around. He says, 'What are you doing? Painting walls? Drinking beer? Listening to music? Teachers don't paint walls in Vietnam,' he said. He couldn't understand how a teacher could paint a fucking wall with one hand, drink beer with the other, listen to music and rap with his students. Get students to help paint their own school. It was unheard of. You know what he was afraid of?"

Calvino looked at Josh's bloodshot eyes and saw a lot of pain which the booze was keeping just below the surface. This was what running a bar entailed—listening to other people's suffering as they drank your booze, thinking that somehow, between the talking and the drinking, some of the pain should drain away.

"What was he afraid of?" asked Calvino.

"He was afraid that the school might be success-ful. His message was pretty clear. Keep it dirty and ugly. Don't paint the fucking place. You might make the government school look bad. We can't have foreigners doing things to make us look bad. He didn't give a fuck that the school would help the students or his country. All he cared about was what was in it for him. He was motivated by greed. All of Saigon is motivated by greed. After you take out one of those government assholes for dinner you want to wash out your mouth, ears, nose, throat and hands. You don't want their scent stuck to your body."

He leaned across the bar.

"Another beer, if you please," he shouted.

Sitting at the bar on his right, a fat American from South Carolina carefully balanced beer bottles onto ashtrays, creating a pyramid. He was like a fat man in a circus act. A cigarette was hanging out of the corner of his mouth. The fat man, who looked about the same age as Josh, said, "Josh, well, he's drunk. You are drunk most of the time, tell the man. But that doesn't mean he ain't telling the truth or that I can't balance these fucking beer bottles. Look at the waitresses, they love this. Some excitement in their lives. The thrill of broken glass. All those years and years of things falling out of the sky, of things breaking, shattering. Well, sometimes, I think it gets a little too quiet for them."

"You plan to break those bottles?" asked Calvino, as if it were his bar.

"I ain't ever broken a bottle in one year, have I, Josh?"

"Charlie never has broken a fucking bottle. That's correct," said Josh.

"That's a fact," said Charlie.

"Once I saw Josh on the hydrofoil to Vung Tao with this beautiful Vietnamese girl. It was early morning and he was drunk. And you know what Josh was doing?"

"I don't remember," said Josh.

"You were teaching her English."

"I'm an English teacher."

"You were teaching her the lyrics to Gilligan's Island. That old TV show. And, you know, by the time the hydrofoil reached Vung Tao, she was singing the Gilligan's Island theme song all by herself."

"I don't remember that."

"You were with that lawyer. The one who got himself killed."

"Drew Markle," said Josh.

"He took his job too seriously," said Charlie. Calvino leaned toward Charlie.

"Why too seriously?"

The fat man was concentrating on stacking a Tiger beer bottle. "Sometimes, Drew would complain that there was no rule of law in Vietnam."

"He got that part right," said Josh.

"But you can't go around saying that to the Viet-namese," said Charlie.

"Charlie's right on target. He said it one too many times and they blew him up."

Calvino watched Charlie's fat finger position one empty Tiger beer bottle on top of the other. They were Josh's empties.

"And you can't be too successful in business. Let's say you get a successful bar up and running," said the fat man, who was late 20s and had a deep Southern accent that made him sound like he was from another century. "The Vietnamese will notice your success. They will get together and find a way to take the bar away from you. Why? Because you are a foreigner and you are making money. They don't think that foreigners should be allowed to make all that money from a bar in Saigon. It bothers them. It isn't your country. You're an American. You lost the war. Why the fuck should you come back to Vietnam and take away their money from right under their nose? And then say there are rules to protect them. It don't make sense to them. So they find a way and the rules don't matter. They'll find someone to yank your visa, take away your lease, threaten you, hint they can cause an accident. Like Drew Markle. They got rid of him the old-fashioned way. And he was just a lawyer. Christ, if he had been running a successful bar, they would have dropped an A-bomb on him."

As he said the word A-bomb, his pyramid of empty beer bottles and Q-Bar ashtrays became unstable, collapsed, and fell to the tiled floor on both sides of the bar, showering glass in every direction.

"Christ," said Charlie, his eyes wide.

"That's the first time that ever happened. Tell him, Josh."

"Fuck, Charlie, it happens all the time. Stop jazzing the guy."

"Not that often."

"Who do you think killed Drew Markle?" asked Calvino. Charlie stood, looking down at the broken glass.

"There will be manned colonies on the moon before they solve his murder," said Charlie.

"Point is, no one cares," said Josh.

"The communists got themselves a crippled RVN sergeant. The Americans want to do business here. The sergeant's okay with them. That's the end of it."

They were still talking about why no one had any interest in pursuing Drew Markle's killers when Douglas Webb came into the bar with a woman. The buzz at the bar stopped as the *farang* crowd stared at the woman on Webb's arm. She wore a red, sleeveless dress with a hemline exposing her legs to full advantage, the kind of dress which clung to the body like fresh paint, imported shoes with six-inch heels, and a firm 37" bust was half-exposed as the dress did one of those fashionable U-turns at the cleavage, leaving a shadow large enough to hide a handgun.

"This is Vincent Demato, Darla, he's the client I was telling you about," said Webb.

Darla held out her hand, smiling at Calvino, who had turned around on his stool. Josh's head rose from his glass, his droopy eyes growing larger, and Charlie forgot all about the broken glass, running his thick fingers over his head, slicking back his dirty brown hair from his forehead. Calvino grasped her hand and she pouted her lips into a red, dayglo like kiss. "He said you're from Brooklyn. I think that is so romantic. Barry Manilow is from Brooklyn and I have every one of his records."

"I'm opening a bar in Saigon," said Calvino, shaking her hand.

Darla moved in close enough that he could smell her perfume. "Once I had this dream that I was giving Barry Manilow a blow-job," she whispered. "I had him in my mouth, you know. He was pushing my head back and forth like he was really into it and everything. Then there was this loud bang."

"And?" asked Calvino.

She pulled away from his ear.

"I woke up. It was someone setting off Chinese firecrackers outside my window. In Bangkok, where I live, the Chinese are always throwing firecrackers. I think they think to make lots of noise late at night makes their cock hard. Otherwise, why would they do it?"

"Enough," said Webb, his hands around her waist and pulling her back.

Webb stepped forward and put his arm around Calvino's neck.

"Hey, sorry buddy, about being late and all that crap. But you know...," he glanced over at Darla and then winked at Calvino.

"Let's take a table. I want to talk to you."

"Here's the guy you should be asking about who killed Drew Markle," said Josh.

Webb looked around at Calvino.

"You do business in a city, you wanna know why people get killed."

"Here, they do what they want," said Charlie. "Isn't that right, counsellor?"

"You certainly do what you want, Charlie," said Webb.

"That I do."

"You need a beer?" asked Webb, turning away from Charlie and toward Calvino.

"I always need a beer."

Webb gestured to the bartender and slipped away from the bar.

Calvino followed Webb over to the table as Darla walked with her arm wrapped around Webb's. They sat in the corner. Webb waved a waiter over and ordered a round of drinks.

"Look, I've got a meeting set up for you," said Webb.

Calvino waited, saying nothing for a moment as he watched Webb's eyes.

"What are we talking about? Meeting about what?" asked Calvino.

His eyes glanced at Darla and then back at Webb. This made Webb break into a wide smile. "Not with Darla. But with a guy who has a property for lease. It was a bar until the police shut it down a few months ago. He had leased the ground floor to some Australian who drank too much beer. He was married to a Vietnamese whore. The Aussie had a permanent hard-on. You know the type, Darla. But this Aussie rubbed the local police the wrong way. He hit one cop in the face, knocked him out, stole his sidearm. Sure he showed up an hour later at the police station and gave the gun back. But hey, I'm sorry, but you don't punch a Vietnamese cop in the mouth and make yourself popular in Saigon. I told the owner you wanted a class place. There wouldn't be any trouble with the police. You had something like the Q-Bar in mind. And that you would be willing to fix it up so long as he gave you a three-year lease."

"Where is this place?" asked Calvino.

Webb smiled again, leaned forward. "That's the beauty of it. It not that far from the Q-Bar, the hottest bar in Saigon.

You can draw the same kind of crowd. Saigon is big enough for two first-class expat bars. I think enough of the idea to even put some of my own money in if you want. You know, just to show good faith."

"When's the meeting?" asked Calvino.

"At eleven. About twenty minutes from now. It was the only time Mr. Tang had free."

"Tang? You mean like the orange drink?" asked Calvino. This made Darla laugh.

"You are funny," she said. "I like men who make me laugh."

"Tang like the soft drink. It's called Karen's Bar and it's about a ten minute walk," said Webb. "Go have a look around with Mr. Tang, if you like the location and see the possibility, then come back. I can draw up the contracts tomorrow and you are in business."

"What if I don't like the place?" asked Calvino. "Then we'll find another one, Vincent."

Darla sighed, "I just love your accent, Mr. Demato."

"And I love your dream about the Barry Manilow blow-job," he said.

"Funny thing, most men like that dream a lot."

According to Calvino's law, you need to know two things about your enemy: what he wants and what he fears. You can't deliver what he wants, any more than you can put the ocean in a bottle, but you can do something about the fear. You study the mechanisms of his fear, study the wires, then disconnect, if you are right, you are alive, if you are wrong, then you are dead, like Drew Markle. Calvino was banking that what Webb wanted was money. Above respect, above his career, above any sense of right and wrong. He had given him an opportunity to have a great deal of money.

CHAPTER 9

THE LAST RAT OUT

CALVINO FELT THE weight of the Smith & Wesson hugging his body like a lover comforting him, snuggling real close as if nothing in the world was strong enough to come between them. But he knew this was a lie with a woman and a lie with a gun. In Vietnam, a handgun worked like an infant's security blanket, something better left behind once one left childhood; a handgun was about as much use as a security blanket in a firefight where the other side was armed with combat zone fire-power. But a small argument against the forces of dark and evil was better than no argument at all.

He stood on the pavement, the fountain to his back, and glanced through the window of the Q-Bar. In the far corner of the bar, still seated at the table where he had left them, and in full public display were Webb and Darla. He saw Darla's long, wet tongue move between her teeth and touch the tip of Webb's nose, and then her tongue entered his mouth like in a porno film or a horror film, a devouring kiss which unleashed a monster. He turned and walked away. He had seen enough. Calvino's law said that any woman who loved Barry Manilow's music and dreamed of going down on him was still stranded circa 1969 in a Sport's Illustrated Swimsuit issue. A time-warp baby. He had a fix on Darla, pegging her as that unusual brand of hooker—a Zone freak, a hardcore regular one ran across now and again—a genuine romantic in a mechanical, functional profession which was built on the illusion of romance and the reality of commerce.

Calvino moved quickly past the line of cyclos parked outside the Q-Bar; some of these drivers worked as undercover security agents, police, military and God knew what from other intelligence organizations. Chinese, Korean, American. Others worked for the privatized sector of the local mafia. He avoided them. A couple of ragged cyclo drivers pushed their cyclos away from the curb and rolled as if to chase him, running and panting, crying, "Mister, where you go?" Calvino waved each of them away, and their smiles vanished like a series of light bulbs as they explode one after another until there is nothing but complete darkness. But they finally got the message, peeled away, turned and walked back to their space in front of the Q-Bar.

He walked along the street, dodging cyclos, motor-cycles and cars for some time, trying to figure what Webb's angle was in setting up a meeting at night. Maybe he was hungry for that two hundred grand, thought Calvino. On the main road, he flagged down a cyclo and told the driver to take him to a street a short walk from Karen's Bar. The driver looked at him, sizing him for the fare.

"Two dollars," said the cyclo driver, climbing off the bicycle seat.

It was one of the few places on earth outside of America that drivers quoted fares in dollars.

"Five thousand dong," said Calvino. He climbed into the seat.

The driver, who was no more than a boy, stared at him before climbing back on the bicycle seat behind Calvino.

"One dollar," said the driver, immediately dropping his price by half.

"You don't like dong?" asked Calvino.

"Dong no good. Dollar much better."

"Okay, one dollar."

The cyclo driver smiled, then not long afterwards, the cyclo turned left onto Hai Ba Trung Street, then made a right, not stopping for the light to turn green, at Le Thanh Ton Street. No one stopped for traffic lights or stop signs unless there was a policeman standing on the corner. The cyclo passed Don Dat Street. Calvino motioned for the driver to pull over to the curb. He climbed off the cyclo and paid him. He stood in the street until the cyclo disappeared from sight, then walked into Don Dat Street, and, a few minutes later, he cut down a small lane. It was as dark as inside the elevator during the power failure. There were no street lights. Calvino kept on walking, feeling his heart beat increase, the weight of his shoulder rig and the Smith & Wesson, whispering a lullaby, in a sweet voice.

"You're gonna be just fine, baby."

He stopped and stared down the street and made out a dimly lit rim of light framing a few windows here and there. As he approached the lights inside the buildings showed the shadowy outline of windows, doors, roofs; the street was lined on both sides with old, cramped, dark shophouses, smelling of dry rot, backed-up sewage, and street garbage. Behind the padlocked gates some dogs barked. Nothing moved along on the small lane. He stood on the broken pavement, thinking how this was like Bangkok. In the distance, he could make out the sound of one of the Chinese soup boys beating bamboo sticks. Some traffic passed on the street, a cycle, then a motorbike, then an old man pushing a cart. He kept on moving ahead, almost stumbling over a woman who looked about eight months pregnant sleeping on the sidewalk beside her man. Their bed was a piece of cardboard. Bamboo stick music filtered through her dreams, he thought. The general wretchedness of the neighborhood would have made the lower East side of Manhattan look like Singapore. A hell'va place for an expat bar, he thought, as he stood listening and watching on the street.

There was unusual silence for a huge, slummed-out Asian city that had people swarming and crawling over every square inch of the place, picking over the scraps like junkyard dogs. More pregnant women camping on bamboo mats shifted in the shadows. He walked on until he came to a row of shophouses. He looked up at a painted sign that read: Karen's Bar. Behind him a cyclo driver called out, "You, you. I take you now. Go find girl. Make love, good. Not expensive. Drink beer. Take girl. Can."

Calvino shook his head and watched him pedal away, thinking he should call him back and make the call in the morning. He tossed a coin in his mind's eye. Heads he stayed, tails he left. It came down heads. He thought about two out of three, then he walked three more steps and pounded on the gate of the vacant bar but no one answered from inside. He kicked the door out of frustration, wondering what Webb's game was and why he was hanging around the Q-Bar every night and how such a lawyer had ever been hired by Winchell & Holly. He was about to leave when a Vietnamese leaned out of the window two floors over his head and shouted down.

"Take the staircase on the side. I'm up here."

Calvino stepped back and saw an old skinny Vietnamese man in a dirty singlet leaning out the window. Behind him a naked light bulb hung from the ceiling. He had pillow hair matted on one side like he had been sleeping. The other side was bald. Some men had that kind of hair they had to parcel out over the skull in a thin layer for maximum coverage.

"You Mr. Tang?"

"That's me. You Demato?" Calvino nodded.

"Webb said you had a bar for rent." Calvino stood back in the street and tried to imagine a bar in the shophouse. Bright lights, prostitutes, loud voices, a jukebox, and the smell of cigarettes and beer.

"You're looking at it."

There wasn't much to look at. No wonder the former owner had gone out of business. Prison must have been a holiday camp after this neighborhood. Just finding the place required persistence and courage. Tourists taking one look at the street would have headed for the high ground of the Rex and Continental Hotels. Keeping in the circle of light like moths happy with the heat of the flame.

"Why don't you come down and open up?"

The old man shrugged.

"The rats..." Then he stopped himself.

"What about the rats?" Calvino sensed the landlord and forgot himself for a minute. Having stopped short of explaining the rat problem was a good sign, thought Calvino. If you are trying to rent a bar, then you leave the rat problem for the new tenant to discover for himself after he has signed the lease. That's why he wanted him to come upstairs. He probably had someone to go down and clear the rats out before he allowed Calvino to go inside.

"I'm from Brooklyn. I grew up with rats. I had two hundred kills with an air-rifle the summer I turned eleven. I had two hundred notches on my rifle butt."

There was a light to the old man's back making him look about a hundred years old but, in reality, Calvino guessed he was about sixty, with a couple of missing teeth, flabby arm skin and weepy eyes that looked like yellow piss holes in the snow. By the time he got down to street level, he was coughing, one of those deep smoker's hacks. Calvino watched him bring up a lunger, and spit the contents of his lungs into the street. Stepping on a landmine or one of Mr. Tang's lungers would be registered about equal on the horror meter. At ground level, Mr. Tang looked like he had shrunk to half size. His skinny legs stuck out of baggy shorts. He carried an oil lamp with a broken glass pane on one side and a large metal ring with keys. He didn't look like a landlord, a man of means.

"You own this building?"

Mr. Tang looked up from the keys. "I am the manager," he said.

"Who is the owner?"

His face turned to a Halloween black tooth smile.

"Someone from Hanoi. I rent it for him."

"Beautiful place like this. You shouldn't have any trouble."

"In Vietnam there is always trouble," he said.

Mr. Tang turned back to the key chain and the padlock which was in the middle of a fistful of chains pulled around the metal grates in the shophouse gate. After he unlocked the padlock, he unwrapped the chain and pulled up the metal gate. Then he reached down and picked up the oil lamp.

"Remember, watch out for the rats. The Australian was no good with rats. Mr. Evans complain very much. Say too many rats. Too much rent. Say Mr. Tang no good. He fight with everybody. He fight with police. No good. Police beat him up, break his balls, and take away his wife. She's in prison. Next month she have baby," said Mr. Tang, making a gesture over his stomach to show how fat she had been at the time of her arrest. "But he was the bad one. Not her. The police let him go. Said she was selling girls. Communist don't like prostitution. Say old regime have

Saigon girls fucking foreigners. No good. Fucking no good, they say."

"I don't plan to run girls from the bar," said Calvino.

Mr. Tang looked him up and down. "Yeah, if you say so."

He didn't sound so sure and snorted back a laugh and brought up another lunger which he coughed up in stages, dragging it like a snake from his lungs, before spitting it on the sidewalk. Then he stepped inside the main room. Calvino followed a step behind. The oil lamp cast light about the height of a man against the floor, falling just short of the bar.

"How much is the rent?" asked Calvino.

"Very cheap price. Three thousand dollars a month. Two years paid in advance."

He rolled off the finance part of the deal straight away without blinking an eye. He wouldn't have been surprised if the old man had pulled out a lease and pen and asked him to sign it on the spot.

"You want it?"

"And you will throw in rat traps as fixtures?" asked Calvino. The old man pretended not to hear him. He looked at Calvino as if he had already decided it was a mistake to come down and open up for him. But he had gone this far and decided to go ahead and show Calvino the premises.

"You fight with police, they break your balls," he said as a kind of half warning. "The police come here and break Evans' balls."

Drew Markle had more than his balls busted, thought Calvino.

What had been on the diskettes? And why had he asked Mai to keep copies at home? Why didn't he ask Jackie Ky to help him out? She was American... The thoughts crashed through the gates of his mind, and ran, and ran. He was distracted, lost in thought as Mr. Tang crossed the floor and put the oil lamp on the bar. Out of the corner of his eye, Calvino caught a movement as the light danced in the mirror behind the bar. A quick blur of motion which pulled him out of his thoughts and back into the moment. In the stinking, dark bar. The flash of motion could have been anything. A head, shoulder, arm or an extremely large rat standing on its hindlegs checking out a potential new owner. In less than a second Calvino dived out of the light, rolling over the floor and aiming for cover behind an over-turned table outside the arc of the lamp light. He crawled on his belly as the first shots ripped through the darkness. Tang groaned, said something in Vietnamese, then thumped like a fish that had taken a hook deep in its gut, and disappeared under the surface for one last, final dive. Calvino wasn't sure how many of the shots had been fired, and whether all of the shots were intended for Tang. The firing stopped, and silence engulfed the bar. A long, tense quiet waiting for someone to make the next move. In the darkness he pulled out the Smith & Wesson from the shoulder rig. The feel of a gun was as good as the feel of a woman, and gripping the gun in the expectation of killing, choosing the moment, waiting with a finger pressed against the trigger, was unlike any other wait on the planet. A death watch. He won the advantage, and whoever had shot at him was exposed with the light to their backs. But, as in his worst nightmare, they had enough fire-power to blow him across the street.

He didn't have to wait long before he saw a head pop up from the side of the bar. "Rats," he thought. "Big, motherfuckering rats." Calvino watched as the barrel of an AK47 came around the corner. The gunman exposed his head slowly, then he rose shoulder high, directly putting himself in the line of fire. Calvino squeezed three quick rounds, hitting the man in his left eye, jaw and the last round passed straight through the neck and shattered the mirror behind the bar. Seven years bad luck, he thought. There was silence for a moment which was broken by two male voices exchanging orders in Vietnamese, as he moved back from his firing position. Halfway down the bar, another figure rose up as if he were immortal, an automatic rifle tucked in close to the body and began firing, sweeping the darkness. AK47 rounds ripped into the wall several inches above Calvino's head. The table top was metal but that didn't stop a slug from passing clean through. A second burst split the oil lamp in half, and the oil splashed across the bar carrying a wave of flames. Calvino counted one, two, then flipped around the table, his hands around the gun, took aim and dropped the second gunman with two rounds. The man's head jerked and he fell onto the burning counter top, making a gurgling noise as blood filled his mouth and lungs. The last gunman had meanwhile circled away from the bar, and the fire. Coughing from the smoke, he rolled right in front of the doorway. Smoke had got into the gunman's eyes, half-blinding him, instinctively, his hands had come up to rub his eyes. Three blind mice. See how they run. Calvino didn't wait for him to take his hands away from his eyes and back to his gun. Calvino shot him four times and the third gunman fell against the side of the metal gate and was dead before he hit the cement.

Calvino found a handkerchief stuffed in his jacket pocket, pulled it out, and covered his nose and mouth as he slowly rose to his feet. He edged forward, stopping to check the two bodies of the gunmen who had died at the bar counter. The interior temperature of Karen's Bar was rising. He turned over the first gunman, who was obviously dead. Then he pushed over the second man whose head was split open, leaking blood like engine oil, bone and brains mixed with the blood. Blown apart by a high-tech piece of plastic in the shape of a gun. Both of the gunmen were young Vietnamese, early 20s, plastic sandals, not badly dressed. In terms of tailoring, the dead men were several cuts above the average cyclo driver parked in front of the Q-Bar. The hitman who was dead at the entrance was older. Calvino made him somewhere in his mid-30s when time had stopped forever. It didn't matter, none of them were ever going to see forty.

In front of the bar, Calvino stopped and knelt beside the body of Mr. Tang who had been hit by a couple of AK47 rounds and most of his head was gone and his brains were splattered across the floor. A couple of slugs from the AK47 had torn away his face; no one, not even his mother, would have recognized whether this was an old or young man, or if it were a man at all. Tang's clothes were on fire. There was the sickening smell of burning flesh. Calvino was shaking and angry, thinking how Webb had sent him and this old man to get themselves killed in Saigon. A moment later, he was out the back door, keeping to the shadows, climbing over a wall to the adjacent shophouse. He looked back at the flames leaping into the night. Below the wall, in the light of the flames, he saw dozens of rats were running out of the door. Jesus, he thought. How could one place have so many rats? He knew that the street was no longer silent and empty, but teeming with people running in every direction. These people had heard gunfire, seen bodies with bullet holes, and watched the flames of destruction before. The nightmare had returned to their lives and they rushed to see the carnage and to celebrate that once again they had survived. What they didn't know was that Calvino was already over one wall, and scaling a second wall, taking evasive action under cover of darkness.

Calvino, smelling of smoke and fire, stayed on the back streets as he walked back to the Q-Bar. He hoped that in the tropical heat of the night he would lose the smell of death. At the Fourth of July picnic, he had worn the cheap cologne. He admitted to Pratt that he had no sense of smell. But he had been wrong, he couldn't get rid of the scent of death, burning flesh, which clung to his nostrils. After scaling several more walls, he came to an alley and kept on moving low to the ground until about a kilometer later he finally came to a main street. He ignored a succession of cyclo drivers who came alongside, looking at this man in the wrinkled, soiled suit, smoky hair, and unknotted tie. They just kept on pedaling. He didn't look like a passenger they wanted to deal with. His return journey to the Q-Bar, with all of his diversions, took about forty minutes and by the time he arrived, he had worked up a sweat, his shirt was soaked, sweat dripping off the end of his nose and chin. Webb had gone and so had Darla. But the Q-Bar was packed with people three deep around the bar, drinking and talking business. Funny thing was the music. The Miles Davis tape Jackie Ky had been playing earlier that day rose above the background chatter around the bar. One of the bartenders had cranked up the sound.

"What sauna did you find?" asked the school-teacher.

Calvino sat down at the bar. "It never gets this hot in Brooklyn."

The schoolteacher laughed.

"You looking for your friends?" he asked.

"Well, you won't find them. Webb's probably fucking her. I wish I was fucking her. Everyone at the bar wishes they were fucking her. But we ain't. Not tonight. So we are getting drunk. You want a drink?"

"Yeah, I want a drink," said Calvino.

"So how did Karen's Bar look to you?"

"A little on the rundown side. Bad neighborhood, too," said Calvino.

"You smell like you've been eating at a beggar's barbecue."

Calvino took a long drink out of the beer the bar-tender handed him.

"You like Webb?" Calvino asked.

The schoolteacher 's forehead wrinkled.

"Let's put it this way. If he were on fire, I wouldn't piss on him."

"Did you see Webb leave?"

He smiled, taking a long drink on his beer.

"Not long after you took off."

"Do me a favor."

"What kind of favor?"

There was an edge of suspicion in his voice.

"In case anyone asks, I was at the bar all night. I left for five, ten minutes, then came back, bitching I couldn't find Karen's Bar. Can you do that for me?"

"A real mystery man we got here. What happened? You get in a fight or something?"

"Something like that," said Calvino.

"Hey, you've got yourself in some shit. That goes with the territory of Saigon. And you need someone to cover for you, right?"

Calvino smiled.

"How about another beer?" he said.

He gave the schoolteacher a couple of twenties.

"Take care of my bill."

"Where are you going?"

"To see if Webb is on fire. Unlike you, I would piss on him." Calvino had pulled real hard on the reins of his rage but the four horses kept galloping full speed ahead, cliff or no cliff, those ponies weren't stopping for any one. The man had sent him out intending him to get killed. Setting him up for a hit. Pratt had said it was going to happen, he had set himself up by handing over that much money as if he had a death wish. His cover was that of a *farang* who didn't know the story of how things worked in Southeast Asia, but Calvino had been in Asia for years and years. What he hadn't known for all his years in Asia was the kind of love for a woman that made a man think stupid things such as love was powerful enough to have won a foothold in the world. Of course it hadn't even come close. It was novice thinking; the kind of thinking that got you killed. By the time he had walked out the door of the Q-Bar, he had convinced himself not to go straight to Webb's apartment and kill him. That had been the temptation. He wouldn't really kill him, but he would make Webb wish he were dead. The sonofabitch, he thought, had finally figured out that Demato was Calvino, a lawyer, who once, in New York City, had represented an English grifter named Gentlemen James, the bed wetter, who had got a huge settlement from Webb's client.

§ § § § §

AT the reception desk of his hotel, the room key was gone and the young clerk with thick, black hair had a large grin on his face. Behind him on a Sony TV, a Chinese kung-fu film was playing from a VCR hooked to the TV, and three hotel staff sat on the floor watching an action scene. Two more had sheets pulled over their bodies, curled up, sleeping against the wall. They looked like corpses and the lobby looked like a public hospital morgue. Motorcycles were parked all down the first floor corridor.

"I give your friend the key," said the clerk. "What friend is that?"

The clerk winked. "You know. Your American friend. She's very beautiful. Very big."

With his hands he gave the universal sign language for very large breasts.

All the way up in the elevator he was trying to figure out how Webb's mind worked. Expat lawyers in Southeast Asia, the local hires, were a breed apart from their brethren in America. Those lawyers, who survived on the edges of a world closed to foreign lawyers, made themselves useful because they had learned to understand the importance of the unwritten code of fear and face. How a deal would blow; how someone could get a bullet in the back of the head. Guys like Webb had usually developed a specialized taste, and their experience turned them away from a part of themselves, alienated some inner core, made them hard like steel, not just ruthless, but the moral compass which pointed to right or wrong got smashed along the way. They were usually smart, street smart, that is, they knew where young girls or boys could be found at bargain price. Or who had to be paid to fix a problem. They knew how to work the Zone to their commercial advantage. They were loners who stayed out of the limelight because that kind of attention made them nervous. However, that didn't make them killers. Killing a man was easy enough to talk about but, even for the hardcore guesthouse lawyer, working the fringes of small-time deals, it was a rare thing for a man to find enough courage to pull the trigger. They worked a bloodless line of words and phrases, making paper trails. This wasn't just crossing some line drawn in the sand, this was crossing a void with no name, a void which entered the man, and became him in a way he never anticipated. Taking another man's life marked a separation from everyone else who lived on the other side of the divide; and once that happened, there was no turning back, no return to the paper trails. Gentleman James had pissed in the richest beds for a living. It was the one link to the past that Webb shared with him, thought Calvino. But Calvino had crossed that line. What would it take for Webb to kill a man? That was the question.

The elevator door closed behind him as he knocked on the door to his room.

When the door opened, Darla stood in black high-heels, six-inch heels, and she was wearing one of his shirts unbuttoned to the navel, the sleeves rolled up. She put her arms around him and kissed him hard on the mouth. He held her arms under his own, keeping her hands away from the gun he was carrying.

He kept his eyes open, looking behind her. The bathroom door was half-open. She opened her eyes and moaned.

"You taste good," she said, pulling back.

Calvino pushed open the bathroom door with his foot, looked inside.

"Where's Doug?"

"Not in your bathroom," she said, laughing.

"Then where?"

"He went to the office. Where else? All he does is work, work, work. He lives for his work. And it can make him so boring."

She walked back to the double bed, took a cigarette out of her handbag, lit it, raised her head, and let the smoke coil out of her thin nose.

"I always charge lawyers in six minute intervals. It makes them feel, well, homey. Hey, you look kinda beat up. Are you okay?"

"I am having a great night. Does Doug know that you came here?"

She shook her head.

"It's none of his business."

"Why are you here?"

"Why, your charm, of course." She inhaled on the cigarette until the ash grew long and gray before it fell onto the carpet. "And Doug said you are opening a club in Saigon. I started thinking. Yeah, a bar in Saigon run by an American. It's romantic. Plus I am getting bored in Bangkok. So I am thinking to myself, Darla, here is a chance for a new start. Everyone knows that Vietnam is about to take off. The Vietnamese love Americans. Don't ask me why. After all we bombed them for years. But they love us. I want to live in a place where people love us, Mr. Demato."

"You want a job," Calvino said, sitting on a chair opposite the bed.

"Exactly."

"And this is your idea of an interview."

"If you are shy, then no one is going to notice you."

"That rule wouldn't apply to you."

She let the shirt open and expose one large, firm breast with a pink nipple.

"They aren't silicon. They are real. Natural. No sag. You can touch it. Go on, it won't bite you."

Calvino sighed and leaned back.

"What are your other qualifications?" he asked.

This made her laugh, her red painted lips pulled back, showing some very expensive dental work. This woman took care of herself.

"Any other man would have been all over me. Are you gay, Mr. Demato?"

"Cautiously heterosexual." And incredibly in love, he thought. Why is it after you fall desperately head-over-heels in love, you find a Darla standing in your hotel room door, wearing your shirt, showing her breasts, promising every last single Zone fantasy in the privacy of your own hotel room? Why was the universe o rganized to create such misery and confusion? Was it that the world hated love, and whenever it struck, a Darla strike was launched to rub it out?

"Let's see, I was born in Seattle. I am twenty-four years old. I am 37-23-34, and five foot seven and one half inches. I am university educated. I worked as an RN in Seattle. One night, on the graveyard shift, I read a magazine article about Russian hookers who were getting four hundred dollars a night to fuck Chinese-Thais in Bangkok nightclubs. I was taking home fifteen hundred a month after taxes. I've always had a head for numbers. So I worked out the figures. It was startling. If I worked double shifts in Bangkok like I was working in Seattle, then it would take about two years to make the same money as thirty-three years in Seattle. When it comes right down to it, is there that much more dignity in a bedpan than letting a stranger make love to you?"

That was one of those Zone questions that no one ever had an answer for.

"How long have you worked in Bangkok?"

"Eighteen months."

"How long have you known Webb?"

"About a year. He pays like everyone else. I want you to understand that."

"Why give up a good thing in Bangkok for a bar which isn't even opened in Saigon?"

She leaned forward off the bed, wrapping her arms around his neck.

"Because I've had it up to here with Bangkok. The traffic on Sukhumvit and Silom. The air pollution is so bad I can't breathe. Bangkok is turning every call girl I know into a raving environmentalist. What I am saying, Mr. Demato, is that it's time for me to make a change."

"Bangkok's definitely not Seattle, and neither is Saigon," said Calvino.

He got off the chair, walked over to the small fridge, knelt down and took out a beer.

"Want one?" he asked over his shoulder.

"Honey, I would love one."

He took out two cans of 333 beer and snapped the tabs, handing one to Darla on the bed. She had the figure of a catwalk supermodel. The woman didn't have a bad angle, he circled her looking for that one ugly profile to make him feel that he wasn't giving up that much but, all he ended up doing was pacing, and working himself up into one of those blacked-out moods that he poured booze into. She leaned forward on one arm, her legs crossed, a relaxed smile on her face, as if she were right at home, no hang-ups, no stress. Good ole West Coast Pacific Northwest ease and grace. She took the beer and drank straight from the can.

"I'm trying to imagine you as a nurse in Seattle," he said. "You know, as part of the American health care problem."

She held up the beer can.

"I'm trying to imagine you as my boss," she said. "And I don't see any problems."

He liked that about her: she was quick off the mark.

"The other night in the Q-Bar Jackie Ky was giving Doug a hard time," he said, watching her on the bed.

"That bitch," she said, the fire flashing into her eyes. "Whoa, why do you call Jackie a bitch?"

"Doug probably didn't tell you. But Jackie Ky is a prime suspect in the murder of that lawyer who was killed here. I liked Drew. He was a nice kid. You know the type. Decent. All-American values. Knew how to treat a woman right. He was much too nice for her, that much is for sure."

"Why would she kill someone?"

Darla rolled her eyes like she had to explain two plus two.

"Because she found out that Drew was having an affair with some Vietnamese girl named Mai. She's a secretary or something at Winchell & Holly. Drew had something going with her, I guess. Well, I don't know how much clothing they had on, but one night, Doug caught them late at the office. Let's say in a com-promising position."

He swallowed hard, his face and throat were burning. I don't believe it, he said to himself. Was this one of Webb's crazy lies? Or a weird kind of sexual foreplay he used to stoke the fires with Darla?

"And he told Jackie Ky about it?" asked Calvino.

"I don't know who told her. Does it really matter? She found out. Women don't like cheating men. Men can't seem to get that message in their head or in their balls. So, if she killed him, then, even as much as I liked Drew, well, he got what he deserved."

"You've been working in the Comfort Zone too long."

She laughed, and gave him a flash of recognition.

"Yeah, you got that right. I was a Zone chick. But Jackie's not. If she were a Thai Zone head, then Drew would still be alive but minus his dick. What do you think is better. Dead? Or dickless?"

"Wanna another beer?"

Calvino pulled two more beers out of the fridge. He flipped the same mental coin in his head. The same one he flipped before he went into Karen's Bar. This time it came down tails. Tails Darla goes... Two out of three, he said to himself. I should have done two out of three at Karen's Bar, he thought. After two more imaginary flips, he went into the bathroom and hid the Smith & Wesson under a pile of dirty clothes. Thank you for saving my ass tonight, he thought, giving a kiss to the plastic barrel. He showered, combed his hair, looked in the mirror, thinking about Mai with Drew. It made him crazy to think of that possibility. He turned out the bathroom light and walked out wearing only a towel wrapped around his waist. The main overhead lights were off. Only a side light near the bed illuminated her standing naked looking out from the balcony at the night. The sound coming back was from the bamboo sticks of a Chinese soup boy.

"Soup's ready," whispered Calvino, as he came up behind her.

"Good, because I'm real hungry," she said, turning around

and flipping the towel away from his waist.

He took a deep, deep breath, moved slowly away from her, put the towel back around his waist. She didn't fuck Markle, he said to himself. Faith, he said. It was an old-fashioned word that hadn't crossed his mind for years. Faith was for fools, for people who lived outside the Zone. It was also for lovers, which was just another word for a fool. If he did not link faith in Mai with his love for her, then it would be lost; it wouldn't matter. None of this would matter, and he would go back to Bangkok, his slum, his office, his Zone haunts, his missing person cases, and pass time until time finally passed him. He said the word, faith, over and over again, as he walked to the French doors to the balcony. Below, the boy with the bamboo sticks walked across the parking lot, making music. Behind him, Darla dressed and a couple of minutes later she let herself out without saying another word. Four dead men were in a burning building. The woman he loved was at home in bed. He was still alive. Looking into the night, he told himself that in life you needed some act of faith. Something beyond yourself to believe in. There was so much static misinformation in the world, crossing through computers, conversations, entering minds slightly altered, perverted, shuffled along the network, splitting into fragments along the web. This is what Drew Markle and Mark Wang and the men he killed tonight no longer have.

CHAPTER 10

FIRE ON COMFORT ZONE ICE

"YOU'RE NOT MAKING a lot of sense. Jackie gave you a gun. Mai is going to give you a diskette with Drew Markle's private files on it. You used the gun but don't know if you can get the diskette. If I didn't really know you, I'd say that you have been babbling," said Pratt.

"*Mai dtem baht.*"

"I know I sound like I am operating at fifty satang. Let me start over, bring in the other fifty satang," Calvino said. He knew this Thai expression. There were a hundred satang in one Thai baht, about four cents US. Thais used the money metaphor for the slang expression to describe defective mental facilities or full facilities but flawed reasoning.

Shakespeare had lots of minor characters who were mai dtem baht. Like the fool in King Lear who was whipped by the daughters for telling the truth, thought Pratt. Calvino looked like a whipping boy, sitting too far forward from the edge for his own good. The fool in Shakespeare was the man who told the truth and suffered because only a fool does not understand how truth can inflict misery and pain more damaging than the most gross lie.

Pratt waited as a silence fell between them. Calvino sat, shifting from one side to the other, not feeling comfortable and not saying anything. It was like he was thinking, straightening out the sequence of events, the order of how the horror had grown legs, crept up on him and grabbed him by the throat.

Calvino sat forward, rocking, his arms folded around his chest, staring down, his legs dangling over the edge of the scaffolding with a solid air of defeat about him. Someone or something had knocked him into a hyperstate where depression and rage commingled. Pratt had gone easy on him; a *farang* on the edge could be unpredictable, which made it all the more unnerving since *farang* claimed some monopoly on logic, control, analysis, so when that snapped, and they looked over the edge at a floor four stories below, a Thai didn't know what firework of intellect and emotion was at work, if the *farang* might jump or was content to just think about jumping.

If Pratt could have looked inside Calvino's mind, he would have found him thinking about a Vietnamese girl named Mai, and wondering to himself really how little he knew who she was and how little that seemed to matter; it defied every rule he had laid down, applying to a man's relationship with a woman. Love did that kind of thing, shattered rules, common sense, and then there was duty. He had started to keep things back already, and he was going over in his mind whether to break this cycle, and level with Pratt about Mai's possible link to the double murder. Easy to think about doing but much harder to do. He wanted to protect her, there was no reason for her to have told him about the diskette, he was certain that she hadn't told anyone. If he was right about her, then he was the only one other than her who knew about Drew's legacy.

Looking down at the stage, he thought about the three men he had killed inside the old Karen's Bar, an abandoned rat infested room that was on fire as he ran out. Tang's brain gook on the toe of one shoe. Afterwards, he had vomited in the street. Then, what? Yeah, he remembered. Darla had been waiting for him to return, all nice and cosy inside his room. A Seattle nurse turned high-price call girl to the wealthy businessmen in Bangkok, and their friends from the neighborhood—Japan, Korea, Singapore, Hong Kong and Taiwan. She had yanked off his towel and he had pulled back from her. Sitting in the dark beside Pratt thinking about that scene, it was like it had happened to someone else. Why had he done that? It wasn't because she was a *mem*-farang; was it simply because of Mai? So far with the Hanoi girl, nothing had been simple. Chipping through the deep ice in Zone haunts like Patpong all the way to the Q-Bar, he had emerged with Mai at his side. No one would have believed this was something that Vincent Calvino would have done. Not even Vincent Calvino could quite believe what he had turned down in the name of love. Next he would be thinking of a building an up-country cottage, white picket fence, and having kids and a dog.

These were some of Calvino's nonlinear links that threaded his thoughts together as he sat on the edge of the scaffolding. The ability to weigh and value events had been blasted apart, he couldn't think straight, it had been a night where death and sex had been strung together like the rough cuts in a dream. He was floating out in the middle of the stage, seeing himself out in the center of that empty place, surrounded by the darkness, with nothing below him and no one in the audience, suspended, wanting to fall back to earth but unable to move. It was no wonder that Pratt had questioned whether he was playing with a full deck.

All he wanted to say to Pratt was he had this ache deep inside and he no longer knew who he was, what really mattered.

"Did I tell you that Darla came to my room?" asked Calvino. He looked down at the stage, the exhaustion of the night slamming into him like a sumo wrestler dropped from a crane.

"Who is Darla and why did she come to your room?" asked Pratt.

"Darla's a ten thousand baht a night call girl from the high-priced ice end of the Zone. Webb treats himself to her once or twice a month. Flies her into Saigon and puts her up at the Rex."

"Lawyers are paid that well in Saigon?" asked Pratt.

"That's what I'm getting to. If you dip into the cash, then you can fly someone like Darla in every other day."

Pratt had the attitude of an interrogating officer, that same tone in his voice that Calvino had heard him use after collaring a suspect. He deserved this, Calvino thought. He had brought it on himself, walking straight into an ambush. He should have known better.

"This happened after you went to Karen's Bar?"

He repeated the name to himself, thinking of Mr. Tang with his funny hair standing in the window and, a few minutes later, part of Mr. Tang's head had been blown away by an AK47.

"And?" Pratt asked after Calvino had gone silent for a minute.

"You know, she's resourceful. Must be that nurse's training. She got the key from the front desk. She was already in my room, wearing one of my shirts and nothing else."

"Why would she do that?"

Calvino grinned, turned and looked at Pratt.

"She was applying for a job in my Saigon club. Webb told her about it. He went back to the office, left her off at the Rex, and she...Well, she has native skills that go beyond the normal interview."

"Or Webb used her to set you up like he did Wang," said Pratt.

"I thought about that. But I had the feeling she was for real."

"Right, you're an exception to the rules of the game. From everyone else she demanded money, but she really liked you. The money was a side issue."

"I am not that crazy. She was playing an angle." Pratt was only half buying the response.

"Did it occur to you she might have had the same effect on Mark Wang? She could have gone to the hotel, walked straight in, no one would have stopped a *mem-farang*, maybe he was waiting for her because he had this feeling she was for real, then she pulled the gun, shot him twice, cleaned his computer hard disk, took the back-up diskettes, and then disappeared. She sounds like a pro to me. Webb hits Markle in Saigon; she takes care of Mark Wang in Bangkok. It's a nice fit. They split the money."

All Calvino had to do was to agree and that would have been the end of it. He would be finished with the case, he could get on with his life. Pratt only wanted him to say that was how it happened. Wang's family would take care of Darla, the heat would be off the Thai Police Department, no small army of reporters fanning out through the Zone to bring international disgrace down on their head. He knew how badly Pratt wanted to put an end to the case. But he couldn't and, deep down, he knew that Darla, whatever else she was or had done, hadn't killed Mark Wang or anyone else.

"She was a nurse, Pratt. In the healing profession."

"A nurse has never killed anyone? Is that what you think?"

"I'm saying Darla didn't kill Mark Wang."

"Then who killed him?"

Calvino shrugged drank from his can of beer, swung his legs back onto the scaffolding and faced Pratt. She had said that Drew had had an affair with Mai, the Hanoi girl. The words were in his brain but he couldn't make them come out. He didn't want Pratt to start on

Mai. And he would have had every right to do so. If she were having an affair with Markle, and Jackie Ky found out what would Jackie have done? She would have had a motive to have him killed. Markle was going to meet her at a restaurant on the river on a road where getting in and out fast was possible that time of night.

"Wang's family would kill Darla. I know that and you know it. We got to be certain before you make that phone call. I know they have turned up the heat on the Department. They want a quick fix. I am not all that happy working on the case. Believe me, it would make my life a lot easier to put this case in a closed file. So, it kind of depends on who we really are, Pratt. If we want to deliver up a head, no one is ever gonna know except you and me that Darla had an opportunity, she had a motive. But there is not one piece of evidence to show that she took the opportunity or was even aware of the money that Wang had stashed with Webb."

Pratt shook his head and opened an envelope he had been holding.

"What'cha got there?" asked Calvino.

"Some footage of the audience the night of the Thai-Vietnam friendship concert. The Saigon concert where everyone sat in the same row. A friend of a friend had a camcorder and filmed the audience. Markle, Webb, Wang are on the tape. Three men. Two of them are dead."

"I killed three men tonight, Pratt."

Pratt ignored the comment. His mind was still on live suspects. "Webb is still my first choice."

"He was mine, too. But now I'm not so sure. There's something that doesn't come together about Jackie Ky. I

215

don't know what it is. But that pack of condoms falling out of her handbag the other night in my room."

"She's being careful, Vincent. Condoms are practical."

"Inside, she's got the wiring of any other American woman. If she really had been that tight with Drew Markle, someone who's been dead less than two weeks, I can't figure where she's coming from. Living in a villa confiscated from her uncle. She has a lot of money and connections. Home delivery of handguns."

Pratt nodded.

"She looks in love with Markle on the tape. And the other woman on the tape, the one with Webb, she most likely is the woman who was in your room tonight."

"Something, isn't she?" asked Calvino. "A Zone queen bee."

"I could've..."

"What?"

"What time is your appointment at Winchell & Holly tomorrow?"

Pratt handed Calvino the envelope. "Ten in the morning."

"Meet me for lunch afterwards," said Calvino. "The Italian restaurant at the Continental Hotel."

"One more thing, Mai, the girl who has got you acting like a teenager on hormone injections, she's on the tape. She's sitting beside Markle. You tell me what you make of the body language between them."

Calvino nodded, leaning forward on his hands.

"I forgot. I'm having lunch with Mai tomorrow."

Pratt rubbed his eyes. "Never mind."

"Don't say, never mind. Thais say never mind when they are totally pissed off."

"I am Thai."

"Do you know she studied nineteenth century Russian literature at the University of Hanoi? How can you not love someone who did that? She's never heard of an MBA degree. She's untouched, unclaimed. Innocent, Pratt. She thinks the Zone is a place you park your motorcycle."

"The claims come later."

"Don't sound like a cynical, married man. I love this woman."

"We'll get together after lunch. The courtyard of the Continental Hotel at two. If that gives you enough time for lunch."

"No problem," said Calvino.

"Thais say that whenever they really have a problem," said Pratt.

"But I'm not Thai."

"Sometimes I'm not so sure."

"Never mind," said Calvino.

This crack—the English translation for *mai pen rai*—made Pratt laugh. "You should be dead."

"I know. It feels great being above an empty stage when I should really be in a morgue. I am going to miss this scaffolding after you leave."

"What do you mean after I leave? You're staying in Saigon?"

"It's starting to look like a possibility."

In two days they would leave Saigon. Pratt would then meet with his superiors in the Department and they would take a decision. Then, a general would make a call to Wang's family in Hong Kong. They would take care of the rest. Your relative gets whacked in Bangkok, what do you do? Call the police? Ask for justice? There was no rule of law. There was only a closing of ranks. Whoever killed Mark Wang would receive a visit from someone with excellent skills in dispatching members of the human race to the other side, joining the ranks of all those dead Chinese ancestors. Calvino only hoped that Markle's killer was the same person, or persons. Because this was as rough as justice got, and Pratt and he were all the due process the killers would get in this life.

"Mai knew Markle was scared. I think I can find out why," said Calvino.

"Tomorrow I have another meeting with Khanh. The Vietnamese lawyer who doesn't much care for Thais or Chinese or Americans. He might know why Markle was afraid."

"Markle might have been afraid of Khanh, for all we know."

"Khanh is playing everything very close to his chest," said Pratt.

"I saw your friend Fred Harris at Winchell & Holly," said Calvino.

This caught Pratt off guard. "Doing what?"

"Remember Marcus Nguyen's card?"

"The financial consultant card." There was a snicker in Pratt's voice.

"Well, your buddy Fred had the same kind of card. Only his name was Daniel Bryant. I thought he worked for the American Embassy."

"He does," said Pratt.

Calvino's law said anyone who makes more than one international flight a month in Southeast Asia is on a mission of either conversion or subversion.

"Before tomorrow we should have a talk with him."

"Why before tomorrow?"

"Tomorrow is the launch party for this Vietnam Emerging Market Fund. Remember, he had you checking out the security for the investors who were going to be in Phuket? Same guys will probably be at the party. Remember the sting like a bee, float like a butterfly outfit he wore at the Fourth of July picnic. He's a party animal."

It was Pratt's turn to go pale and silent. There was even less to link Harris to the murders, thought Calvino. He was just another of the free-floating suspects in a sea of suspects. He guessed that the Fund was cover for some kind of black-bag operation but that had been American policy toward Vietnam since the time of the French reoccupation after World War II. Covert actions, war, more covert actions. It was a cycle, like the weather or the stock market and, like each of them, you never knew what exactly would happen next because chaos prevented any ability to predict with any degree of accuracy. Guys like Harris believed and had absolute faith in predictability and charting the future. That was what separated them from the old hands of Asia who gained that status only once they put predictability behind them like the toys of a child. Murder was a snake's head that usually rose out of hate, anger or another strong emotion or it rose out of a cold-blooded business decision to eliminate a competitor. Principle was sometimes used to justify murder in either case. Khanh hated the Chinese and he hated the Americans. He could have accumulated enough hatred to have both Drew Markle and Mark Wang killed. If Mai, the Hanoi girl, had been tempted out of Winchell & Holly and away from Saigon, that would be enough reason for Khanh to kill.

"In Saigon, there is no shortage of suspects who had a reason to kill both Markle and Wang."

"Let's give it a rest tonight," Pratt rose to his feet. It was nearly three in the morning.

He should have been tired but he wasn't. For some reason, he didn't want to leave the inside of the empty theater. He liked the feeling of isolation and quiet inside. It was a good place to play cop, jury, judge and executioner, talk about what character might have done what to whom. The theater was a place where people came to work out their doubts through the players, who let them into the story and, if they were good enough, then the characters would keep them awake for nights afterwards. The Opera House had the ghosts of the past, returning back with an accusing finger and saying, you got the wrong man and the wrong government. Or, Calvino thought, the ghost might say, he had fallen for the wrong woman.

"Pratt. What do you make of the Vietnamese?"

"They live in a no-man's land. Between peace and war. Between communism and capitalism. And between revenge and forgiving. That's what I make of them."

"People focused on killing foreigners and each other. People addicted to the absolute power that killing gives. Living like that for more than half a century gives them an edge. That's what I make of the Vietnamese," said Calvino. "That's what makes me uncomfortable trying to find a killer in a place where so many people have killed and been killed. Saigon is filled with too many ghosts. It makes me uneasy."

"The *farang* disease is not believing in ghosts," said Pratt.

"Maybe you're finding a cure in Saigon. Talk of ghosts. Talk of love. I am discovering a whole new side to you."

§ § § §

CALVINO shoved the videotape into the old VCR and turned down the volume on the TV set. He collapsed in a chair, holding an open beer in one hand, the remote control in the other. Okay, entertain me, he thought. The tape had been brought to Saigon by Pratt's contact who had flown it in from Bangkok tucked inside a diplomatic pouch. The tape flickered with some numbers and weird spots, then a wobbly pan shot of the audience came onto the screen. It had been shot on video and had a cheap, porno- like quality to it. Yet it was the ultimate music video: no performers, no stage, no light and smoke show. Instead what you had was stripped down to the audience reaction to the music being played off-camera. He found the volume button on the remote control and increased the sound. He could hear a male vocalist singing the song "Cocaine," the unofficial national anthem of the

Golden Triangle, shared with a few Latin American republics. Whoever was behind the camcorder must have been a male. When he spotted Darla the wobbly camera became immobile, still, as if it were resting on a platform, like the camera Andy Warhol used to film the Empire State Building for six hours without ever moving the camera. Darla sat with her legs crossed and her 37" breasts looking like they might be ready to climb the fence and make a break for freedom, jump right out of the top of a low-cut, red blouse and she was wearing the translucent pants of an ao dai . Her long thick blonde hair cascaded down her shoulders in waves. The camera eye stared at her with the intensity of a voyeur. Whoever was holding the camera must have forgotten he was at a concert, on the job for his TV channel. He no longer cared, he just wanted an excuse to watch this woman, to take the film back and show his friends what he had discovered in an audience in Saigon. It was obvious from the way she glanced at the camera, smiling, that she was fully aware of what the camera man was doing, and that she was loving the attention.

The camera was positioned far enough back to pick up those seated around her. Webb had a hand on her left thigh, massaging it to the tune of "Cocaine" and smiling at Darla who was looking at the stage. On her right, Mark Wang sat motionless, as if in some deep, meditative stage where a series of tiny Alpha waves lapped softly against the shores of his consciousness. What images were rolling across his brain? Cocaine memories? The business in Hong Kong, Saigon, or

Bangkok? On Webb's left was Jackie Ky and next to her was Drew Markle. Two dead men like bookends and sandwiched between were two beautiful, young and desirable women and Douglas Webb, who was looking pleased with himself for securing what was probably the best seat in the concert hall. A few seconds before the sequence ended, Mai came into view: she was sitting in the seat next to Drew Markle.

The emotion in Jackie Ky's face turned sour like she had drunk some bad gin, blinking her eyes as if she might be going blind. Drew acknowledged Mai by brushing his hand against hers, and in a quick reflex action she pulled hers back, her face flushed. She smiled at him, ignored Jackie Ky's presence and then stared straight ahead at the stage.

Calvino ran the video two more times. Second time around, he punched the still, freezing Darla's mouth in a provocative half-open position as if she had just spotted Barry Manilow on stage. He studied the row, going over each face, looking at the hands, the legs, trying to read the language of the body. Who was relaxed, laid back and into the music? Who acted like they belonged to someone seated next to them? Where were the loyalties running? Markle was between two women who refused to look at each other. He studied the way Markle's hand touched Mai's and Jackie's reaction. Some adrenalin kicked in. He could tell by the way her breathing changed. He watched her chest. Her breathing was heavier. Where were her hands? She was squeezing Drew's hand. This is mine, she was saying. Calvino kept track on the touching, the shoulder rubbing, neck positioning. The way a person sat in a public place spoke volumes about his state of mind, his intimacy level with the person next to him. The camera panned the audience beyond them but the lens found its way back to Darla and Jackie as if it were steel filings flying into the head of a magnet. There had been three women at the concert. And three men. The women were doing a whole lot better at not getting whacked.

A picture was two things. The fine details of the scene and the larger perspective of all the details included in the scene. And one more thing often overlooked. What was absent, what was the missing element which should have been in the scene? he wondered. Calvino studied the TV image and asked himself what was missing. It was like the Caravaggio on the walls of the Q-Bar. Something had been left out by the painter. There was not a single woman in the scene. Caravaggio was gay and liked painting tragic, young men from the bars and streets. Images of angels could be found in the gutter. What wasn't in the picture was the most powerful message and the answer to what had been excluded colored the painter's motive. Khanh was excluded from the video. He hadn't been at the concert. The key Vietnamese lawyer at the law firm had missed a chance for an all expenses paid night on the town with Darla. His absence didn't make sense.

Calvino lay back on the bed and hit the off button on the TV. There was a sliver of light under a blanket of gray sky outside his balcony. There was that sound again. The beat of the bamboo sticks as some soup boy looked for the first sale of the morning or the last sale of the night. The sound made him smile because, for the first time, the bamboo sticks reminded him of the slaughterhouse birds with their eerie death shrills from a pig being killed. Could you teach a slaughterhouse bird to made the sound of the bamboo sticks? Of course you could, he thought. You could teach it to make the sound of a two-stroke motorcycle, why not the bamboo stick melody that the soup was ready? This was the kind of moment which cut between those times in Bangkok and his life at that second in Saigon. Just like there was a moment that cut between the living and dead. A realization of a state of being that was passing from one form to another. Lt.Col. Pratt said they would have to make a choice. The case had become "political" and somewhere high in the chain of command, out of sight, out of mind, a decision would be made. Whatever his superiors decided, that would be the end of the Wang murder case. All that anyone expected was for Lt.Col. Pratt to do his best. File his report. He had other work in Bangkok. Other murders, other crimes that faded the memory of those that came before. Harry Markle wanted the ass of whoever killed his brother. Marcus would do the job. Assuming the same person had killed both Drew and Mark Wang, Harry would be satisfied if the Triad would do the job for him. Like Lt.Col. Pratt's superiors, Harry asked for no more: Do your best, he had said. In Asia, doing your best was pretty much always good enough to pass for doing it right.

Again he watched Mai on the video and each time she had withdrawn her hand from Drew's touch. Calvino remembered touching her hand in the restaurant, and she had responded with a warm, encouraging smile. The Bangkok Comfort Zone—that strip running between Patpong, Soi Cowboy and Nana—was a huge bank of ice, thick as a glacier. Only you had to be around the scene for years and years to see and feel the deep chill, and by the time you had, it was too late, the glacier had already dragged you under. Then you could never escape the gravity of the place that pulled them back from all over the world. Comfort Zone ice like a narcotic made you feel invincible. Zone veterans lived inside a solid block of ice. Zone workers, who were teenagers in chronological years, were soon aged inside the ice. The night ice crystals formed a thick fog over the Zone veterans and workers, creating an ice bridge; these ice people knew they could no longer live outside the Comfort Zone. They looked as normal as anyone else on the street because no one can see the ice, it's carried inside, around the heart.

Calvino had gone through the event horizon of the Comfort Zone, and lived in the Zone's ice age so long that it had become a habit. Addiction, baby. He had become Zone dead like the others. Ice so thick that nothing touched the heart: the slaughterhouse birds' death cries, child beggars, child prostitutes, broken bodies on the road. It don't matter, none of it, drink your drink, eat your food, buy out your women by the hour, read your paper; and remember that ice shields you from pain, from expectation, from any anguish or worry. Some entered the Zone looking for a wife or a relationship. Opinion was divided. Some said Zone workers could never shed the ice; others said they had thawed out a Zone worker, turned her into a wife. Yet others said the Zone was like a black hole, once a worker was sucked in, her fate was sealed and she was lost forever. All that Calvino knew for sure was the Comfort Zone shielded him from what non-Zone people called love. You checked love at the door. And, by the time you checked out, you forgot about it. One day it was gone. Love vanished. You couldn't take it back. He looked inside himself and found an ozone hole above that Zone ice which Mai had formed with a look, with a touch...and when she pulled her hand away from Drew Markle on the video, yeah, he felt a chunk of the Zone ice slough off. He experienced some feeling in that region called the heart, and the downside of that feeling—of being vulnerable to some force one could never control.

The beer can fell out of his hand and hit the floor.

As he reached down to find the can, he heard a noise, looked up and saw someone behind the bar counter, moving fast. He rolled behind a round table and flipped it over so that the surface area faced the bar. In the mirror he saw old Mr. Tang, combing his hair and smiling. The comb was missing as many teeth as the old man using it.

"So what's your problem, Calvino?" he asked in perfect English.

"Who you got back there with you?"

"Rats. Didn't I tell you to watch out for the fucking rats?"

"That you did, Mr. Tang."

"But you didn't fucking listen."

Darla walked across the room, hands on her hips, wearing a white nurse's uniform. She carried a syringe with a large needle. Walking straight up to Mr. Tang she plunged it into the side of his neck and pushed the plunger down. The old man's face froze in the mirror and he collapsed behind the bar.

"What are you drinking, Vinee?" Darla asked him.

He pointed his Smith & Wesson at her, fixing a target about nipple high on the right side. She leaned over the bar and smiled.

"You're gonna kill me? That's a mistake. It's this bitch who killed Markle."

Jackie Ky sat on the bar, legs crossed, smoking a cigarette.

"Darla," said Jackie Ky, coming out of the shadows.

"Ask sweet, perfect, Mai, where she was the night Drew died."

Mai looked icy cool, as if one of those Zone breezes was blowing over her as she sat on a bar stool.

"I was still at the office," Mai said. "You've got to believe me, Vinee. I love you."

"Love. What a joke. What a great alibi," said Jackie Ky.

"So you let Khanh kill him for you. He never liked a nice Hanoi girl playing nurse with an American."

Mai came off the stool and pushed Jackie against the wall. It was a sudden, unexpected action.

"Like all overseas Vietnamese," said Mai, "you think you were the only ones to suffer. That's a lie. We suffered as much as you. No. We suffered more. We don't go throwing money around, pretending we are better than anyone else. You Viet Khieu aren't real Vietnamese. You aren't American. You are nothing. That's what eats you. Your California university education, your perfect English. So what? This is Vietnam; it is my country. You don't belong here in Ho Chi Minh City. It is no longer your place."

Mai sighed and drank a straight orange juice from a straw. With her free hand, Mai took an AK47 from her handbag. Calvino kept watching as the long automatic weapon slowly came out of a bag a fraction of its size. She sprayed the mirror with gunfire. Darla reached out and pulled the AK47 away by the barrel. Mai didn't put up much of a struggle. Basically, she just let Darla have the weapon.

"You get to choose, Calvino," Darla shouted from behind the bar. Then she aimed the AK47 and fired a burst at the table.

"Did you kill Markle?" he asked, sitting behind the table. He caught her image in a fragment of the mirror.

"Why would I do that? Dead men don't use my services."

"Jackie?"

She started to cry like at the temple in front of Drew Markle's photograph.

"I loved him," she sobbed. "I told you it was Webb. Why don't you believe me? He killed Drew because he was going to tell New York about the money from Mark."

Tan skated across the bar top on his wooden platform and skidded to a stop right next to one of Darla's huge breasts.

"It's been a long time since I have been that close to heaven's gate," said Tan, looking up at the breast.

Pratt stood in the door, looking at his watch.

"Time's up, Vincent. Who is it gonna be?" asked Pratt.

"I know that Thai game. You assign me the responsibility. You're off the hook. If there's a mistake, then, it is the *farang* who takes the fall."

Pratt smiled, then started playing the saxophone real mellow and smooth like a single malt scotch that had been inside a barrel for thirty years. Bamboo sticks picked up the beat. Darla tapped a series of glasses with a spoon, blending into the rhythm.

"Soup's ready," said Tan.

"You gotta believe me, buddy," said Webb. "I didn't kill Drew."

"Time's up," said Pratt, lowering his sax.

Calvino rose up from behind the table, holding the Smith & Wesson out, pointing at everyone behind the bar. Sweat rolled down his face, stung his eyes. Someone had to die. He swung around and aimed at Pratt.

"Don't make me do this, Pratt."

"I'm not making you do anything. It's the way of the world." The handgun turned into a sword with a long, sharp blade.

"The blade of Solomon," said Darla.

"Where's the baby?" asked Tan.

Each of the women held out a newly born infant and Calvino raised the sword above his head, weeping as the blade started down. The loud cracking sound made Calvino turn. Again the pounding thundered and he opened an eye. He was still fully dressed, his necktie half undone, and he had a gun in his hand.

Someone was at the door to his room. He put the gun under this pillow and went to the door. It was the cleaning woman, small and serious, in a gray uniform.

"Can I clean your room?"

"No," he said, slamming the door and leaning against it, his head up, looking at the ceiling. He looked down at his watch, swallowing hard. It was nearly eleven in the morning. Pratt would have already had his appointment with Khanh. He himself would, with any luck, soon be having lunch with Mai. He wanted to tell her about the dream. And he wanted to know if she would have the diskette with her.

CHAPTER 11

FEE FOR SERVICES RENDERED

WATCHING HIS EYES, Mai handed a photo-graph to Calvino at lunch. She wanted to judge his reaction and then she could decide what to do next. She had retained vivid childhood memories of living in the countryside and the terror she felt upon hearing American bombers approaching. This had been the first time she had ever revealed that time to anyone outside of her family. She had been evacuated by her parents from Hanoi when the bombing made life too dangerous. Her father had been a MIG fighter pilot. At age twenty-seven years, he was killed in action; in the same year, Mai turned five years old. An American fighter had shot down her father's plane. He had been a hero of the People's War of Liberation; a handsome, young man, eyes squinting a slight smile as he looked into the camera for his official photograph. Then he was gone. Only the photograph remained. She sometimes dreamed of seeing that face trapped inside a MIG at the exact moment it exploded in the sky and, in an instant, the face was replaced by twisted metal, burning flesh, and shards of bone raining down on the jungle canopy. Her mother, a practicing Catholic, still lit candles in his memory at the church. Mai thought of her mother praying, kneeling before the altar, eyes closed. It had been a long time since the war, since his death, since she had moved to Ho Chi Minh City. She was now older than her father had been when he had died, but the thought of this young man in his flight uniform in the photo never left her for more than a few days. She had quickly wiped away a tear as Calvino studied the photograph, finding a hint of her father 's face in hers.

"You're on a flight path that would have made him proud," he said.

She took back the photograph.

"Sometimes," she paused. "I don't know. I think I feel him nearby."

"Watching over you."

"That's it."

In the middle of eating a piece of pizza, Mai slipped a brown envelope across the table. He already had come to recognize the meaning of the smile: The one that says, 'I'm taking care of you, baby. Making my man happy, giving him what he asked for and feeling good about it.' He took the envelope, folded it in half, feeling the plastic diskette inside and put it into the inside pocket of his jacket.

"You like pizza?" he asked her.

"I love pizza. Not as much as Chekhov. Maybe not as much as you. But I love pizza," she said, covering her mouth as she giggled.

Markle had been five years or so older than her father when he died. He couldn't help himself from wondering what had been the nature of their relationship. He had gone through every frame of the video from the concert, asking himself one question.

"Did Drew Markle ever hit on you?"

It was the question he had wanted to ask from the moment she sat down at the table. The image of Markle reaching for her hand at the concert had burnt into his memory.

"Hit?"

"You know, make a pass at you."

As the message sank in, it wiped away the smile.

"He wasn't like that with me."

"All I am asking is, did he have a thing for you?"

She thought about this, as she used her fork and knife to put another piece of pizza on Calvino's plate—serving a man food was one of those things a Vietnamese woman did to show her feelings toward him.

"I will be honest with you. He was very smart. And in his legal work he was totally honest. He was straight with the clients. He wouldn't have anything to do with dirty money. He said that a lawyer had to put ethics first. Even above his client. No Vietnamese thinks like this and I think it caused him some trouble. But with women, he had no honesty or ethics. He was a playboy. He had money, a good job, he was single. So he had lots of girls chasing him. Why not? For me an unethical lawyer and ethical lover is much better than an ethical lawyer and unethical lover. I think commitment to the woman is more important than to the client. What do you think?"

In the Zone, deep inside the ice, seven days a week, such a distinction made no sense—the premise contained in the question exploded like Mai's father and his MIG. Love, ethics, devotion, loyalty were slipped under the glacier wall of ice maids, ground into a fine dust, blown into a storm of lust and passion. Comfort Zone hearts, all cold, hard, and dead had crashed, and the ash was carried inside the chest of people neither living nor dead. Could a sense of commitment ever return to someone who had lived that long inside the Zone? What did he think, he asked himself.

"I think you and I...you know, should get married."

She blinked, her hands holding the fork and knife suspended over her plate.

"Are you proposing?"

He swallowed hard.

"What I'm saying is: You're single. I'm single. What do single people do when they have certain feelings?"

"What do they do?"

"I don't know. I guess they get married."

She looked at her watch. "It's late. I have to get back to the office. Since I met you, I am always running late."

"Aren't you going to answer my question?" She was already on her feet.

"I need some time."

Next thing he knew she was gone, floating into the traffic stream on her Honda Dream, turning on Dong Khoi where it converged with Le Loi Boulevard. Outside the restaurant window, a boy walked past carrying a wooden model of a seventeenth century sailing ship on his shoulder. The ship had masts and sails and the wind caught the sails. The model ship dwarfed the boy. Another street kid ran up with a tray of American attack helicopters and F14 fighters made from empty Tiger and 333 beer cans.

Calvino wondered what went through Mai's mind when she saw a Tiger beer can replica of the fighter which had killed her father. Maybe she didn't make the connection, or something inside her refused to allow her to make a connection. There were no MIGs being hawked on the streets of Hanoi. Saigon had been liberated but there was no tourist market for souvenir MIGs formed from discarded beer cans. Marcus Nguyen, the financial consultant, had lost a villa and, having returned to Saigon, Calvino had begun to wonder if a second liberation of Saigon was under way. Everyone needed time in this divided city. He had proposed to a woman and she had answered with a request for more time. With enough time old wounds healed, enemies were reconciled, but, somehow, he had a feeling that not enough time had passed in a divided city, among a divided people, for the woman he loved to make a choice she knew that she would never be able to change.

§ § § §

CALVINO had half an hour to kill before Pratt arrived at the hotel for their meeting in the courtyard. He had re-run the videotape of the concert inside his mind. Pratt would want to know what he thought about the row of the living and dead. Calvino paid the bill at the restaurant and walked through the reception area. Two *farang* stood together at the front desk and one was saying to the other in an American accent, "You got to know the date of the first recorded blow-job in Saigon after 1975." His friend didn't know. Calvino slowed down to catch the answer.

"The first post-fall of Saigon blow-job took place inside the Casino Bar. That's a bar opposite the square from the Rex. It happened on the staircase of the Casino at six pm on March 14th, 1979. That's a little known fact. But it's true. I was there. The guy who got the blow-job was a friend of mine. We wrote it down in his journal. No one should forget the important stuff." Comfort Zone talk, thought Calvino. Cold enough to ice the wings of any approaching lover.

Calvino kept on walking, letting the conver-sation between the two *farang* fade into garbled, white noise as he reached the waiting area in the lobby. He could feel the ice... Bangkok Comfort Zone ice, an avalanche of snow tumbling from the front desk. He stood in the doorway, looking out at the courtyard, there were a few people at tables. It was hot in the courtyard. He decided to wait for Pratt in the air-conditioning and read a newspaper.

The small waiting area in the main lobby had a few cherry wood ornate benches with small, flat red cushions that looked like too many fat people had sat on them and they hadn't been changed since 1975. Fresh cut flowers were on glass tables. Persian carpets had "Continental" stitched in a blue weave pattern. This part of the lobby was empty. He sat down on one of the benches and opened a copy of the International Herald Tribune. This was not the place nor the newspaper one would expect to conform with the image of a wiseguy from Brooklyn, who was going into the Saigon water trade. One of the Calvino laws, written in large print in the expat bible, was this one: To stay alive you keep the other side off-balance. Every time they think they have you figured out, you throw them a curve ball, pushing them back from the plate.

He spotted Fred Harris as he walked across the lobby. Harris had passed him as if the guy behind the Herald Tribune didn't exist.

"Staying in the Graham Greene suite, Fred?" Calvino asked. Harris stopped, turned around, not quite believing his ears.

He took a couple of steps down to the lobby and pulled down the newspaper, exposing Calvino's face.

"Jesus Christ, what are you doing here?" asked Harris.

"Catching up on the financial news," said Calvino.

"What did you say to Webb about me?"

"That I thought you were a G-man."

"What did he say?" He sounded guarded, not sure whether Calvino was being ironic, or whether he was telling something that approximated the truth.

"He didn't believe me."

"Your problem, Calvino, is that you are way over your head. And that's not healthy."

"I didn't know you were concerned about my health," he said, folding his newspaper.

"Why don't we go out into the courtyard and have a friendly cup of coffee?"

What was Fred Harris going to say?

"No, I don't have time for coffee, asshole."

He could have said that, but he didn't and instead he said, "Calvino, what the fuck were you doing at Winchell & Holly's?"

"You will get your salary docked for using such language."

"What's with the Demato bullshit?"

"Danny Bryant, come on, baby. You are asking me if I'm having an identity crisis. I didn't hear you call-ing yourself Fred Harris, Central Intelligence Agency, Bangkok Bureau."

"Will you lower your voice? I am here on a routine investigation."

"Yeah, is that so? It seems like a long-standing routine."

Fred Harris looked around.

"Let's get some coffee," said Calvino.

Harris followed Calvino out of the hotel lobby and into the courtyard. One step out of the lobby and they were hit by the wall of afternoon heat. The next thing they hit was Pratt seated at a table near one of the large gnarled trees festooned with Christmas tree lights.

"Look who's here, Fred Harris," said Calvino.

Calvino pulled up a chair and sat down. Pratt said nothing as Harris pulled up another chair. A waiter arrived and took the order for two black coffees.

"It's a Fourth of July Bangkok picnic reunion," said Calvino.

"Lieutenant Colonel Prachai, good to see you," said Fred Harris. Calvino sat back in his chair.

"You didn't say you were glad to see me, Fred. I'm hurt," said Calvino. "Never mind, it is not healthy to walk around with a hurt heart."

"I want to thank you, Colonel Prachai for your co-operation in Phuket," said Fred Harris, ignoring Calvino. In the courtyard of the Continental Hotel, suddenly, Vincent Calvino no longer existed. Harris sat talking with Pratt, using his rank and formal first name, as if the two of them were at the table planning an official operation. This was standard operating procedure in the Zone when a Zone worker pushed her way between two friends, looking for a lady's drink. Calvino smiled at Harris. The man had tried to break his face.

"Mark Wang's name was on your list of people going to Phuket," said Pratt. "But we've drawn a blank on who killed him."

"So have we, Lieutenant Colonel Prachai. But we will find whoever did it. That much you can count on. We have deployed resources. Military and security resources. Wang's case, like Markle's, has the highest priority."

Fred Harris was starting to sound like an asshole again. All that was missing were the black and yellow Bermuda shorts.

"What's the official theory on Markle's murder?" asked Calvino. Harris forced a smile, but didn't look at Calvino. He addressed the response to Pratt as if he had asked the question. "Saigon has its problems. Along the river you have a turf battle between some veterans from the North and some locals who fought for the South. It's no secret there's no love lost between these two groups of people. It was just a matter of time before something like this happened. Someone made a move. The night before Markle was killed, there was a fight along the river. A guy from the North had a knife. He used it. No one was killed but one guy got himself cut up pretty bad. The next night was revenge time along the river. Markle just got in the way. No one was looking to take out an American. Are you kidding? The Vietnamese have been on their fucking knees for years for us to lift the embargo and now they are going to set back their economic development ten years for what? To hit an American citizen in the middle of Saigon?"

"So if you've got it all figured out, why have you deployed resources?" he asked, trying to sound like Harris.

"And what are you doing in Saigon working for a mutual fund company under a fake name?"

"Let me ask you something, Calvino. Are you an American taxpayer?"

Calvino brushed off the question and looked away.

"No, I am serious. Do you pay taxes to Uncle Sam?"

"Since when does the CIA care who is paying taxes?"

"You don't pay my salary. That's what I'm getting at. You're a civilian and you are in the way."

"Let me apply my civilian's way of thinking to what is happening in Saigon. Big business interests in the States are sniffing around Vietnam. Looking for a way back in. There is a consulate in Hanoi, putting out feelers for them. These are the same people who set up mutual funds. Funds like the Vietnam Emerging Market Fund. And who is their financial adviser? A CIA Bangkok Bureau man. Interesting, don't you think, Colonel Prachai? These are the kind of conservative business types who don't want the boat rocked. Washington says they want Markle's case closed because they want to turn on the tap pouring out ten billion dollars of aid. Aid is linked to business. Business to profit. Markle's murder is a political embarrassment. And there are those who are investing millions of dollars in private deals. No one wants the gravy train derailed. Now that it is back on the tracks. Saigon turf war makes great newspaper copy back home but you know and I know that it doesn't hold a teaspoon of 333 beer."

"You've been away from the States for too long, Calvino. You don't have a clue how things work there any more, assuming you ever did."

"Maybe I need some education. That's why the Lieutenant Colonel and I thought we might go along to the launch of the Fund tonight," said Calvino. "Mingle with all those who know how things work in America and Vietnam. It will be like a graduate course. My continuing education in American foreign investment. I saw a list of the Fund directors. It reads like a Who's Who of those in America and South Vietnam who lost the war. So they are bringing their money back. Interesting. Makes me wonder what they are going to do with that money in Vietnam. Using a financial adviser who is CIA makes me real curious."

Pratt played it real cool, the smile never leaving his lips, looking out at the courtyard, the ancient trees, the staff on the second floor balconies, the ghosts of those who had come and gone, dreamed and lied, promised and retreated for all those generations. The weight of history fell all around them, and Pratt wondered if they felt the burden of all that destruction, death and loss arching like a streak of lightning against a pitch black sky. Only it wasn't a sky, it was a landscape of an entire people that had been shattered.

"Is that right, Sir?" asked Harris.

Pratt nodded. "Did Drew Markle do legal work for this Fund?" This was a question he had expected from Calvino. It caught him off guard.

"Yes, Sir, he did. He was a fine lawyer. Without Winchell & Holly's help we wouldn't be as far along as we are. Markle did his part."

"And what part was that?" asked Calvino.

"Take some friendly advice. Go back to Bangkok. Do your skip chasing cases. Find someone's missing husband. But get your nose out of this case."

Harris was rocking and rolling with rage. He stirred three teaspoons of sugar into his coffee and the spoon just kept moving like he was on automatic pilot. Calvino thought about how far he should push him.

"The advice doesn't sound all that friendly."

"Don't underestimate what can happen."

"Do I look like a guy who underestimates the forces of big money? I hope not. I remember you at the Fourth of July picnic. You were wearing those funny Bermuda shorts, black with yellow bumble bee stripes and white jock socks up to your knees. You were selling lotto tickets. Free tickets for two to Singapore. Free dinner for two at the Oriental Hotel. Three nights in Phuket. Shaking hands, showing the world how friendly and down home Americans overseas can be in the middle of Bangkok. Anyone who can pull off that act deserves respect, Fred. So don't worry about me spoiling the quarterly report of any American company doing business in Vietnam on account of someone getting themselves whacked. In Brooklyn, people get whacked all the time. It's mostly turf wars over the drug concession. A man's got to protect what's his. If he don't, then who will?"

"Exactly, Calvino. Then who will?"

"Mr. Harris, did Mark Wang or his family have money in the Fund?" asked Pratt, as Harris got up from the table.

He leaned back over the table. "Yes, Sir, he did. That's on the record."

"Thank you, Mr. Harris. You have been very helpful."

"Thank you, Sir." He glared at Calvino, then turned and walked across the courtyard.

"He stiffed us for the bill," said Calvino.

"It may have been worth the price," said Pratt. "He didn't say anything."

Pratt smiled. "He said a lot."

"Like what?"

"He didn't want us going to the Fund reception tonight."

"Because he's afraid we'll start calling him Fred Harris."

"There's something else he's afraid of."

"What?"

"We might find what we have been looking for."

Pratt sat back in his chair, looking at the bill as a waiter ran over. Calvino snatched the bill away and handed the waiter a twenty dollar bill.

"It's my turn," said Calvino.

"See you at the reception," said Pratt.

Calvino watched him leave, thinking that he had the Markle diskette in his pocket and he hadn't mentioned it. He felt guilty, like he was withholding evidence from him. They had worked cases before and this was the first time he had held out on something as important as this. It wasn't that he had forgotten the diskette and what it might mean for breaking the Wang case as well as his own; some instinct had made him hang back. He knew it came down to a conflict of loyalties. Mai on the one side, Pratt on the other. She had trusted him. Giving him Markle's computer diskette had been a major risk. Whoever had killed Markle and Wang had been doubling up their risks as well. Harris and company were involved. The Thai Police Department. International investors, Hong Kong, and that was only the start of the list. What link between the two men could have been so important that both died within twelve hours of one another? In his Bangkok hotel room, Wang's computer hard disk had been wiped clean. No floppy diskettes had been recovered. In Saigon, the Vietnamese were inside the law office and onto Markle's computer files and hard copy print-outs within hours of his death. Coordination. People in two cities, two countries, had to be working together toward a common goal. Calvino asked himself if it had been the Vietnamese Security and Intelligence Police who had taken the files. Fred Harris had people on the ground in Saigon, old regime operatives who might have impersonated the Vietnamese security people. It was something to think about.

As Calvino walked out of the Continental Hotel, he remembered how Harris had been sweating in the courtyard. He had the face of a deeply troubled man with a slow burn swelling inside. Harris had little patience in explaining his actions to outsiders, to civilians—a word he used like an obscenity—someone like Calvino who was on his turf, threatening to stake a claim to a higher moral ground. He had wanted to ignore Calvino, who was unaffiliated in a world where affiliation was power, authority and respect. Calvino didn't exist within the bounds of Harris's world, Calvino was another *farang* in a deep Zone sleep, no compass, no direction, no way of escape.

Calvino thought about Harris's treatment of Pratt. He had been quick to recognize Pratt's official position, his connection to power and authority. Pratt had arranged the security for the Fund directors in Phuket. After Wang's murder, that wasn't a hard sell. Was Harris throwing up a smoke screen at the Fourth of July picnic, or had Harris been tipped that something was going down? Context. The request hadn't come out of the blue, it was part of a much larger package. It had bothered Calvino at the time, and as he walked along the road, the same questions came back. Why hadn't Fred Harris set up an official meeting with Pratt, or better yet, gone to one of the generals or someone in the Ministry of Interior? Exactly who was at risk in Phuket and why? Why raise a sensitive security issue at a social function, the Fourth of July picnic of all places? Was it a coincidence that only hours afterwards Mark Wang, who was on his way to the meeting in Phuket, was murdered in a Bangkok hotel? Was Harris using the chance meeting with Pratt to cover himself, or to stage a performance for someone who was watching him?

His mere presence had annoyed Harris, thought Calvino. But the distaste Harris had shown covered a deeper anger, that he was in Saigon on official business, something was about to happen and this civilian was getting too close to whatever it was. Harris didn't like it, and Calvino had begun to wonder if the Karen's Bar trio had been arranged not by Douglas Webb but by Harris and friends. Having missed the chance to take him out, Harris had to endure the humiliation of sitting at the same table with the man who just would not leave well enough alone. Let's say then, thought Calvino, passing the fountain opposite the Q-Bar, that Harris was the guy who killed Wang. Maybe he didn't pull the trigger but he had the hit carried out. The irony of Pratt's situation was he was to deliver the name of the person responsible for Wang's murder. To accomplish his mission, he had to write a name on a piece of paper and send it up the chain of command. His job would be finished. He could return to Bangkok, Manee, his kids, his life, and whatever happened to that name and piece of paper would happen out of his sight, out of his knowledge. Was this any different from what any political commissar was assigned to do: purge an enemy who threatened the system, the structure, the organization? You closed ranks and acted whenever an external threat occurred. Who wasn't guided by this principle? The police, State Department, investment banking house, law firm, Zone people? It was the way of the world. Pratt's piece of paper with the name would be the same as a judge's death sentence, delivered to Wang's relatives, the designated executioners. Whoever touched that kind of power was tainted, thought Calvino. Vietnam was a place which had sucked out the moral core of many men and governments, leaving that dry rattle of numbers, the body count. This time they were returning as investors in a mutual fund, crunching numbers and being tracked by guys like Fred Harris. The entire group had checked into the Continental Hotel in Ho Chi Minh City. Saigon was dead, buried, and the twenty year anniversary had been celebrated. Was Harris in Vietnam looking for a way to reconfigure the winners and losers in the Vietnam War ?

§ § § § §

ONE can learn a great deal about the character of a man in listening to what he chooses to reveal about the past. The same rule applied to countries. Countries distorted, withheld information, and outright lied about their past. After leaving the Continental Hotel, he walked down Le Loi Boulevard to a newsagent's stand opposite Ho Chi Minh Square. The stand was no more than a cubbyhole and loaded with foreign newspapers and magazines. The owner, a slender Vietnamese with a thin, black mustache and gold wire-rimmed glasses, stood out front, keeping an eye on the Square and the Rex Hotel on the far side of the Square, calling out to foreigners who walked past to buy a newspaper. His English was street-smart American accented.

"I heard there was a big fire last night in Saigon," said Calvino. The owner sucked on a cigarette, nodded, looking at his feet.

"People are careless in Saigon. There are fires every night," he said with a nervous, forced laugh. "People cook over fires!"

"Anything about a big shophouse fire in the newspapers? Some people found dead inside?"

Questions about fire and death made the vendor nervous. He took refuge behind his well-worn street vendor's smile which said get the fuck out of my face. "No time to read every newspaper. What you want? Time magazine. Newsweek. Far Eastern Economic Review." He held up one after another from the counter sticking out on the sidewalk.

"No, forget the international magazines. A Viet-namese newspaper is much better."

"Can you read Vietnamese?" He pushed his glasses up and took a closer look at Calvino.

"There should be a picture," said Calvino.

"Here," he said, handing Calvino a two-day old English language newspaper. He glanced at the paper. It contained news about rice export goals, the meeting of the People's Committee, and a story about a Korean managing director who had humiliated a Vietnamese worker. Food, politics, and anti-foreigner stories. Communist newsspeak stories, control and restriction in every sentence. Calvino laughed, wondering how he had ever been so crazy to think that the press in Saigon was like the press in Bangkok. Bad news stories about crime were counter-revolutionary sabotage and incitement and a journalist would go to prison for the crime of having leaked State secrets. Who gets killed in the street is a State secret. You didn't have to be a graduate of a school of journalism to see that the barcodes of daily events were perfectly matched to the vision of State policy. Calvino gave the vendor five dollars and he started to make change. If you wanted to know what really happened, you had to tap the bamboo telegraph at street level.

"Keep it," said Calvino. "Tell me something, was there anything in the Vietnamese press or on the radio about a fire last night?"

The vendor was frowning as he looked at the five-dollar bill. Calvino laid another ten-dollar bill on top of the five and this brought a slight smile.

"Shophouse fire. Someone said it was in a shut-down bar. I think it was called Karen's Bar. It's history. Dust and ashes, like the old regime," he said. "In Vietnam, everything is history, even today will be history by tomorrow."

"What's it say about the fire?" asked Calvino.

"Oil lamp got knocked over."

Calvino nodded.

"An oil lamp was knocked over? Careless people. I think they will go to prison for a very long time. Burning down buildings is no good for investment. When they write the history of today, you know what they are going to call it?" asked Calvino.

The vendor shook his head.

"The day when everyone in Saigon became an investor."

"Boring title," said the vendor, grinning.

"That's because the investors are people who ultimately win all the wars, and they are boring."

The story had been twisted, compressed and buried. The distance between Fred Harris, Winchell & Holly, and the People's Committee was getting smaller and smaller as everyone started to count profit margins above all other margins. Like the margins for justice, the margins for doing right, the margins for honesty—those margins had been eroded, torn down with the Berlin Wall, and what was left on the landscape? People on someone else's turf at the wrong time of day.

He heard someone calling his name. As he turned around, Marcus Nyugen was removing his aviator sunglasses and leaning out of the driver's side of a new red BMW convertible. He had the top down and in the passenger's seat was a Vietnamese woman, mid-twenties, tall, angular, with an ice skater's figure and MTV presenter's face, dressed in a top-of-the-line tennis outfit, with her hair pulled back into a ponytail.

Calvino walked over to the car.

"Heard about the fire last night," said Marcus.

"Someone knocked over an oil lamp is what I hear," said Calvino.

"Maybe it was a cow. Or a ghost."

The supermodel Vietnamese girlfriend slowly lowered her sunglasses. She looked like she never sweated and never got any further than the inside of a BMW with her tennis racket.

"Accidents happen everywhere in the world," he said, glancing over at his girlfriend.

"This is Diep. Beautiful, don't you think? And she fits within the seventy-five year rule."

Calvino hadn't heard of this rule, and Marcus was pleased to see the puzzled look on his face.

"You don't know the seventy-five year rule? It works this way. I add my age to the age of the girl, and the total number can't exceed seventy-five years. I am fifty-three and Diep's twenty-one, so it's a perfect match."

Zone speak, thought Calvino. Zone rules.

Diep hadn't said a word. She sat erect, smiling, holding her racket in one hand and her sunglasses in the other.

"I think Webb set me up last night. Sending me for an appointment at Karen's Bar."

Marcus looked back. "Who else knew you were going to Karen's Bar?"

"I can think of a couple of other people."

"All you have to do is give me the word. I'll do the rest. I promised Harry Markle I would look after it personally. If it's Webb, just give me the nod. That's it, you've done your job. You can go home."

"She understand English?"

Marcus shook his head. "Not a word. Beautiful, isn't she? And you are wondering what she's doing with an old guy like me? There's a Vietnamese saying that translates roughly into, 'one night leaning against the royal barge is worth more than a lifetime inside a fisherman's boat.' "

He switched on the ignition, slipped his aviator glasses back on, saying, "See you around."

§ § § § §

DARLA stretched out on the beach chair, chest pointing toward the sun with the swimming pool a couple of feet away. Calvino walked along the main walkway leading up to the Floating Hotel. The hotel had been built on a barge which floated up the Saigon River. The hotel floated. In an emergency it could be sent down river. A dozen tourists were sunning themselves around the pool. Some kids splashed at the shallow end. Two of the kids wore the inflatable water-wings that kept their heads above water level and allowed the mother to sit calmly at the edge of the pool, her toes submerged in the water as she read a book. Calvino walked past the mother and sat down in the beach chair next to Darla who wore a bikini so small that her name in eight point type would have spilled over the edges and onto her flesh. She was parked under a large, sun-faded pink and gray umbrella. She had fingernail polish, manicure set, mirror, brush, eyeliner, lipstick laid out like an operating room nurse who had adapted her skills in setting up the surgeon's operating table. The only operation going on at the pool was cosmetic.

"How you doing, Darla?" Calvino asked, folding his hands behind his head and leaning back in the chair.

She lowered her sunglasses and smiled.

"Vincent, you're not going to believe this. But I was just thinking about you."

Across the pool, a Japanese business type was staring at her. "Yeah, what were you thinking?"

"About last night. I wanted to keep it strictly business. I hope you don't hate me for wanting to make love with you last night. I have been thinking ever since: what happened? I have never, I mean not ever, had a man who said no to me unless he was gay. And I don't think you are gay. So I don't get it."

"I would hate to take advantage of my professional position. I like to separate business from pleasure. Otherwise, I would be out of business before I started," said Calvino.

"Really? I've never known a *farang* who separated business from pleasure in Bangkok," she said, pulling one of her long legs up and examining the painted toenails.

"You ever kill anyone, Darla?"

The question didn't unnerve her as she un-screwed the cap from the fingernail polish. "There was a German once. You know, we were doing it. Mixing business and pleasure. And he had a heart attack. I guess you could say I killed him. But then, at the same time, you could say he killed himself. I went to the German Embassy for an interview and explained what had happened. He wrote down in the space for cause of death—Act of God. Who said the Germans don't have a sense of humor?" She had finished painting the nail on her big toe and was blowing on it.

She had some professional delivery, cool, controlled and smooth.

"But if you were going to kill someone, how would you do it?"

"What do you mean?"

"A gun, a knife, drug overdose?"

She thought for a moment.

"You mean just kill someone?"

"Just like that."

"I don't know. Maybe poison. Snake venom. You know that little green snake in Thailand that, after it bites you, you have about forty-five seconds before you go into shock, then your heart stops? I'd probably use that snake."

"That's dangerous. The snake might bite you," said Calvino, watching her on her middle toe with the tiny, wet, red paint brush.

"That would be a bitch," she said.

"You wanna go up to my room for a drink?"

She looked up from her toes.

"I want to go to your room... but I gotta see someone about the club."

"Maybe later," she said. "When you're not so busy."

He got up from the chair.

"One more thing, Darla."

"Yeah?"

"After that Thai-Vietnamese concert, did you make it with Mark Wang?"

She shook her head.

"But I think Jackie Ky fucked him."

§ § § §

SHE had done what he had asked of her on the phone. When he arrived at the villa, she had a fresh battery pack loaded into a laptop computer. They only stayed long enough for Calvino to check out the software, and then turn it off, and slip it into the carrying case. Jackie Ky was not all that happy walking beside Calvino in Cong Vien Van Hoa Park. On a Sunday afternoon, the park was filled with people. The masses came to eat, talk, walk and watch each other. It was a perfect place to get lost in a huge crowd of people. A gray pony pulled a wooden cart, the blue tassels on the canopy flopping as the cart wheels rolled over the pavement. A tangle of children and adults were inside looking like they had just transferred from one of those overcrowded Bangladesh ferries that sink a couple of times a year. As they walked to the right, they passed a roller skating rink with hundreds of kids skating inside a small enclosure. A chain-link fence made the rink look like a minimum security prison. Jackie Ky stopped next to the fence. She looked angry as she watched the skaters try to gather enough speed to climb a small, plastic-moulded hill. They hit the hill in waves. Some wouldn't make it, falling back and knocking down others behind them. Sweaty, determined, exhausted like the Caravaggio faces, they had a doomed, haunted expression as they approached the hill. Another wave hit the hill, knocking and bumping against each other, tripping and falling like soldiers mowed down by a machine gun. They came back around again and again, never stopping, a relentless wave of bodies. It was difficult to defeat such people in a jungle war. They skated through the jungle. They skated through the tunnels. They never gave up.

Jackie Ky turned away from the fence and stared at him.

He wasn't sure whether it was her reputation she was worried about, as the Vietnamese eyed them as they passed along the pavement, or whether it was the stifling heat or the hopelessness of the young skaters.

"I don't understand. You said you wanted to use my computer, not take it."

"I said that I needed to borrow it."

She sighed. "We should have stayed at home," said Jackie Ky.

"Drank some white wine. I hate this park. This skating rink. And the people who come here. They smell."

Calvino moved away from the fence and started walking across the park.

"You know that was what Harry said about his brother. He should have stayed home," said Calvino, as she caught up with him.

"I hope they don't end up saying that about you," she replied. If it hadn't been for the Smith & Wesson she had delivered to his hotel room, that is exactly what they would be saying in Bangkok today, as the news whipped through the Bangkok Comfort Zone like one of those forest fires, leaping from Washington Square bars, to Soi Cowboy, over to Soi Nana, and breaking out from the Zone and jumping to all the other clubs like the Sports Club, the British Club, the Foreign Correspondents Club and spreading through the halls of various embassies.

They followed the paved path toward an elevated shrine. A small building painted white and red was on a raised platform. Calvino walked up the steps and through the entrance first, then Jackie Ky followed him to one side. A woman who was kneeling at the shrine held up between her clasped hands several incense sticks, the smoke curling lazily above her head. Her offering tray of fruit, flowers and tea was between her and the monk, an old man, who sat on a stool beside a bell. He rang the bell as the woman prostrated herself on the bamboo mat.

As the monk rang the bell, Calvino turned to Jackie.

"Did Drew know that you screwed Mark Wang the night of the Thai-Vietnamese concert?"

She dropped her head as if someone had whacked her on the back of the neck. She stood still on the grass, her head slumped and her hands balled up into fists. A paleness spread across her face. She had lost her edge. He had kicked an emotional stool from under her and she swung back and forth as if she were suspended at the end of a hangman's rope. Calvino had scored a direct hit and he knew it.

"Who told you that?" she asked. "Doesn't really matter, does it?"

"Webb told you."

Calvino shook his head. "No, it wasn't Webb."

"I want to go back home."

He reached for her wrist and she pulled away, walking fast.

"Just let me go, Calvino."

He kept pace with her as she cut through the grass and broke into a run.

"You slept with Wang because you thought Drew was making it with Mai."

This time it was as if he had hit a deer with a single round and the 30.06 slug passed through the lungs and heart, tearing them into shredded, useless pulp, causing the legs to go out from the body. Jackie Ky stumbled and fell on the grass outside the shrine. Calvino ran after her, then knelt beside her, listening to her sob. She buried her face in her arms, whimpering and moaning, like she had been mortally wounded.

"He was so stupid. Men are so stupid about women. They can't see when they are being used. Mai only wanted to use him. She wants to find a way out of Vietnam. I told him that. I was the one who came back to Vietnam. I was the one who had made a commitment. She was the one who wanted to use him to leave. He wouldn't listen. He wouldn't talk about it. I talk openly about my feelings. But Drew closed down. The more I asked him to be open, the more he ignored me. We had a fight the night of the concert and he asked why didn't I let him lead his own life? Why was I always pushing him? He said, I never push you. I give you freedom. Why do you want to take mine? During the concert he was pawing Mai right in front of my eyes. Do you know how that hurts? The man you want to marry is making a play for a woman right in your face. What I did was stupid and wrong. Fucking Mark Wang meant nothing."

She raised up on her arms and looked at Calvino. "You believe me, don't you?"

Calvino didn't know what, or who, to believe in Saigon, whether truth was left at the doorstep as if the entire city operated on make-believe stories like the kind told inside the Zone. The way Jackie Ky could turn on and off heavy emotions and hand out state-of-the-art handguns made her difficult to put in a pigeonhole. Her eyes were wet and red and she had some grass stuck to the side of her cheek.

"In Bangkok, a woman has been known to kill an unfaithful boyfriend."

"This isn't Bangkok. And I'm not a Thai," she said.

"But you wanted to hurt Drew."

She sighed as if filled with frustration.

"No, you don't understand much about relationships, do you? There's a big difference between a woman wanting to get back at her man and wanting to kill him."

"You didn't kill Drew Markle?"

"No, I didn't kill Drew Markle. I know how it looks. He was coming to meet me when he was murdered. We had this big fight. I slept with that yuppy. But you goddamn know well that I didn't kill him. I loved Drew. I told him things he would never have known to show that I loved him. The sonofabitch didn't deserve my love, but what kind of strong emotion ever makes any sense?"

Calvino helped her to stand and brushed the grass off her cheek. He wished he knew that for sure. But he owed her the benefit of the doubt. Without her gun, there would have no consciousness of the realm of benefits and doubts. He would have been dead in a place once called Karen's Bar.

"What kind of things did you tell him?"

"None of your fucking business." Her anger flashed, hot and raw.

"If that's the way you want to play it."

She wasn't sure how she wanted to play it.

"The night Drew died was the worst night of my life," she said.

Somehow he believed her.

"When someone makes you feel small and dirty, you sometimes act irrationally. It's a mistake. Mark Wang was a mistake."

She started to laugh as her mood swung back to the top of the pendulum.

"You know, I made Mark Wang use a condom. I bought a package before I went to his room. He said he had never used one before. Here was a guy going off to Bangkok who had never used any protection. I told him he was insane. I asked him if he had a death wish. But you know how guys are. I'm sure next time he's in Saigon he will phone me. Oh, remember me, this is Mark Wang. Why don't we have dinner for old times' sake?"

"Mark Wang's dead."

She grabbed his arm and made him stop and repeat what he had said.

"Dead? But how?"

"Someone shot him."

"I don't believe you. You're trying to fuck with my mind."

"Ask your uncle Marcus. I'm surprised he didn't tell you."

"God, that's awful."

Jackie Ky had no idea Mark Wang was dead. Why should she? It wouldn't have been in the newspapers in Saigon. Harry Markle would not have mentioned anything. Score one in her favor. Also, she had no idea that Calvino was going to Karen's Bar. Drew Markle's killer would have had access to that information and a reason to stop any further investigation into the circumstances of the murder.

"Why do I get the feeling Marcus doesn't like me?"

"He's never said anything bad about you. Except for one thing." She had caught his attention, distracted him.

"Yeah?"

"Nothing really. Only when Harry mentioned your name, he made a remark about your initials being 'VC'. He said it was a bad omen."

"If it makes him feel any better, my undercover initials are 'VD'. You really didn't know about Wang being murdered?"

Whatever control she had over her emotions fell apart and she stepped away from him. She stared at him as if he were dangerous, someone to avoid, to fear. "Why are you trying to hurt me? Hurt my uncle?"

Before he could react, a group of kids cut between them.

"Hello, how are you? Where you from? What's your name?" A rapid-fire of questions from the faces gathered around him. Before Calvino could respond, both Jackie Ky and he were surrounded by a half-dozen youngsters who came running up with cameras, wanting their photos taken with him. He clutched the computer in one hand and stood in the centre of the group as one boy looked through his camera. After the boy snapped several shots, he shoved the camera into a friend's hands, ran toward the circle of kids surrounding Calvino, grabbed Calvino's arm, demanding his turn to be photographed with the foreigner. Jackie Ky slipped away and when Calvino looked around, he saw her running across the grass toward the far gate. He lost sight of her as she passed a row of cyclos.

CHAPTER 12

DOI MOI

A BONY-CHESTED Vietnamese man, a cigarette dangling from his lips, massaged Marcus Nguyen's neck. The masseur 's hands and fingers were knotted by highways of tendons and veins as he worked them deep into Marcus's muscles. Pratt sat at the outdoor table opposite Marcus, a plate of untouched rice and chicken in front of him. The masseur was tiny, whiplike, thin like a jockey, though his hands were out of proportion to his body, as if they belonged to a much taller, bigger man. It was late Sunday afternoon and the street was choked with cyclos, bicycles, motorcycles, heavy Russian-made trucks, and a few cars honking at anything that moved. Pratt thought this place was much closer to Calvino's world in Bangkok than anything in his own world; Thais didn't frequent the *farang* ghettos.

On one stretch of Pham Ngu Lao Street, the shophouses had been converted into cheap, rundown expat restaurants and bars with bright neon lights, tables and chairs on the pavement. *Farang* customers in shorts and T-shirts sat at the tables eating hamburgers, talking, watching the street action, scoring drugs. These were the same backpacking travelers who checked into the cheap guest houses around Banglamphu in Bangkok, thought Pratt. One or two of them turned up dead every year. There were investigations into the cause of death—drugs, a knife, a gunshot, a twenty-five year old loaded up with enough speed to fly to the moon and back. Patches, as Calvino said the Zone people called them. They hit the Zone looking to patch into overload, all circuits opened on amphetamines, searching for that final tap pushing them over the top. Patches on their clothes, nervous system patched together with a combo of designer drugs, speed, bring- me-downs, grass, and hatched from broken families which could never have been patched back together. They patched into the Zone. They patched into Saigon.

Pham Ngu Lao was littered, noisy, dirty, a strange place to suggest as a business meeting area—no privacy, for instance. None of this computed, thought Pratt. On the telephone, Marcus had said he had something important he wanted to talk to him about, that is new information, which Pratt might find useful. He had used Pratt's police rank on the phone. Just dropped it out there, no follow-up, leaving Pratt to make the next move.

Marcus's eyes were half-closed, a purr of enjoy-ment in his throat, as the masseur worked him over.

"During the war, Dung worked for me," said Marcus. He pointed up at the masseur.

"That's Dung. When the end came, he didn't get out. He spent almost four years in a re-education camp. That's where he lost most of his teeth. Every time he smiled, they hit him in the mouth. But he kept smiling for almost four years. Isn't that right, Dung?"

Dung, his narrow shoulders hunched over, looked up, nodded, the gray ash from his cigarette falling and grazing Marcus's shoulder before hitting the pavement. The small masseur wiped the ash away. A cyclo driver in the street below took the distraction as a chance to scoop two large spoons of rice and chicken from Pratt's plate into his mouth. Marcus yelled in Vietnamese at the cyclo driver who laid down the spoon, grinned and walked back to his cyclo.

"And Dung is the reason you asked me to come here?" asked Pratt.

Marcus, his eyes narrowing as the strong hands worked on his shoulders, nodded his head. "In a way, yes. Dung works for me. During the war, Dung went down tunnels armed with only a .45 and a knife. He's killed a lot of VC in the dark, smelling the earth, far away from the surface. Now he gives tourists a massage for one dollar and a bottle of local beer."

He watched as Marcus succumbed to the pleasure of the deep massage. Ever since he had first met Marcus at the restaurant with Calvino on Dong Khoi Street, he had started re-reading Coriolanus. While the *farang* had gone around raving about The Quiet American as the embodiment of the truth about the tragedy of Vietnam, they had missed a genuine masterpiece. Marcus had banished himself just like in Coriolanus and was one of literature's first modern anti-heroes. To update the story, this Marcus returned to Saigon but was he a pawn of Rome? Substitute Washington, D.C. for Rome and the drama became closer to the original, thought Pratt. Although he knew his Shakespeare, the more difficult part was to know whether the man at the receiving end of the massage, who sat opposite him, was leading an army inside the city. Was he simply following orders? Or, as Calvino assumed, was he a friend in need who had been set in motion by Harry Markle?

"Much bitterness remains after any war. '*You souls of geese, that bear the shapes of men, how have you run from slaves that apes would beat!*' " said Pratt, quoting Shakespeare's Coriolanus, as if the Saigon Marcus would see the reflection of himself.

"Was that English?"

"Shakespeare."

"Tragedy? Or comedy?"

"Tragedy."

"That reminds me of Calvino. Tragedy in the making."

"Vincent can take care of himself."

"We are Asians, you and me. Military men. We think like Asians. No one can take care of themselves alone in Asia. Without friends, a network of friends, where would you be in the police force? You don't have to answer because I already know. You would be nowhere."

"Who said he was without friends?"

"Harry Markle tells me you work for the police. I respect that. I wish we had something like a real police force in Saigon. Instead we have an occupation army strutting around with AK47s, big swinging dicks, looking for ideological infractions. You Thais are pragmatic. You don't vote on principle. You don't choose your friends or enemies on principle. Whatever fits and works becomes the automatic choice."

"Asians never talk about automatic choices," said Pratt.

Marcus let his face break, counted to ten as Dung's hands worked the muscles in his right arm.

"I want to explain why I asked you to meet me here. It is ugly, smells of exhaust fumes and the people are poor. So why did I invite you to such a place?"

" '*So, now the gates are open,*' " said Pratt, quoting from Coriolanus as if he were ordering another bowl of rice.

Marcus gave the impression that he had missed the connection. "Gates, fuck the gates. Pham Ngu Lao is controlled by a certain mafia, and they are safe in this part of town. They don't leave unless they have to or someone gives them a real good reason. And that usually means a lot of money stuffed in a duffel bag. They stay tight with each other, look after each other like family. The man who ate out of your rice bowl would go to your room at the Saigon Concert Hotel, open and close the door real quietly, and slit your throat before you had a chance to say William Shakespeare. The man Calvino's looking for, the one who killed Drew Markle, works on this street. He's the one Calvino's looking for, the one he's been hired to finger. And that's all he's gotta do. Just lift his arm and point the finger. A reflex..." He began to purr as Dung, who was squatting down under the table began to work his fingers on the outer edge of Marcus's left calf. "...action. But Calvino isn't necessarily a difficult man; he's a man who is overloaded by Saigon. So, I thought, if his friend Pratt could listen to the killer confess here. The local mafia runs this street like it's their own private country. Even the police are afraid of them. Asians don't come here but foreigners like it. Webb, for instance, likes the action here."

"What do you want from me?" asked Pratt.

"Straight to the point. We Vietnamese like that quality. I figure that if I can explain to you what happened to Drew Markle, and you are convinced, then Calvino will believe in your judgement."

"If it is logical, without holes, without agendas behind it, then he might think about it," said Pratt.

"Calvino told you about his little problem the other night?" Pratt remained expressionless, not knowing how much Marcus really knew, nor how much he was testing to find out the gaps in his knowledge. Dung was down on his knees, the sweat rolling off his chin and nose, as he massaged Marcus's leg. His hands were dark, swollen, obscene appendages that looked non-human. He had used those hands inside dark tunnels to slit throats. No massage, just the passage of a sharp blade across a throat, sending the warm blood over his hands.

"Calvino killed three men in some old abandoned wreck of a bar. He had no choice. I mean, it was self-defense. But, if he hadn't been supplied with a certain weapon, he would be dead now. And if you ask him how he came to have such a weapon, I believe he will confirm that I played some small role."

"What does this have to do with Douglas Webb?" asked Pratt.

"The men Calvino killed were the same trio who took out Drew Markle."

Pratt contemplated the possibility.

"The word on the street is they were working for Webb."

"Why would Webb want to kill Markle?"

Marcus opened his eyes, removed a cigarette from a pack. It had a broken filter, he smiled, and flicked it toward the street. As soon as the cigarette hit the street, two cyclo drivers made a dive for it. The victor tore off the broken filter and came up with a short cigarette in his mouth, spitting out pieces of tobacco.

"A vertically challenged cigarette," said Marcus, pulling out a second cigarette and handing it to Dung whose huge hands pushed the cigarette into his tiny black hole of a mouth.

"What does that mean?"

"You can't say broken or damaged in the States any more."

Closing in on two decades, thought Pratt. Marcus was showing off his knowledge of America, letting Pratt know who was current and who was living in the past.

"As to why Webb would have Markle murdered, several reasons spring to mind. Webb had been going out with my niece, Jackie Ky, before Markle came on the scene. They hadn't been going out all that long. But sometimes a man marks his turf and once marked any other man stepping onto it finds himself with a serious health problem. If the people running Pham Ngu Lao

Street thought I was coming to take away what they saw was theirs, I would be dead. I would expect to be dead. In Bangkok, I am certain there are similar places where you could get yourself dead very fast by moving in on the wrong people."

The cyclo driver smoking the discarded cigarette butt made another swipe at Pratt's plate, but this time, Pratt half turned in his chair and handed him the plate. The driver took a couple of steps back, squatted down and ate the rice and chicken with his fingers, taking a puff of the cigarette, his mouth ballooned up, chewing the food and the smoke curling out of his nose. The videotape he had flown in from Bangkok of the Thai-Vietnamese concert had shown Webb sitting with an American woman named Darla, his hand finding her hand. If he was suffering from rejection and jealous over Jackie Ky's involvement with Markle, Webb was doing a very good job hiding it.

"You see, with the way people live here, mostly unemployed, dirt poor, it doesn't take much to find a man, or three men, to kill someone else for very little money. And if you are willing to pay a little more, then you can find men with a talent for killing. There are many men like that in Vietnam. The only talent they ever had a chance to develop when they were young was a talent for staying alive and killing other men. Important qualities to be sure."

"Have you told Calvino this theory?"

"It's not a theory."

"And Webb would have access to such people?"

"Indirectly, yes. There is a younger, wilder crowd that hangs out at the Q-Bar, they are there every night. They speak Vietnamese. Webb speaks enough to get by, but his friends are fluent. One or two introductions and he was in business."

"What proof do you have to connect Webb to the three gunmen?"

Marcus had been waiting for this one. Dung finished the massage and rose to his feet, taking the cigarette out of his mouth long enough to reach over the table and take a large bottle of beer. He tilted back his head and the beer emptied from the bottle straight down his throat without Dung ever stopping to take a breath. As they watched, the cyclo driver handed back the plate to Pratt. The plate was clean as if it had come out of a dishwasher. Finally, Dung removed the bottle from his mouth, the sweat dripping from his face, smiled and popped the cigarette between his lips. Marcus reached into his pocket, removed a roll of dollars, and peeled off a one dollar bill. Dung accepted the dollar and pulled up a chair and sat down. Marcus reached into his shirt pocket and removed an envelope.

"Have a look at these," he said.

Pratt opened the envelope and removed some pictures. There was one of Webb and Jackie. Another picture of Webb with three Vietnamese, all young men in their twenties, dark shirts and trousers, tough, serious, fit like a commando unit fresh from the field. Webb was in half profile as if he were talking to someone off-camera.

"It was dark in the bar, Vincent didn't get a good look at any of the men."

"In other words, Calvino thinks that we all look the same," said Marcus.

Pratt started to hand back the photos but Marcus waved him off.

"Keep them. Give them to Calvino. They are the same men. If he sees the photo it will come back to him. You don't kill a man up close and forget what his face looks like. Even if all you see are his eyes for a moment. You don't forget that instant when he dies."

"Webb seems like the kind of man who likes women. Lots of women. That's why Vincent may find it difficult to believe that this kind of man would kill because someone else came on the scene. Remember Webb is a *farang*."

"You are a wise man, Colonel Pratt. I didn't say that the only reason he killed Markle was because of my niece and Markle. He was a good company man. An American company man. Things were done according to the rules. Webb is wired a little different like many foreigners who spend too much time in Asia. He was, shall we say, flexible. Winchell & Holly have been working on a mutual fund."

"The Vietnam Emerging Market Fund."

"You've done your homework. So you will know there's a pipeline of money that will be flowing into Vietnam through the Fund. What will happen to that money? It goes into investments. Land, companies, resources. Drew Markle was doing due diligence, making sure that the companies the Fund might invest in were keeping the books rather than cooking the books, they owned what they said they owned, they had no problems with taxes or the government. That sort of thing. Webb had connections inside one Vietnamese company, one of the State enterprises. Only Markle found out that this company wasn't really a company at all. It was just a name on a card. It was a division of a State enterprise. Now this defect didn't bother the Japanese, the Hong Kongers, the Thais. They did business with this non-company as if it were a company. You understand what I am saying, they were flexible. Markle was legalistic. He said this non-company was in violation of Vietnamese law and he would recommend that the Fund not invest any money in it. Markle told all this to Jackie after work. How he had these big fights with Webb and how Webb was starting to get nasty. Push was coming to shove, as Markle told her."

"How much money was involved?"

Marcus shrugged, stretching out his shoulders and arms, feeling the warmth of Dung's massage. He gave Dung another cigarette, lit it, thinking about the question, letting it hang in the air as a loud motorcycle shot past.

"Markle told my niece that Webb stood to get about a hundred grand from the head of the State enterprise. But only if the Fund invested in the company. Say, at least one point five million. That was the deal. The one Markle was blowing off over a stupid American technicality."

"Calvino was a lawyer," said Pratt.

"Yeah? Then he should appreciate the dilemma Markle faced."

"Who took the picture?"

Marcus tapped Dung on the shoulder.

"Show my Thai friend your camera."

Dung, a cloud of smoke obscuring his face, produced a small camera from his pocket and set it on the table. Another bottle of beer appeared on the table and Dung helped himself.

"Webb's one of Dung's customers. One dollar for a massage like Dung's is exceptional value. And Webb is a man who appreciates value. Another dollar he snaps your picture. Sometimes he takes a photograph on the side and sells it to other people. Like me."

"When did Dung take this photo?"

"A few days before Markle was killed. Here on Pham Ngu Lao Street at this restaurant. Look at the background. See that TV, the fridge, the potted plants with those same huge green leaves against the ugly gray cement. It's the same."

Pratt matched up the background in the photograph with the restaurant. Webb had been sitting in the same seat that Marcus now occupied. Dung must have been seated across the table where I am sitting, thought Pratt. On the street side, a beggar 's hand reached away from the table. Only Webb wasn't looking at the camera, the only one who didn't know that a photo was being taken. Dung was Marcus's man on the street, his source of intelligence, making contact with foreigners, and probably selling his photographs to the police, local mafia as well as to Marcus. The way the man guzzled a beer, he demonstrated a powerful appetite that needed feeding and one dollar and a lot of sweat giving a massage wasn't exactly the most efficient way of doing it. The Vietnamese in the photo didn't look like the kind of men who had to steal food off foreigners' plates. Young but hard, beyond hard, scary eyes with that dull, dead look. Marcus's version of what happened had an internal logic, it was a serviceable, workable explanation. Men had been hanged in a hundred countries for a thousand years on less evidence, thought Pratt. And more than one innocent man had been hanged on far less circumstantial evidence. That was the way of the world. You could never be sure, thought Pratt.

"You are friends with Harry Markle, I believe. Vincent is working for Harry. Why not simply go directly to Mr. Markle and explain to him what you have told me and let him decide?"

Marcus smiled. "I already have. Harry and I go back a long, long way. Before he ever heard of Calvino."

"He's leaving it up to Calvino," said Pratt.

"The *farang* stick together," said Marcus.

Drew Markle did get himself killed on Marcus Nguyen's watch. If Marcus had the photograph before Markle had been murdered, then why hadn't he taken steps to warn Markle, protect him, get him out of the country? These were some of the questions which Pratt thought that, if he were Harry Markle, he would be asking himself. Why wasn't Harry Markle in Saigon himself? Calvino had said Harry had a work commitment. Are *farang* that different in their feelings when a brother was killed? he wondered. How could work ever come before seeking the murderer of one's own brother? How could money and career ever be valued above family? Pratt had had these questions from the start.

Behind him in the street, voices were raised in anger. A fat, young American stood beside an empty cyclo and ten Vietnamese formed a circle around him. The men closed in with clenched fists, one held a metal pipe, another a brick and they were moving fast, shouting at the large *farang*. The *farang* was shouting back in Vietnamese and waving a five-thousand dong note in one hand.

"Street theater," said Marcus.

"Starring a character named Charlie who is from South Carolina."

"You know him?"

"Everyone knows Charlie."

Marcus had begun to rise from his chair as the angry crowd pressed in on Charlie. At the same moment, Charlie stepped forward and hit the largest of the cyclo drivers smack in the face with a fist that looked like if you cut it off and tossed it on a scale, it would have weighed no less than ten kilos. The fist drove into the driver's face, smashing his nose; his legs buckled and he dropped to his knees, blood gushing everywhere. The others in the crowd froze in their tracks, looking at the damage inflicted on the largest man in the group.

"He carries a real punch," said Marcus.

Charlie put an arm on the shoulder of a young kid, gave him the bloodied five-thousand dong note and the kid took off running. And as Charlie faced off against the cyclo drivers, the kid returned with a soldier in camouflage uniform, steel helmet and carrying an AK47.

"This should be good," said Marcus.

A couple of minutes later, the soldier led away the cyclo driver, his face still leaking blood, his nose flattened to one side. The other drivers drifted away and Charlie climbed up the steps to the restaurant and sat down at the table next to Marcus.

"Sorry, I'm a bit late. I had a little trouble over the fare." He was shaking his right hand, rubbing some torn skin over the knuckles.

"This is Colonel Pratt," said Marcus, nodding in his direction.

"My name's Charlie in desperate need of a Tiger beer. I'm a South Carolina boy. Sometimes you get these basic misunderstandings over money. I said five thousand dong to Pham Ngu Lao and sure as hell we arrive and he demands five dollars. I speak reasonable Vietnamese."

"Perfect Vietnamese," added Marcus.

"So I am pretty sure I got the message across that the fee was five thousand dong. Now he has a lot of people who are backing him up. I ain't been in three fights in my whole life. But I remember what my daddy told me, you get a group of 'em comin' at you and all you got to do is find the biggest one and hit him as hard as you can in the nose. You break his nose. He's gonna have blood flying every which direction."

"What did you say to the soldier?" asked Marcus.

Charlie smiled. "The driver said I stole his cyclo and he had ten witnesses to back him up. So I thought to myself, it's my word against theirs. Who is the soldier gonna believe? I said to the soldier, he's right, I took the cyclo. But under Vietnamese law, only the rightful owner can file a charge. Now this caught everyone off guard. I was running a risk. But I know for a fact more than half these cyclos are stolen and I figure if this guy had tried to cheat me on the fare, he probably stole the damn cyclo somewhere down the road. I said to the soldier, if this driver has the papers, then you arrest me. Put me in jail. I won't complain. But if he doesn't have the papers, then he's the thief, and you arrest him. Well, that boy didn't have the papers. I gave the soldier five dollars just so he would know how grateful I was for him enforcing the laws of Vietnam. That boy's cooling his heels in jail now. And, damn, I think I might have broken my hand hitting him so hard."

"The reason I asked you to meet me, Charlie, is for you to tell me again that story about Webb and Markle getting into a fight in the Q-Bar. The night before Markle got killed."

"Jesus, that was quite some night. Crazy stuff was in the air," said Charlie. Then he started speaking to Dung in Vietnamese, and Dung examined his hand, each knuckle at a time, finding one that was dislocated, he popped it back into place.

"Goddamn that hurt and felt great at the same time."

"Crazy stuff in the air," said Pratt.

"Douglas Webb sat at the Q-Bar with a small audience around him. He has a lot of friends who drink there. They usually get drunk together. Well, that night, Webb was getting himself drunk on premium whiskies and was feeling no pain. Drew Markle shows up with Jackie. Kin of Marcus here. And Drew makes the big mistake of pushing into the bar beside Webb. He accidentally hit Webb's arm, and bingo, knocks the drink out of his hand and all over his suit. The color drained right out of that boy's face. Drew tried to say he was sorry and all but it was too late. Webb hit him. Not so much as a hit but a slap. Bang across the face. The kind that leaves five red finger marks. Drew looks dazed then he takes a swing at Webb and misses. He was a nice kid but no fighter. Webb ducked, came up with a right hand into Markle's gut, which knocked the wind out of him. Next thing Webb is saying, 'Keep out of my way or you will be put out of the way.' But Webb was kinda drunk, Markle had tried to punch him, so I didn't think too much about it. Then Markle is dead the next night. Lucky for Webb they caught that ex-RVN sergeant or his tit could have been in the ringer."

"What kind of work you do in Saigon?" asked Pratt.

"I am a consultant," said Charlie, smiling. "Same business as Marcus here."

"You think Webb killed Markle?"

"I've lived in Saigon long enough not to know what I think any more. He might have done it. He was pretty pissed off that night. But who knows how pissed off you have to be to kill someone? I've never done that. Hitting that driver in the face is as close as I ever hope to come to murder."

CHAPTER 13

SAIGON CONCERT

BRUTALITY IS THE way of the world. At first this Marcus twist of phrase had sounded like one of those T-shirt sayings. But, on reflection, Calvino had been thinking there was some basic truth in what Marcus had said. Brutality wasn't an isolated exception, floating to the surface now and again and dragging down the less fit, the less prepared. Brutality was the main operating procedure and, if there were a lull in the blood and violence, the nightmare had not ended, the silence which fell was a rest between rounds. Then a bell rang, and a deeper mechanism of cruelty intervened, and blood and bodies, the visible evidence, the trail of death, began all over again. Brutality was like one of those creatures in a horror movie that had been eliminated only to return again in the darkness of night. Markle existed half of the time on his information superhighway out there, somewhere, making new hook-ups, establishing connections, surfing in cyberspace, but in the electronic world there was nothing that could ever pave over that mud road of hatred, jealousy and greed which ended at some juncture in death and violence.

"Corruption is a necessary evil to fight brutality."

Another one of Marcus's sayings. Without corruption, the brutality would have been much worse. There would be suffering, more bodies, more grief and despair. "You Americans don't understand this. You call us corrupt. You want to eliminate corruption. You don't understand it is our shield, a way for us to survive. When America ends brutality, then come and talk to us about corruption. The time will be right then. So we make you a deal. We leave you with all your guns and you leave us to make what payments have to be made."

His arguments rumbled through Calvino's mind as he walked back to his hotel. He was reasonably certain that Marcus's discussion about brutality and corruption was intended to explain how Markle got himself killed in Saigon. He was a young American who simply didn't understand the nature of the game and when the brutality machine descended on him, it was, of course, too late. What Marcus didn't know, however, was that Drew Markle had left a trail on the diskette.

Calvino wanted to read the thoughts of a man who had been stalked, who knew that the veil might be lowered at any time, a young man, an American, who had been raised to believe that brutality could be mastered, tamed like a wild animal.

At the same time Calvino arrived at his hotel, Marcus and Pratt were sitting at a table on Pham Ngu Lao Street, listening to Charlie's version of what had gone down in the Q-Bar between Markle and Webb, on the eve of Markle's death. Calvino paid his cyclo driver, an attendant opened the sliding glass door, he picked up his key at the desk, walked through the lobby and straight into the elevator. As the elevator doors opened on his floor, he stepped out, carrying the laptop in one hand and his room key in the other. The corridor was empty. As he set down the laptop on the old carpet, a strand of wire caught his eye. The copper wire stretched about four inches above the floor and had been strung tight, spanning the base of the door. It was a professional job, the kind of trip-wire anyone going through the door wouldn't be able to miss hitting. Open the door and take one short step forward; one last step forward and the big sleep, he thought. He was on his hands and knees, his eyes following the thin, copper wiring.

"Brutality is the way of the world," the words ran through his mind like a mantra, and when it comes from you, then you are surprised because you think it doesn't belong to your world. But what other world does one live in? he thought to himself. His heart was racing. Had whoever done this job might also have booby-trapped Pratt's room? He sat on the floor, staring at the wire, slowly he leaned his head back against the wall, took a deep breath. He stared at the wire. One more step and...the void. He saw himself coming out of the elevator, his mind somewhere else, back in the Winchell & Holly elevator when the power had cut out. If he hadn't been carrying the laptop and hadn't bent down as he set it on the floor, he would have opened the door, taken that one step forward over the threshold and tripped the wire. Would the local police have arrested another one-legged ex-RVN sergeant on crutches?

Now what? Go down to reception, and do what? Lean over and address the young girl in the white ao dai, "Excuse me, could you have the maid remove the bomb from my room?" Then they would phone the police, and that would start something he didn't have time to finish. The investment fund reception was starting in a couple of hours. Leaving the door wired was not a good idea. A maid might go through the door with his laundry. He tried to imagine if there was more than one way to trip the wire. He rose from the floor, his legs still shaky and tried the door to the room next to his. He knocked once, then again, but there was no reply. With a Swiss army knife he picked the lock, let himself into the room. There was a plastic cup of half-eaten rice and lentils overrun with ants. He quickly crossed to the French doors, slipped out onto the balcony and climbed over the railing to his own side of the balcony. He let himself into his own room. He set the computer down on the bed on his way over to the door. A grenade had been fixed to the inside wall and a wire was attached to the pin. The wire would have yanked out the pin if he had tripped over it, or if he had opened the door. The force of the blast would have unleashed hundreds of jagged metal fragments, scattering the shrapnel with enough energy to dismember legs, hands, arms.

Some thought had gone into this fail-safe system. He leaned down and marveled at the mechanism that had been intended to end his life. The grenade was a newer pin type, the kind with coiled springs inside, and the explosion shattered the springs along the score marks, releasing the bits of spring out as deadly shrapnel. The first thing Calvino did was to check the pin—it was a cotter pin with the shaft pressed together. A little tug on the wire and the pin would have pulled out. With the Swiss army knife, he bent each end of the cotter pin, folding each shaft back. Then he sliced the electrician's tape and carefully pulled the grenade away from the wall, releasing the tension of the wire, then he cut the wire. He stared at the grenade, wondering whether the fuse had been removed. In a normal booby-trap, the fuse was removed, the cotter pin was pulled and the grenade blew up immediately. Calvino looked at the door. Chances are enough fuse would have been left to let him go through the door so that his body would take the full impact of the blast. He was betting three to four seconds of fuse had been left in the grenade. If he were right, the grenade might come in handy later; if he were wrong about the fuse, then the grenade would explode in his face. He looked at the door one more time and then slipped the grenade in the pocket of his suit jacket. It was heavy and made his jacket sag. He looked at himself in the mirror. Here was a man with a .40 caliber Smith & Wesson slung in a leather rig on one side and a grenade stuffed in his jacket pocket on the opposite side. He looked like an Orchard Street merchant on a chilly New York afternoon in late November, standing in the doorway of his shop with a thermos of coffee shoved deep in one pocket.

He sat on the edge of the bed, flipped open the case of the laptop, hit the power switch and watched the screen come alive, scrolling protocols, before the windows filled the screen with icons. Calvino then inserted the small plastic floppy diskette in to the side of the computer. He looked at his watch: it was nearly five o'clock. He opened the Word Perfect program, changed to the floppy disk drive. There were dozens of files arranged in a methodical order: Saigon.1, Saigon.2 and so on. Then the numbering skipped, went out of sequence, jumping from Saigon.24 to Saigon.33. Either files had been deleted, or he hadn't had time to download them. Saigon.33 had last been opened and saved on the day of Markle's death. Over two hundred thousand bytes combined in all of the files. Saigon.33 was the Fourth of July file and bore the time marker 6.32 pm, followed by the notation: 9,762 bytes. Markle must have updated the diskette and given it to Mai just before he left the office, an hour before a grenade had blown him apart. Calvino opened Saigon.33 and glanced over the text which appeared like a conversation that Drew Markle was having with himself. Calvino started to read the file on the screen: SAIGON CONCERT.

"By the time you have gone through Saigon.1 to Saigon.24 you will have the evidence to support the conclusions contained in this final file. And also my personal observations, for whatever they are worth. Winchell & Holly was instructed to do the due diligence on several Vietnamese companies on behalf of the Vietnam Emerging Market Fund. My task has been to coordinate the due diligence, not a term which has much history and even less meaning in Vietnam. I scratched the surface and what I found were bad loans, bogus bookkeeping, and directors whose only quali-fications were their mafia connections. I am told by Webb that a lawyer can't apply the same standards of due diligence in Vietnam otherwise the Fund would have not a single company which would meet the test. He's probably right. The investors are a cosy, small club of people who have a history of doing business in this environment. They know what they are getting into. It's a commercial decision where no one expects transparency. Jungle law! You fly over the jungle in a chopper and you look down and what do you see? asked Marcus. Just a lot of green. You know there is a hell of a lot happening on the ground but you can't see it, man, sez Marcus. Emerging markets, but emerging from what?

"Since April when Harris starting coming in every two weeks from Bangkok, he's been dropping some big hints..."

"And Marcus's name came up? "

"As a matter of fact it did. He sez Marcus and some ole buddies from the pre-1975 days have been talking about old times and what they might do to bring the old times rolling back again. One of those ole buddies is my own brother. If Harry knew what was going on... I tried to phone him all afternoon, and then remembered it was the Fourth of July and he was probably at the picnic. Harry never missed a Fourth of July. It is just as well, the news I have would only spoil his celebration. Mark will get hold of him if I don't and let him read the Saigon files. He has the key files loaded on his hard disk.

"And I came to Vietnam because I wanted to prove myself, like Harry had proved himself. Harry once told me that he grew up in Vietnam...he grew down as well. Harry smiled when I asked him what he meant. He said you find the heaven and hell, the animal and the angel walking a jungle path... Frustration, boredom, and death in the 90s isn't in the jungle; it's in a law office, my law office...

"I talked with several people in New York City. Excuse me, I am a lawyer. I didn't sign to be a live feed to the CIA. You hit that web and you never get unstuck. Like a fly waiting for big momma spider to climb down for her dinner. It's just a matter of time. And what does Wallace, my mentor, in New York say? He doesn't say, 'Fine, son, we understand, we will pull you out. Fly you home. Go to the airport, we will have someone waiting to escort you home.' Or he could have said, 'We are on your side, fuck Harris, ignore him, forget him. Do your job as if you were sitting on the twenty-fourth floor of our offices on Park Avenue. And I am one hundred percent behind you.' But what he does say is something altogether different, 'Drew, sometimes a lawyer has to act on faith. This is one of those times. I didn't have to double check on Harris. It wasn't necessary. I know his boss in Washington. Way back when you were in grade school we worked together.' Worked together! Shit. I should have been doing due diligence on the partners in Winchell & Holly. Revolving doors are sometimes attached to companies you would never think of. 'Harris,' sez Wallace, 'is not involved in some rogue operation. That's TV-land stuff. Our interests are his interests. And the interests of our client. The Fund. You have to do what you think is right. But helping Harris is the right thing, otherwise, I wouldn't be asking you to give a hand. This is your first really big deal. You pull this off and you will be a partner of this firm.'

"Give them a hand, no problem. A hand I would give, but Harris wants a leg, arm, the head, the soul. Do I want to be a partner in this law firm? The answer is hell, yes, I want it. To say I don't would be bullshit. Christ, I would be Webb's boss! That alone would make it worth the effort. But there are so many problems to overcome. Every time I turn around there is one more new hitch. For instance, to complicate my life, Jackie Ky is Marcus's niece. She's living in his old villa. Basic information for anyone winging through the background of Saigon.33. That's what Marcus calls this crazy plan. Saigon Concert.33 to be precise. It's perfect, he uses a code word based on a cheap beer that isn't even called 33 any more. It's called 333. The number 33 is also printer's talk for the end. Throughout the Vietnam war, someone was saying at the Q-Bar the other night, thousands of reports were filed with 33 at the bottom. It was a number that journalists used and the Vietnamese thought this was a lucky number so they named their beer after it. Of course, it is a bullshit story, but it sounds good. Kind of like the stories Marcus tells or a lot of the other vets who are still living twenty, thirty years ago in the past. All this goes to show how far in the past Marcus is living, out of touch with reality. Harris doesn't really know what Marcus is planning. If he did, then he would shit himself.

" 'Jackie Ky knows what her uncle is up to,' sez Harris. 'Use her,' he sez. 'It's for the good of your country. Too many bad things have happened between Vietnam and America. You have the chance to do what few people ever have offered to them: You can make a difference in the history of millions of people. Think of it, Drew. What you will be doing for your country is right and moral. Something to make up for the damage my generation did to the people here.'

"Does that mean the CIA will make me a partner? I

thought." 'You have the run of Jackie's place. Sooner or later you will find something,' sez Harris. I found it sooner, and what I found was Saigon Concert.33. A cell of three men who had missed the final evacuation and were left behind on 30th April 1975. All three are Viet Khieu who later escaped on boats. They kicked ass together in the old days in something called SOG. Special Operations Group is what SOG means. Someone told me at the Q-Bar. The villa was a perfect place for them to meet. A perfect place for me to plant a listening device. I had access to every room in the place. I had Jackie's trust. No one would suspect...Drew Markle, a lawyer, Jackie's boyfriend. What a joke that turned out to be. You know why I decided to help Harris? Jackie was using me to feed her information about the Fund. Tit for tat. All is fair in love and war, they say. Also, I have this fear that somehow my brother is connected to this crazy thing. I've got to know, find out before Harris does. When I finally get the tapes from the villa, what do I find? A lot of the conversations are in Vietnamese. I can't understand anything they are saying. Marcus would sometimes switch into English. I think there is someone in the room who doesn't understand English, an official, a mole in the government and he wants to keep that person in the dark. Or maybe he is showing off, the Viet Khieu thing equivalent of the big swinging dick act. Hey, man, I speak English. I am not just some local cyclo driver talking out of my ass. I am special. I can talk about taking out a man in his own language. He said that on tape. You shouldn't kill a man unless you know his thoughts and his dreams. Otherwise, what have you destroyed? It is like cutting down a tree, sez Marcus. I don't understand him any more than I trust him.

"Bottom line is that Marcus Nguyen has planned to kill an ex-Deputy Director of the CIA, named Rodney Judson, who had a significant connection, a personal pipeline into SOG during the war. Twenty years after leaving Saigon, Judson will return as one of the directors of the Fund. Twenty years before, Judson had run away from Saigon and left Marcus and a lot of others hanging out to dry as the NVA were at the edge of the city. 'What price has Judson paid? He landed on his feet. He's coming back to Saigon as a hero. Think of that! I think we will have a welcome for him. I intend to blow the motherfucker away,' sez Marcus on the tape. Marcus's story was simple. Judson had promised that Marcus would be airlifted out of Saigon on April 28th but it seems that Judson left without him. Left without two of the other men in the plot as well. Rather than a simple bullet in the brain, Marcus wants to plan a big, grandstand play. Saigon Concert.33 has coordinated the assassination of Rodney Judson the night of the Fund launch. Marcus will shoot him as he gets out of his limo at the Continental Hotel. This was the place Marcus had gone to meet him by prearrangement twenty years earlier. This was the place he wanted to kill Judson.

" 'I will kill the sonofabitch,' sez Marcus on the tape. 'Rodney Judson threw us away like a piece of shit. You know how some of the GIs called the VC monkeys without tails. Hey, man, I gotta tell you the VC were Vietnamese. I am Vietnamese. I wasn't living in some kind of fucking zoo, man. I was putting my ass on the line because I really believed that Judson would be behind us, no matter what happened, we were in it together. If it turned to shit, then, we were knee deep in the same shit. On April 28th, what do I hear? Oh, Judson, well, Sir, he's not available, Sir. What do you mean not available? He's on a carrier conferring with his staff. What the fuck does that mean? I am part of his staff. He's not conferring with me. Well, Sir, all I can say is that Judson isn't in Saigon any longer, and, no, he didn't leave a message for you. Next.'

"Some real anger was working in that part of the tape. The

heavy, black clouds you would see roll in on East Hampton Beach just before a major storm would blow out the lines on every beach house for miles.

"There is one concession to something called conscience. Doing the right thing. I am going to tell Jackie tonight that she is in grave danger. I don't think she knows how far Marcus has gone and is prepared to go. She may have fed him some information I gave her about the reception in Saigon. I knew she would pass it along so most of what I told her was misinformation about the arrival of the directors. It doesn't matter. Marcus would have other sources to double, and triple check against one another. But she needs to cut loose from Marcus before he drags her down with him. He has been using her from day one and she should know that...if she doesn't already know. Her voice never appeared on a single tape. If I had to make a call, I would say, she really doesn't know the full extent of what her uncle has planned.

"Marcus has several rooms overlooking Dong Khoi and Le Loi Boulevard. The night of the Fund reception, he will be there. He will take out Judson. Pick him out on the nightscope. Watch him between the cross-hairs on the pavement in front of the Continental Hotel, and squeeze the trigger. That's for leaving your friends on April 28th, 1975.

"A copy of the Saigon Concert files are on Mark Wang's laptop. He will get them to Harris in Bangkok. Then it will be done. I can't believe this is happening to me. I am a lawyer. I keep saying that as if I still believe that nothing has changed in my life.

"Harry once said, do the right thing, and don't ever forget right stays right wherever you are, wherever you go, whatever you do—foraging for food, nesting, mating. There is right in the world. Don't lose your moral compass. Because if you forget north, south, east and west, you will wander without direction, not knowing where you are, where you are going and where you have been. Not knowing who you are. Without that compass, you become the man in motion, the man who travels a path suspended by lies, attached to no one, and detached from meaning or value. It 's up to you, he said. Find something of worth you can hold onto or go nowhere. Go to hell.

"At the end of the day who can I trust? A Hanoi girl. The only person in the office, maybe in the city, that I can trust. FOR YOUR INFORMATION. WHOEVER IS READING THIS TAPE. Please be advised that Miss Mai did not ever read the contents herein. She gave her pledge. She is a woman with integrity and honor. I warrant and represent that her word is not only her bond, it is more than that. It is beyond price or ideology. Her father was killed during the war. She has only one or two memories of him. He would have been the enemy that my brother Harry would have been sent to Vietnam to kill. How does it turn out that his daughter, Mai, is the one I can rely upon? And my own brother is at a fucking Fourth of July picnic. It's time for dinner. I must sign off and give this diskette to Mai, my Hanoi girl, the only one I know who will keep this record of what I found, what I have done, and the reasons for it all.

Drew Markle, Esq."

§ § § §

RODNEY Judson was one of those vaguely familiar names like the off-brand name of a cheap whisky one had drunk to excess and the next morning couldn't quite recall. Deputy CIA director, Vietnam War. A cog in the memory wheel moved. In the late 60s, at Columbia University, there had been a mock trial and a number of American government officials had been tried by law students from Columbia and NYU. Judson had been one of those charged and convicted of war crimes, crimes against humanity. A journalist for one of the wire services testified that Judson was the operational guy for SOG, and that SOG was little better than the Gestapo in their use of tactics, which included assassination, the two in the morning knife at the throat call. True or not, the law students convicted Judson in absentia. The sentence they handed down was death. But it was all a long time ago and it was play- acting by students on a university campus. Marcus was not playing or acting, if Drew Markle was to be believed. And his death was convincing evidence that he should be believed. Drew Markle, Esq. He had signed off using his title.

There had been a time when "Esq." wasn't a designer label, it meant something, a warranty of honor, dignity and loyalty. Drew had signed off in the old-fashioned way. He hadn't known that "Esq." would be the last thing he would leave behind. His last mark on the sands. A scrawl less than one percent of the population of the planet would have registered as carrying any meaning. Calvino scrolled back to the top of the file and began re-reading the opening when someone started knocking on the door. He unholstered the Smith & Wesson, and moved from the bed to the corner away from the door. Calvino waited until the second series of knocks started. In the background, the sound waves registered a familiar voice. A soft, hushed plea to be let into the room.

"Vincent, it's me. Mai. Please open the door."

He slowly shouldered the Smith & Wesson and moved across the room, standing to one side of the door. He swung around and faced the door. If he was making a character judgement then he would rather have blown himself straight to hell by opening the door. It was the Thai way: What will come in the future is not a surprise, it is precisely tailored to

291

match your karma. Twist and turn, duck and dodge, wait or charge—it is all figured in, calculated. No matter how many times you spin the possibilities, it won't affect the final outcome. The door was open and Mai ran to him, both her arms squeezing, pulling him in, clinging like a frightened child on the wrong edge of tears.

"What's wrong, Mai?" he asked, pushing the door shut with his foot. He leaned back against the door, rocking her from side to side.

"I am very afraid for you," she said.

"How did you get past the front desk?"

"I work for Winchell & Holly. You are a client. I have an important message."

"What's the message?"

"I think I should throw away the disk I gave to you. I think that maybe it was wrong to give it to you. It is dangerous. You might be hurt."

"I was just reading it now. Did you read it?"

She shook her head, lifted her face off his chest and looked up at him.

"Mr. Markle, he gave me the disk then he died. I am afraid for you," she said.

Calvino smiled, pressed his lips to her forehead. "I am afraid for me, too," whispered Calvino.

Talking so openly in this way was taking a lot of getting used to. Life outside the Zone had all kinds of trip-wires, the emotional ones as dangerous as the others. He kissed her gently. This was the one, he thought, the woman who could break him free, melt the ice. He had lived so long with that coldness. Like drugs, it numbed the brutality of the world, as Marcus had called it. He had no more than pulled his lips away from her forehead when the laptop computer exploded. The blast shattered the glass windows in the French doors to the balcony and blew out the mirror and the TV screen. The air was so thick with mattress filling that it looked like it was snowing inside the room. Someone had wired the computer, timed, set and ready for any user who had not punched in the correct sequence of letters and numbers, the code sequence, which separated the living and the dead. Or the computer had gone on fail-safe once he had inserted an alien diskette, any unauthorized diskette lacking a source code. The alien user was to be returned to his basic fundamental, molecular state. Blood and microchips sent to hell for using a system dedicated to a single master. Instinctively, Calvino grabbed Mai, pulled her down and hunched over her, waiting for any secondary explosion. There was none. She was shaking and crying. The sound waves of the explosion echoed deep inside the skull, a dull ringing noise that stayed behind the eyes like someone had struck a huge gong. They only had a few minutes before the room would be crawling with maids, staff, and police.

"We've gotta get out of here before the police come," Calvino said, rising to his feet.

Mai was coughing from the blue smoke and a million bits of matting and feathers.

He shoved opened the door and half-carried her up to the fifth floor, unlatched the small, secret entry door and led Mai out onto the scaffolding. She froze as she looked down at the stage floor a long drop below. When they reached the place where Pratt and he had conducted their off-the-record discussions, he stopped and squatted down.

"I had this feeling. I knew I was right," she said, choking out the words.

"Your timing was perfect. We'll rest here."

"I feel so cold."

"It's the shock."

"I was thinking of my father in the airplane."

"I'm going to marry you," he said.

"I know," she said, kissing him on the nose. "And I am happy."

A couple of minutes later and he would have been hovered over the laptop and would have taken the full blast from the explosive device inside, and the room would have been filled with blue smoke, matting, feathers, and bits and pieces of Vincent Calvino, private eye. He looked at his watch. The invitation card to the reception had said seven-thirty. He had another hour. Sixty minutes to make the difference in the lives of strangers whose names he remembered from the Vietnam Wa r. Americans who, as Drew Markle had said, were returning businessmen, ex-CIA and military types who had turned in their uniforms for suits. Across the street, Marcus Nguyen waited behind a high-powered rifle, peering through the nightscope sight; the rifle was fixed to a tripod pointed at the entrance to the Continental Hotel. He would wait until Judson arrived, got out of the car, lining up the cross-wire on Judson. Would he aim for the head? The chest? How many shots would he get off before he escaped into the resulting confusion?

In the far distance he could hear the faint shrill of sirens. Police, soldiers, ambulances, they all had their air-raid siren-like alerts, as if the sounds of war had never completely vanished from Saigon. Calvino had no idea how long it would take them to piece together what had happened. The explosion could have had a hundred causes. The consequences were always simpler: death, injury, destruction. The sounds in the Saigon night were not the bamboo sticks calling people to order a bowl of noodle soup.

Blowing up his room was a perfect diversion, thought Calvino. Marcus had not made a mistake from the beginning. The fact that Calvino was alive was hardly a mistake. It was a miracle.

He hugged Mai, kissed her tears, kissed her eyes, swollen and puffy with tears. She trembled like a child afraid of thunder with a violent storm stalled overhead. They sat in the dark trying not to think how close they had come to being dead.

"Remember when the power cut out?" he whispered. That's what death was—one big, final power outage.

"I remember every second," she said. "I can never forget."

"*Anh yew em,*" he said, trying to hit the right tones so that "I love you" didn't turn into something like, "Can I do your laundry?"

She smiled. "*Em yew anh.*"

It had been the first time she had said it in Vietnamese to him. The first time she had ever said it to any man. This was an old, standard, Zone lie. The reflex was to tie those words together with ribbons of hard currency. The more you pay me the more I love you. Zone bumper sticker material. Mai wasn't a Zone girl, she had lived protected, isolated, inside a pocket where love hadn't yet been dislodged by money.

Why not just stay together on the scaffolding and wait for the all-clear? he thought. Calvino's law of life was there was never an all-clear siren or signal you could trust. He felt her snuggle next to him, her head resting against his neck. Their touch was light years away from the way people touched each other inside the Comfort Zone; now, sitting near her, in the half-darkness of the empty theater, nothing really mattered outside that touch, that moment, a closeness that shut down the rest of the world while making it seem distant and insignificant at the same time. If he closed his eyes, held her tight, and pretended hard enough that they were once again trapped in the elevator, then maybe he could navigate through this nightmare. He kissed her softly. Whatever would play out was something between Marcus and Judson; unfinished business from a generation ago and who was he to deny Marcus that sweet meat of revenge, as Pratt sometimes put it. It was as if they had climbed off the wall of the Q-Bar, the Caravaggio youth, the young men of the street, whose sad faces, despite all odds, had escaped death, grown old, world-weary, disappointed but never forgetting a time when they could trust and love.

"I know I asked you before. But are you sure you didn't have a small peek at the files on Markle's disk?" he asked.

She shook her head.

"Then you don't know why he was killed."

"Drew made me promise I would not open the files no matter what. He said I would know the right person to give them to. He said I would know. But he didn't say how I would know."

"He trusted you. It was the one thing that Drew Markle did right. To trust you."

"I knew when I met you. You were the one that Drew said I would know."

It was the simple, direct way she said those words.

The Markle diskette—files and files of detailed evidence—had been blown into byte-size pieces floating with mattress particles inside a huge cloud inside his room. Nothing remained of what Markle had so meticulously recorded except what had been lodged in Calvino's memory; and why would anyone believe him? Why should they trust him, who was he anyway? And what had he been doing to get his room blown up? Near the end of the file, Drew was talking about what Harry had taught him—"do the right thing, and don't ever forget right stays right wherever you are, wherever you go, whatever you do—foraging for food, nesting, mating. There is right in the world."

"I have to go," said Calvino, kissing her forehead.

"Go where?"

The alarm in her voice surprised him.

"I won't be long. It's okay. Everything will work out."

"Drew said that, too."

He started to rise. "I want you to wait here. You can't go back to the hotel. It will be crawling with police."

She grabbed his hand. "I'm going with you."

"Not a good idea."

"You don't tell a woman you want to marry her and then leave her behind."

Calvino didn't say anything because she had taken his Smith & Wesson from his holster.

"I can cover for you," she said.

"You've seen too many movies, Mai. In real life you have to cover for yourself," he said, taking the gun from her, opening his jacket and shoving it back into his shoulder rig.

She had made up her mind.

"You may need someone who can speak Vietnamese. And one more thing. More important than language. Love is what people share. You draw a line on what we share, you draw a line on how we love."

She was part of this, and had been from the beginning. The computer files which Drew Markle had downloaded had been entrusted to Mai. Just in case something should happen to him, he said to her. He was expecting trouble. It was why he had phoned Harry in the first place, a half-hearted cry for help. As Calvino looked at her, he held her tight, then, together, they found a ladder and climbed down onto the backstage. There were stage hands and musicians milling around. One was tuning a guitar. From their appearance and instruments, the band members looked like a rock 'n roll group. Calvino walked slowly as if he had a backstage pass, as if he belonged. He crossed the spot where Pratt had played the sax. Squeezing her hand, he led her down to the stairs and hurried down the aisle to the main entrance. The place was filling up with an audience. Outside it was dark and the street lights had gone on. In half an hour, Rodney Judson was about to have the death sentence of almost twenty years before carried out by a Viet Khieu named Marcus Nguyen. Calvino had gone through the files, opening the last one first, it was all there, laid out by a young lawyer trying to the do the right thing. Saigon Concert was opening tonight. On the banners outside the music was late 60s, Vietnam War era music. Jim Morrison, Jimmy Hendrix...some of the ones who didn't survive...their songs were written on the banners. Sirens wailed. A young boy in plastic sandals walked past pounding out a tune on his bamboo sticks, playing, "The Soup's Ready" song.

As they waited for the light to change on Dong Khoi, Calvino looked up at the giant J&B bottle, three stories high, affixed to the side of the building. Neon lights outlined the bottle. The tall shutters were closed on many of the windows in the enormous stylish building which wrapped around the corner of Dong Khoi and Le Loi Boulevard, providing a direct line to the entrance of Continental Hotel. The shutter on one of the windows to the right of the J&B cap was ajar. The street was filled with jeeps and soldiers carrying AK47s. The hotel blast had brought out several squads of combat ready soldiers. At the intersections, they were diverting motorcycles and cars. They were making it easy for Marcus, thought Calvino. They were creating an uncluttered, free fire zone for Marcus Nguyen who was seated behind the J&B bottle cap, looking through the nightscope mounted on his sniper 's rifle, waiting the last minutes of a wait that had started twenty years earlier. Soldiers watched Calvino and Mai cross the street, hand in hand, staring at them.

"He's my husband," Mai said to a soldier who blocked their way.

"We're going to meet my mother for dinner."

"What's he want?" asked Calvino.

"Just smile," she whispered.

The soldier waved them through.

"You see, speaking Vietnamese helps."

"What did you tell him?"

"That you were my husband."

"You spoke the truth."

§ § § §

MARCUS had been at the mosque when Drew Markle was killed. He had a dozen witnesses. He had been with Pratt on Pham Ngu Lao Street when the explosive device in the laptop blew up, leaving a deep crater in the bed. Marcus was very good at being at places away from where bombs exploded. He was methodical, a planner, who anticipated each move as if he had been playing chess. He was grand master in the chess game which ended in violence. He had learned young, and skills established as a teenager and constantly refined through adulthood created a special breed of killer who was very difficult to detect and stop. Marcus still had made enough mistakes to bring Harris and company to town, looking for someone who they knew was planning a high level hit. Mark Wang must have contacted Harris on the phone, or maybe he reached his secretary, or an assistant. Whoever he talked to, Wang must have given enough away for Harris to know he had a problem. That explained why he had approached Pratt at the Fourth of July picnic. He had probably just received the message and Pratt was the first person he knew that he could trust and rely upon to act fast. Harris had been in and out of Vietnam, watching for something like this to break. Marcus had been lurking around the entire time and he hadn't seen it coming; this wouldn't look good in Bangkok or Washington. Not knowing was the ultimate sin. Markle had found Marcus, a kid lawyer from the States had uncovered what Harris was paid to find out. One chance blown. One dead lawyer. Then he screwed up the relay team member, Mark Wang, who had downloaded the diskette onto his laptop. Get the message to them, Markle must have told Wang. He never got the chance; he never got out of his room.

The touch of excitement and adventure, along with his friendship with Markle, someone of his own generation, doing deals, talking the same language, all of this would have been enough to bring Wang into the loop. Mark Wang was stretched out on the king-size bed with two bullet holes in his chest. Red suspenders and gold-rimmed glasses and a computer with an empty hard disk. Marcus had a hit put on both Markle and Wang to silence them. Whoever hit Wang in Bangkok had to have a good knowledge of computers; that left out the seven hundred baht Klong Toey gunman who never would have got into the front door of the five-star hotel. Funny, Harry Markle was a computer man, and Harry and Marcus went way back to the killing days in Vietnam, fellow SOG members...Marcus had been cut loose, left behind, abandoned. How much guilt mileage could Marcus have drawn out of the bank and laid on Harry Markle? Had Harry done a favor for an old friend?

CHAPTER 14

OPENING NIGHT

THE MAIN BALLROOM of the Continental Hotel was filling with guests, foreigners who had worked the region, experienced in making hot deals and travelling light, travelling fast. The money crowd. Hong Kong, Singapore, Tokyo, New York, London accents filtered around the ballroom, as members milled from one group to another like bees drawn by pollen, the promise of honey. Hung behind the podium was a large, red banner with gold lettering: Vietnam Emerging Market Fund, and underneath were two words which sounded out of a NASA publicity campaign, "The Launch"—something borrowed, something new, something old, something blue. It could have been a wedding. The marriage of vast Chinese and Western money with a willing Vietnamese bride who was tired of being poor. Another half an hour until the formal lift off, thought Pratt, looking around the room, cupping his wine glass between his fingers. The financial astronauts, the Fund's directors, would walk into the room and a small band would play something resembling "Hail to the Chief." He tried to guess who the guests would be. Spot an American. Spot a journalist. Twelve o'clock high a New York investment banker. They dressed and acted as types, performing their expected public role: business people, investors, bankers, lawyers, government people mingling together, a drink in one hand, handing out name cards with the other, drinking and sizing each other up. Pratt had circled the room twice looking for Calvino. The second time around, he found Douglas Webb at the bar ordering a double Black Label on the rocks.

"Have you seen Vincent Demato?" Pratt asked.

Webb took his drink from the bartender.

"You mean Vincent Calvino?"

"I'm looking for him."

"So are we," said Harris.

Pratt's showed no surprise, registered no expression, almost as if he hadn't heard, or if heard, had ignored the fact that Calvino's cover had been blown. Glancing at his watch, he had started to worry about Calvino who was running late for the opening ceremony. At the hotel the staff had been in a panic, police and soldiers searching everyone who came in or out of the door. The key to Calvino's room wasn't at the reception desk, creating an inference that Calvino had not left the hotel. Only his floor had been sealed off. No one answered the phone in Calvino's room. Someone at reception had mentioned an explosion on Calvino's floor. No bodies had been carried out. So far as anyone knew, no one had been killed or injured. Calvino had disappeared into thin air. Pratt assumed Calvino had gone through the small door leading to the scaffolding above the backstage and left through the Opera House in the confusion. It was what he would have done. Had Calvino gone into hiding? Who had set the explosive device? Had Marcus really believed that Douglas Webb was behind the killing of Drew Markle and Mark Wang? If so, wouldn't it be logical to assume that Webb had planted the bomb? Only Webb had been at the reception early. He would not have had time. Could a *farang* like Webb have enough power in Saigon to hire someone to plant a bomb in Calvino's room? These questions circled inside Pratt's mind like ducks at high altitude, looking down at a motionless, blue glass-like surface that was a lake, deciding whether to keep on flying or to land.

"Someone tried to kill Calvino tonight."

"I'm surprised they waited so long," said Webb, sipping his drink.

"It wouldn't have been your people?"

Webb smiled and shook his head.

"No, I missed my chance to get him twenty years ago. About the time of the fall of Saigon."

"You knew Vincent in New York?"

"Perceptive, Colonel Prachai. I was in my first year of practice and as green as they come."

"You've obviously developed some very impressive powers of perception since then."

"There was something about Calvino that stuck after all those years. I will tell you what it is. He's no good at lying. It shows on his face. You know how I found out it was him in Saigon?" asked Webb. He had moved in closer, stopping within whispering range of Pratt.

"Years ago, in New York City, I represented a woman in a divorce case. Calvino was on the other side. His client was an Englishman who made his living wetting the bed of wealthy women. A professional. Of course, he married them first. Then wet the bed. A specialized conman if you like. I got someone at Winchell & Holly to dig out the old files and, sure enough, the lawyer on his side was Vincent Calvino. Last anyone heard, he was working as a private eye in Bangkok. A professional bedwetters' paradise. No offense to you personally, Sir. I have two hundred grand of Calvino's money sitting in my office safe."

"Haven't you just breached your client-attorney confidentiality?"

"Given the two hundred grand is bogus, I don't think so. But it was a good try."

From Webb's blind side an Englishman joined them. He was holding a brandy glass half-filled with brandy, he had a crooked smile and the creased face of a man over fifty. James Lee Fitzgerald worked for an oil company in Saigon.

"Bogus, you say, Mr. Webb. Do you think the explosion at the Saigon Concert was bogus?"

"Mr. Fitzgerald is a client, Colonel Prachai. He is with the Police Department in Bangkok, Thailand."

"A Thai police colonel? How impressive. The Fund is attracting the attention of the Thai police. It must be well connected," said Fitzgerald.

"We foreigners can be out of our element in Asian finance. We are much like the African bushwoman I once took to my room years ago. This was in the early 70s. She had never been in a room in her life. Mud hut, yes, room in a building, no. Of course not. I took her to my room for a screw. I mean, she had a lovely face, a lovely body. She smelled of the bush but her body looked like it had been made from lacquered Chinese figure. I walked over to one end of the room to find my bottle and pour us a drink. As I reached around for the bottle and found the glasses, I turned back in time to watch her to go to the chest of drawers. I didn't think much of it. Then she pulled out the bottom drawer, turned around, hiked up her dress. She wasn't wearing underwear. She squatted over the drawer and took a shit. I poured myself a stiff scotch watching her shit in the chest of drawers where I kept my things. I heard this plop, plop. She had this wonderful look of contentment on her face as if shitting in a white man's drawer was about as natural as peeling a banana. Then she finished and used her foot to shut the drawer. After another couple of drinks, I made love to her. Then I packed up my things, except for what was in the bottom drawer. That I left behind. I checked out of the room. Somewhere in Africa is a chest of drawers that no one wants to talk about or to deal with. It is, I imagine, pretty much the way I left it."

"What did you leave in the bottom drawer?" asked Pratt.

Fitzgerald cocked his head to the side as if trying to remember, his eyes narrowing to slits.

"Two packs of crisps, some letters and a copy of Graham Greene's The Heart of the Matter."

"Are you buying units in the Fund, James?"

"If I knew what they kept in their bottom drawer, I might take a flutter."

Pratt moved away from Webb and Fitzgerald, letting them both see that he held up an empty glass. He walked toward a table converted into a bar and asked for another glass of Bordeaux. Were they going to cancel the opening ceremony or go ahead? This question was being discussed across the room. The explosion across the street had caused chaos among the local authorities, military and the members of the Fund's Board of Directors. What had been planned as a party to celebrate the opening had suddenly shifted to soldiers in the streets and a closing.

At the bar, Pratt found the Hanoi lawyer, Khanh, taking a gin and tonic from the bartender. "I have been looking for you," said Khanh.

"We are all looking for someone tonight," said Pratt.

"One of our secretaries has gone missing. Her name is Mai. I am wondering if you might have seen your friend Mr. Demato?"

Pratt smiled to himself. The Vietnamese were straightforward people, he thought. Calvino was in love, he remembered. He was with the girl, probably with a glass of Mekhong in one hand, explaining how they were going to live happily ever after, and he was going to turn in his keys to the Comfort Zone. And, for the first time since he arrived at the Continental Hotel, Pratt relaxed.

"I haven't seen Vincent tonight. He may miss his chance."

"History is filled with Americans who missed their chance in Vietnam," said Khanh.

Pratt raised an eyebrow.

"Americans had a chance long before the American War to help us. During the King Minh Mang Nguyen Dynasty the Americans had a chance. In 1832, President Andrew Jackson sent Mr. Edmond Roberts to Southeast Asia. He landed at Phu Ye n Port in central Vietnam that December. The Emperor dispatched an official to invite Mr. Roberts to have an audience with the king. Before the official arrived, Roberts's ship had lifted anchor and sailed to Siam. To your country! He could not wait for our king. Four years later, Mr. Roberts returned to Vietnam. The Emperor sent another delegation to meet him at the Tra Son Gulf. When the officials arrived, Mr. Roberts was ill. He couldn't speak. That same day, the ship left Vietnam for America. Mr. Roberts left before we had any chance to talk with the Americans. By the time the Americans sent someone else, it was too late. The French had come with their army and officials. They didn't ask to see our Emperor. They demanded. If Roberts hadn't been sick, then what would have been the course of our history? If he had rallied, met the Emperor 's delegation, stayed for a year, two years, taken a Vietnamese wife, convinced the American Government to trade with us, then think of the possibilities! The deaths averted. The tragedy which would never have been. You see how one man's sickness can change the destiny of history, of people, of nations? The absence of one man can make a ripple in the waters of history for centuries."

"I doubt that Mr. Demato's absence is on the same level as Mr. Roberts's illness," said Pratt.

"How does one know? At the time of Roberts's sickness, who knew that his personal disease would spread a virus of doom down the generations for millions and millions of my people?"

"If Mai is with Vincent, then she is safe," said Pratt.

Khanh shook his head as if he was not believing what he was hearing.

"Her father was killed during the American Wa r. His MIG21 shot out of the sky. Since that time I have been responsible for her. I brought her to Ho Chi Minh City. I promised her mother that she would have a future."

"I am a Buddhist, Mr. Khanh, and a Buddhist lives in the present. To want a future is to invite suffering."

From a door behind the speaker's podium, Harris emerged with two other men in business suits with tiny American flags on their lapels. None of them looked happy, expressions disclosing shadings which ran from fear to anger and crash-landed in resignation. Pratt spotted the tiny wire for an earphone disappearing into the ear of one of the men. One of them shook his head and returned into the inner sanctum of the background; the private room where the VIPs could meet beyond the gaze of the investors who were left to stand around, eat free food, and elbow each other at the bar. Pratt saw Harris take a deep breath and then cross the room, stopping to shake a hand, then another. He walked straight toward Pratt and put his hand on Pratt's shoulder.

"We need to talk," he said.

Pratt looked long and hard at the hand on his shoulder until Harris removed it.

"Sorry, but it is very important."

"Your friends look unhappy," said Pratt, glancing back at the two men, hands folded like church ushers, who continued to watch Harris.

"If you will excuse us, Mr. Khanh. And thank you for the history lesson."

They walked together out of the reception room and into the courtyard where they had coffee that afternoon along with Vincent Calvino. The two men with the unhappy, scared faces were Americans attached to the American Liaison Office in Hanoi. They had been sent to Saigon as a show of support for those launching the Fund.

"They came into Saigon last night," said Harris. "I briefed them."

"Perhaps you might brief me, Mr. Harris."

Harris sat in the same seat as he had sat in that afternoon. The outside lights made the courtyard into a fairyland ancient pavilion and from a bar inside the hotel someone was playing Vivaldi's The Four Seasons on the piano. Harris wasn't the kind of man who liked Vivaldi, thought Pratt; he was a man of a single season, his youth, which he had spent as a soldier in Vietnam, and he was back and in trouble, like before, out of control, confused, without a clue as to what should be done to extricate himself from an impossible situation.

"Calvino's screwing up everything. Why, Sir? What is in it for him? Who is he working for? Why did someone try to kill him at his hotel an hour ago?"

"Those questions cover a lot of territory, Mr. Harris."

Harris covered his face with both hands, leaned forward on his elbows on the table, rubbing his eyes as if he hadn't slept for a week. He took a long, deep breath and nodded.

"Right, I did ask too many questions. Perhaps you might answer only one. Where is Calvino?"

Pratt replied, "I don't know."

"If you did know, would you tell me?"

Pratt weighed the answer in his mind.

"Given what is at stake, I believe that I would."

For the first time Pratt saw a look of relief in Harris's face, who seemed to ease up.

"They have decided to proceed tonight. I think it's a mistake. There is a definite security risk involved. Remember when I asked you to provide security for our people in Phuket?"

"I remember the money people," said Pratt without any hint of irony.

"We believe one of the directors is at risk. He was with the group in Phuket and he is in Saigon now. Nothing has changed. If anything, Saigon is exactly the place a lunatic would want to choose."

"Choose for what?"

"To kill him."

"And you have expressed your concerns to this man?"

"He thinks I am being paranoid. 'Everyone is looking to the future, Mr. Harris,' he said to me. 'Why are you living in the past?' Christ, someone just blew up Calvino's room. Lieutenant Colonel Prachai, I know that he is your friend. Someone out there is trying to create an international incident. To destroy American and Vietnamese relations. Sir, I can't let that happen. Not on my watch. I am asking you to help me bring

Calvino in. Otherwise, he is going to get himself killed. He is in way over his head, with all respect. I served in Vietnam. I know something about how tough these people are. Sir, we are military people and we understand that, in a military situation, you work as part of a team."

"May I speak frankly to you?" asked Pratt.

A broad smile crossed Harris's face as if to say, "Finally, we are getting somewhere."

"Please," he said.

"I believe Calvino is in trouble."

"That's an understatement even coming from you, Sir."

"I want you and your friends to help him if that should be required."

Harris shook his head and coughed out a laugh like he had heard a sick joke.

"Help him? He's done everything in his power to sabotage an intelligence operation we have had in place for eighteen months. Who paid him to do this to us?"

"He has a private client. I can assure you that Vincent, to use your expression, did not set out to sabotage your intelligence operation. If he has caused you inconvenience, it would not have been his intention."

"I can't help a private citizen who has broken the law. Sorry, official policy."

Pratt let a long pause follow as Harris withdrew into his official mode.

"When you asked me to arrange security in Phuket on a moment's notice, I might have said 'Follow the official procedure.' But you said it was an emergency. You didn't have time to go through normal channels. I could have said that was your problem. But I didn't. You asked me for your help. I gave that help to you."

Harris rocked back on his heels, biting his lower lip.

"What is it that I can do for you, Sir?"

"Unofficially, quietly, as a friend. Perhaps you might make an exception to the official policy."

The steam of anger had cooled to a chilling mist in the engine room driving Harris's emotions. He was thinking about this and not wanting to think about it at the same time, a train trying to run the rails of two separate tracks.

When he thought of Calvino out in the night, on his own, or more likely with Mai, he remembered King Richard's words, "Look, what is done cannot be now amended: Men shall deal unadvisedly sometimes, which after-hours give leisure to repent." Shakespeare had the soul of a Buddhist, thought Pratt.

And Calvino, what about his soul? For the first time in years Pratt thought he had seen inside the soul of a man who had successfuly escaped from the Zone. A man who had found a way out, a man who had found himself, a man who was reborn with a new wisdom. This wasn't the time he wanted to lose an old friend. But he knew Calvino had taken flight after the bombing, but what he wasn't certain about was whether Harris, or anyone else, would be useful in helping him find Vincent Calvino in the confusion of that evening. Soon the cars carrying the Fund directors would pull to the curb alongside the entrance to the Continental Hotel and deposit the men who had returned to find some piece of themselves which had been left behind. They had come to find investments for the Fund, they had come back to find themselves.

CHAPTER 15

ROOM WITH A KILLING VIEW

IN THE CORRIDOR, they passed beneath a naked light bulb tangled in spider 's webs and dust, creating a strange yellow halo of light. A halo suspended from an ancient electric cord. The building was of pre-electricity construction, with narrow corridors, wooden banisters with a worn, polished feel. Calvino turned at the end of the corner, looked up at the next staircase, but he couldn't see much because the halo of light did not reach that far, leaving a trail of shadows that terminated in near darkness. He had to make a decision before moving forward. He assumed the clandestine operation organized by Marcus and his friends would have included a contingency plan to deal with intruders. Calvino checked out his .40 Smith & Wesson which had been a gift from Marcus. It had saved his life at Karen's Bar though Marcus was probably as surprised as anyone could be that Calvino had walked out of that shophouse alive. With his free hand he pulled Mai closer, felt her body pressing against his on the staircase.

"Where's an elevator in the middle of this blackout?" he whispered.

"We cannot."

"Don't worry, I was just jesting. Thinking, what's on the next floor?"

"I'm thinking, too."

Like a couple of outlaws on the run, faced with an ugly situation, they stopped at each doorway, listening before going up the next staircase. On the second floor Calvino, had quickly spun around, pushed her down, scaring her nearly to death, as he pointed the Smith & Wesson at each point of the compass; he stared ahead, surveying the corridor, not letting Mai move, as if he had felt the presence of someone following. But the hallway was hot, empty and smelling of cigarette smoke. Politics are local. War is local. And fear is local, he thought. This was the last staircase. Marcus and his team were so close he could almost feel their presence.

"Wait for me here," he said.

She shook her head. "No, I don't wait."

How do you tell someone who has never witnessed the instant of violent death, that pure insanity of the firing, the curses, the awful screams? She had been through the war so she knew fear. But Mai had no idea of how dangerous someone like Marcus was, his guns, his mission, his hatred and, above all, his lack of fear of dying. That was what Calvino felt was waiting for him on the next floor. A man who had prepared himself to die.

"Go to the Continental Hotel. Find Colonel Pratt and tell him that I'm here. Will you do that for me?"

She shook her head.

"Please, Mai."

"You think a Hanoi girl is afraid of anything?"

"Fear is something you should never lose."

"Then you stay and I go up."

She pulled up his hand, the one which was clutching hers, and rested it on her breast.

"I give to you," she said. "All I have inside here, I give."

She pressed her hand, the one he held, against her heart. He started to pull his hand away but she stopped him.

"There isn't much time. You won't even have time to miss me." If Judson was on time, his car would be pulling in front of the Continental Hotel in about ten minutes.

"That is what my father said to my mother the last time they were together," Mai said. "She stayed behind and she regretted that more than any other thing in her life. She taught me many things. But I think the most important thing she taught me was never to live your life with regret. Regret is the only bad thing because, once you have it, then it stays inside you until you die. Do you understand?"

He smiled, leaned forward, kissed her.

"In half an hour we will be out of here, on our way to get married..."

She put her finger to his lips. "Never promise beyond the moment. Because you cannot say what is your future. Or my future. Now we go together. Or we stay together."

A child passed down the stairs as they stood together.

"Let's go," he said.

Marcus would bring to bear all of his strength, intelligence, experience and discipline like a laser beam of light as he stared through the telescopic night sight mounted on a sniper's rifle. Who stayed and who left, who went inside and who stayed outside, the basic, fundamental decisions that separated the dead from the living, soldiers from civilians. What act of biological structure had coded the revenge instinct into mankind? Once the seed of that grudge was born, it grew inside, developing a head, arms, legs, a torso, and was ready to come into the world, ugly, nasty, and mean. Some finely honed survival mechanism was at work. We remembered the wrongs, thought Calvino. Wrongs were used to identify enemies, and enemies were others who were feared and killed. Those who had no memory of wrong, no appetite for revenge, they herded together in the Zone like cattle. They were not selected to survive; they would die out, overtaken by men like Marcus who never forgot. To break free of the Zone, you had to face a man like Marcus. You had to find a woman like Mai, Calvino thought.

§ § § §

MARCUS Nguyen sat alone in the darkness near the window. He quietly smoked a cigarette, flicking the ash onto the floor. Greenish hues radiated off the J&B neon sign outside the window, washing his bare chest and face neon green. He leaned forward, looking down at Le Loi Boulevard. Soldiers, jeeps, police. No private cars, motorcycles, or cyclos anywhere. The street had been sealed. A film of sweat covered his body, dripping from his nose onto the cigarette clenched between his lips. The whisky and oil companies had come rocking and rolling back into Saigon with their big money, projects and neon signs, doing business with the communists as if there had never been a war. He wiped his face with a towel, closed his eyes, breathed in deeply and exhaled slowly. Two bandoleers crisscrossed his bare chest. It was like old times. The companies had come back, he had come back. The twentieth anniversary party had come and gone. Everyone spoke of a fresh start in relations, even the Americans had their consulate in Hanoi. They had forgotten one thing, he thought. A man without dignity is like a company without assets; he is bankrupt. Judson had taken away his dignity by treating him like someone who didn't matter, like a servant, a dog. How do you make a fresh start when you have nothing but your anger to start with?

He had stockpiled enough weapons to start a small war. What he had in mind was to start a very private, limited war. Not even war, he thought. He hated the American word— assassination. It was dishonorable, cowardly—everything a professional soldier was not. But then Judson had not been a professional soldier. He was a CIA operative analyzing and reporting on military intelligence operations. In the end, he ran, turned and fled, leaving behind those he had promised to lead, help, and protect. What it came down to, Marcus thought, was that while a celebration had been held on the twentieth anniversary of the end to the war, this was a fraud. The war had not ended. There had been too much unfinished business in 1975. The cadre who owned his villa, for instance, was the real assassin. By stealing everything he had owned, the communists had done as much as stick a knife in his back. People say it is in the past. But the past, present and future are clumped into one trip-wire of time; hit that wire and everything blows up at once. He thought for a second about Calvino. He had liked him and was sorry he had to be killed. He had warned the man but he wouldn't listen. It had been wrong of Harry to send him in the first place. But, then, Harry fit within a certain class of SOG: a malcontent, misfit, independent thinker, someone who could not be controlled. But Harry had been a warrior with specialized training and skills, someone who worked well with him and other Vietnamese soldiers. Looking through the telescopic sight mounted on the rifle, Marcus thought of himself as a warrior, too. It was one of those terms which had meaning once, before it had been perverted into the same category as a cold-blooded killer. Warriors knew honor, courage, decency and, above all, warriors never ran away, never abandoned a comrade in the heat of battle. His greatest accomplishment was saving a life and not taking a life. A warrior was not afraid to die; he knew fear, yes, he tasted it, Marcus thought to himself as he sat in the dark, waiting.

He had booby-trapped the door to the apartment, using a stun grenade, a weapon designed to immobilize an enemy without killing him. The beauty of such a weapon was that the disabled intruder no longer presented a threat, and, a moment after the explosion, Marcus would emerge into the room and have the pleasure of watching the initial expression of shock, surprise, turn to anguish before melting into utter fear in those final moments before he shot several rounds into the head. There was a purity in that final moment, two men looking at each other with an intensity unlike any other shared moment in the life of two beings, one with the power of life and death, the other powerless, waiting for that long march into nothingness. A soldier's memory. No one who killed another man ever forgot that man's face. Vietnamese practicality welded with American creativity was a powerful combination: invention in the service of a concrete, fixed object. And, above all else, the Americans believed in the underdog, giving the hunted a chance. He could have sent Calvino to Karen's Bar without any protection; but he had Jackie supply him with a .40 Smith & Wesson. Three men with AK47s would easily win that battle. Confrontation is unpredictable in the real world. Who would win was never certain. Calvino, who had no military training, had emerged without a scratch, leaving behind three well-trained, well-armed men. He was almost glad to find that Calvino was that lucky...or that good.

Marcus Nguyen had thought of every even-tuality because he had planned out the moves, countermoves, anticipated the possible mistakes and made contingencies for them, and he knew the strengths and weaknesses of those he hunted and those who had hunted him. No one could trace him to the apartment which was in the name of another Vietnamese, a woman who played tennis and had gone the three hundred fifty odd kilometers to Dalat on a visit to her mother. The visit had been planned months before; the elements of Saigon Concer t had required precision, refinement, back-up systems. He had invested in the Americans, they had returned to invest in Vietnam. They had missed one piece of the equation: Marcus Nguyen had some old war bonds he wished to redeem.

§ § § § §

CALVINO remembered that smell. It was the same cologne he had worn the day of the Fourth of July picnic. He froze for a moment.

"You smell that?" he whispered to her.

In the shadows, a slender Vietnamese male slouched back against the staircase railing, lighting a cigarette as Calvino approached. Mai was a step behind. Before she could answer, the well-dressed Vietnamese male bounced off the railing and made a grab for Calvino. He was close enough for the full power of the cheap cologne to sting his eyes. The Vietnamese, with a fleshy middle-aged face, was half a step too slow to plunge the knife into Calvino, giving Calvino sufficient time to see the glint of a long knife blade. Calvino shot him twice in the mid-section, shoving the barrel point blank into the body of the Vietnamese. Both rounds slammed through his body and passed out the other side. The sound of the two .40 rounds was partially muffled by the flesh. The force of the bullets knocked the Vietnamese back, his eyes full of shock and surprise, blood leaking from the wounds in his chest and spilling out of his mouth as his lungs filled with blood. He was dead before he slumped to the floor.

Calvino looked back at Mai. Her face was expres-sionless.

"Let's go," she said.

They walked past the dead man and continued up the staircase. Mai let go of his hand as he was thinking that, if Karen's Bar was any guide, Marcus had more than one gunman assigned to a job. She doubled back five feet. As he glanced around, he saw Mai kneeling over the dead man. Then she stood up, showing what she had found and smiling like she had won some kind of a prize. The blood, the smell of death had no effect. The man was dead. Death, even violent death, was part of life. Brutality affirmed the nature of the world she had been raised in. And what was her prize? Besides the knife, the dead man had a handgun. In the darkness it looked like an old .38 six shot model.

"Keep it and stay here," he said, his hands on her shoulders.

"I have better idea."

"Yeah?"

"We stay together."

"Marcus is a professional," said Calvino. "Why are you smiling?"

"Because you are a professional, too."

He looked at his watch, thinking that Judson had better be late or he would be dead.

She took his hand and put the .38 into the palm and then walked ahead.

"Where are you going?"

"It's better if I go first. They will think nothing is wrong if they see me."

Who was the professional, he thought, follow-ing behind her holding a gun in each hand. She was right, of course. A sentry was posted near the door to an apartment on the fourth floor. Mai went straight to the Vietnamese who wore a Seattle Mariner 's T-shirt and jeans and started to speak Vietnamese. The man started to smile, then shake his head, looking behind Mai, finding Calvino in the dim light near the top of the staircase. He put two fingers to his nose, squeezed and then blew a line of snot onto the floor. Mai giggled, keeping up her one-sided conversation in Vietnamese.

"He say I a bad girl," said Mai, in broken English. "But I say you drunk and you bad boy, too."

Calvino, watching the man's hands, inched forward, hands in his pockets, a gun in each hand. No heroics, he said to himself. Stay cool, stay alive.

"Come on, I don't have all night," said Mai.

She stepped back and reached for him. Marcus's guard, his last line of defense, started to laugh, hands on his hips.

"Why waste yourself on this foreigner?" he asked.

Before Mai could answer, Calvino had smashed the hard metal of the .38 revolver into the side of the guard's head. It was one of those windmill swings which made a loud crack as the metal struck the skull. Blood splattered across the wall and Mai's face. She touched her face and then looked at her hands, they were sticky wet and red. Slowly she showed her hands to Calvino and though it was dark, he could see that her face and hands had blood on them. They looked at each other for a moment, then Calvino dragged the unconscious man across the line of snot he had shot on the floor to the far end of the corridor and dumped him. He wasn't dead but would have one crashing headache when he finally woke up again. The question was whether he would be facing Marcus Nguyen who would certainly kill him for not stopping Calvino or whether Marcus would be on the other side and no one would ever know, suspect or care that one night he had been assigned to kill anyone trying to go into the apartment. When he came back, Calvino put his finger to his lips, handed her the .38 and ran his fingers along the outside of the door.

"What are you doing?" she asked in a whisper.

"Looking for a wire."

He glanced back at her and then returned to his search.

Her eyes followed the line of the door frame. "Above you," she whispered softly.

He looked at her, then slowly rose to his feet. Sure enough, Marcus had run the wire above the door this time. Through a gap in the upper part of the door, the green neon bled through. As it flashed, he saw what her eyes had seen—a small wire stretched at the top of the door. Inside the apartment it appeared to be dark, empty.

"Amway is gonna love knocking on doors in Vietnam," he whispered.

Inside his jacket pocket Calvino put his hand around the grenade that had been planted inside his hotel room. He pulled it out and looked at the pin.

"What are you going to do?" asked Mai.

He pulled her away from the door and motioned for her to walked down the corridor.

"Make a house call. And hope that I am right about this fuse." He pulled the pin, counted one, then two. And on the count of three he kicked the door with all his strength and tossed in the grenade. He swung back away from the door, his back against the wall, his hands pressed hard against his ears. The stun grenade exploded, making an ear-drum shattering explosion, showering blue flame and smoke through the doorway and into the corridor. Two beats later the grenade exploded, but this time the report was a deafening boom which combined with the other sounds—splintering wood, breaking glass, then in the dark, came screams of the wounded. He had blown up the room. The soldiers in Le Loi Boulevard would have heard the explosions. Calvino rolled through the doorway. His eyes adjusted to the darkness. Some light came through the broken windows. Enough for him to spot two men who were covered with debris and blood.

One man was dead outright, half of his face had been blown away and brains leaked from the shattered skull, his tongue wedged between yellow teeth. Two other men lay with their faces away from the door. They were further inside the room and one of the twisted, broken bodies didn't move. The other man had no leg and moaned, rolling over on his side. Calvino quickly kicked away his gun. There was no fight left in him. Calvino pointed the .38 at the man then lowered it.

"Mercy? Or some other noble gesture?" asked Marcus from a distance.

Part of the room had been barricaded with furniture and mattresses turned on end. From the other side of the barricade was movement.

"Marcus, it's over."

"When Harry said he was sending a pro, I said to myself, Harry is sending some guy from Bangkok. He can call him what he wants. But I gotta tell you, Calvino, Harry was right."

What Calvino remembered next was the mattress flying through the air and the sound of an M60 shooting round after round into the room. If hell had a soundtrack, it would have been the blast of an M60 inside the confines of a small room in Saigon. The M60 stopped and the room became silent, filled with death, smoke, bodies. In the distance he heard voices speaking in Vietnamese. For the first time, Calvino realized that he had been hit; his shoulder was numb, the sleeve of the jacket had been torn away, exposing flesh and bone. Marcus was coming to finish him off, he thought. The shock from the wound ran through his body like a network of electrical charges, short-circuiting the brain. He willed himself not to pass out. The Vietnamese who had taken part of the grenade blast and lost a leg had stopped moaning and lay very still. He didn't want to die like that, he thought. He focused on the voices.

"What mercy did you Americans ever show us?" asked a far away voice belonging to Marcus.

"You came to this country and promised us hope. When you left, you didn't even have the decency to promise us mercy."

Then there was another voice joining Marcus.

The other voice was that of the Hanoi girl, Mai. His vision had gone blurry; he blinked his eyes, focused again, and saw Marcus standing a few feet away with his hand raised. Mai was behind him holding the .38 pointed at the small of Marcus's back.

"If you move, I'll kill you," she said in English. There was no doubt that she would do it.

Marcus stood quietly watching as Calvino pulled himself across the floor until he reached the window. He lifted himself up and looked down at the entrance to the Continental Hotel. He saw a line of limos with doors opened, unloading men in expensive suits. Soldiers were squatting down all around the limos, rifles pointing in every direction, including at the window above with smoke pouring out. On the steps of the Opera House he saw Pratt and, one step below and to his right, Harris stood with a pair of binoculars raised to his eyes.

"How did you get in?" Calvino asked Mai, as he pulled away from the window.

"From the next apartment. They share the same bathroom."

"You came in through the bathroom?" Calvino asked.

"Yes. I did," she said in all seriousness.

There was movement outside. Soldiers were coming toward the building.

"They will be here any minute," said Calvino.

"One night leaning against a royal barge is worth more than a lifetime inside a fisherman's boat," said Marcus, smiling.

"Great pick-up line. But I don't see you sailing away from this."

"Neither do I."

"Enough people have died. So let's leave it alone."

"You can never begin to understand," he said.

"No more than you can ever begin to forgive," said Calvino. That was the last of any English conversation Calvino could remember; the rest was in Vietnamese between Marcus and Mai. Then their conversation stopped. Marcus Nguyen stared silently at Calvino on the floor, walked over to the window, opened the shutters and stood on the window sill. He screamed at the soldiers below. All they could see from the street below was a middle-aged warrior bathed in green neon, wearing bandoleers over his naked chest, his hands raised above his head, screaming at those in the street. He leaned his body halfway out. And when the first rounds from the street hit Marcus, he lurched and fell. Suddenly he was gone. Mai, who was right behind Marcus, stepped forward. Calvino had grabbed her ankle just as an AK47 round struck her in the chest, knocking her back. At first, Calvino didn't know that she had been shot; he thought that he had pulled her back, and it was only as he kissed her cheek and whispered that he loved her, that he knew. The Hanoi girl was dead. He wouldn't believe it, rocking her in his arms, touching her face, brushing away the hair from her forehead.

"Don't leave me," he whispered, sitting on the floor. More rounds crashed through the window, pounding the wall behind him.

§ § § §

WHEN Pratt arrived in the apartment, this was the way he found Vincent Calvino, his head buried in a dead woman's hair. Pratt squatted beside him, reached out his hand and touched Mai's neck, feeling for a pulse. He tried the other side. He looked at her eyes.

"She's dead, Vinee. We must go now," Pratt.

Harris spoke Vietnamese to a ranking Vietnam-ese officer. "Either we get him out now, or it's no go," said Harris.

It may have been the hardest thing Pratt had ever done. He reached down and lifted the dead woman from Calvino's arms. He had no strength to resist, the arm wound was no longer masked with the after-effect of shock and the full brunt of pain shot through Calvino's body, pain beyond the will of a man to control. He fought against the pain, against Pratt taking Mai and against losing consciousness. Then he was somewhere else, a strange desert with a green neon sky. A metallic object flashed against the horizon, coming closer, he could see that it was a fighter plane, a MIG21. Through the cockpit he saw the pilot's face as the plane screamed overhead. Mai's face. He ran over the dunes, chasing the plane. The MIG21 banked right, the wing tip touching the desert floor, and Calvino watched as the fighter did cartwheels, spinning flames and metal across the green sky. He fell to his knees and watched the column of black smoke rise in the distance.

Pratt carried Calvino in his arms down the three flights of stairs to Le Loi Boulevard.

He was glad Calvino was not awake to see the hot tears streaming down his face. When you carry a wounded man there is one thing you can't do: you can't wipe away his tears. There is no wind to dry them, there is no place to hide them. These are the tears which are like a shadow that never leaves you, night or day, for the rest of your life. Then Pratt reached the street where Harris's car was waiting. The last thing Pratt remembered seeing as they put Calvino into the back of the car, was the group of soldiers standing around the crumpled body of Marcus Nguyen in Le Loi Boulevard. Some were smoking cigarettes, others talking. Inside the main ballroom, the Vietnam Emerging Market Fund was being launched.

CHAPTER 16

COMFORT ZONE

VINCENT CALVINO OPENED his eyes in a room filled with bright sunlight streaming through the windows and spreading across the foot of his bed. Outside the window was a garden with tropical flowers and palm trees. Pratt sat in a chair near the foot of the bed, his head slumped to one side, sleeping. At first, Calvino wasn't sure where he was or how he had arrived in this place. All he remembered as he opened his eyes was not of this earth; he had been in the desert running in deep sand toward a column of black smoke. His arm was bandaged and when he tried to move it, the pain shot through his shoulder and bounced off his jaw. A nurse, an older woman with a kind Chinese face, wearing a white uniform, quietly slipped into the room. She set a silver tray down near the bed and poured a glass of water. Pratt looked up from his chair and saw Calvino looking at him. Pratt looked more than ordinarily tired, he had a worn-down, bone-weary expression. Then, Calvino caught him smiling at the nurse; one of those smiles of relief.

"Where am I?" asked Calvino.

"Bangkok Nursing Home," said Pratt.

"Please take these pills," said the nurse in fluent English. "They will help take away the pain."

He put a green and a yellow pill in his mouth and took the glass of water from her hand, raised his head, took a drink from the glass and swallowed the pills.

"How long have I been in Bangkok?"

Pratt glanced at his watch. "About twenty-seven hours."

"How did I get out of Saigon?"

The nurse and Pratt exchanged another glance, the kind shared by conspirators.

"Medical evacuation. The American Consulate in Hanoi processed the papers."

Calvino shifted his head on the pillow, closed his eyes.

"Khun Pongsarn escorts *farang* all over the world. Sees that these wayward *farang* get back to their home. She has seen most of the world. America, Canada, Australia, England, Germany, Denmark. Your case is unique for her in two respects. You are the first non-psychiatric patient she has ever escorted. And the first *farang* who has ever been escorted from another country to Thailand."

"How far did you have to move heaven and earth to get Harris to help?"

Pratt moved closer to the bed.

"He's a fan of yours, Vincent. You saved him from one very large headache in Vietnam by doing what you did."

"When can I leave the hospital?" asked Calvino.

"That's up to the doctor," said the nurse.

"And the doctor will leave it up to you," said Pratt.

"I'm home," whispered Calvino.

"I can hardly believe it, Pratt. You got me out."

"You're home."

Calvino thought about this for a moment as the nurse

left the room. He turned his head on the pillow and looked out at the green garden, he kept thinking about that column of smoke, a mushroom-shaped column pouring out of a crash in a green desert. The pain was like a ragged sound cranked up full volume, blasting and assaulting, bending and pulling, leading him down a blind alley. He waited for the pills to kick in, to pull him back, turn down the volume, slowly until it was a muffled noise lost in the buzz of all the other sounds of living. It was so quiet and peaceful, he thought. Then he turned his head back to Pratt, looked at him hard before he reached out with his good arm to Pratt who bent forward, taking his hand.

"Pratt, thanks." It was all that he could say.

The tears swelled in Calvino's eyes and spilled out, running onto the white pillow case. He wanted to say more, a lot more, but he couldn't speak, he didn't want to remember, and he didn't even want to ask. He squeezed Pratt's hand and didn't want to let go.

§ § § §

ON the top floor of the shophouse where Harry Markle had his office, Calvino stood in front of a wall looking at the citations from the Vietnam War which Harry had framed and hung in two rows. There were two Purple Hearts, a Bronze Star, campaign ribbons and, in the center with nothing on either side, was the Congressional Medal of Honor. Marcus Nguyen had been right about Harry being a warrior, a man of honor and bravery. Harry's study was a private place and after all the years they had known each other, it was the first time that Harry had invited him into this inner sanctum, a place which Harry Markle had reserved for himself against the rest of the world. The room was filled with computer equipment and a huge screen flickered on his desk, the screensaver images were naked mermaids swimming and cavorting across the color screen. Harry had taken him surfing on the Net, locking into Vietnam vet discussion groups and data bases.

"The first time I was shot here," said Harry touching the back of his right thigh.

"Some sonofabitch almost hit my ass. Eight inches over and it would have been goodbye to my balls. Instead the round hit flesh, passed right out through, missing the bone. I was out of hospital and back in the field in two weeks. You know what I lost that first time I was shot?"

"No, but you're gonna tell me, right?" asked Calvino.

"I lost ambition for anything more than to survive. Monkey brain ambition. To survive and fuck. That's what being in the field did to you."

Calvino turned away from the wall of medals, his arm in a sling, and looked at Harry sitting behind his desk. He had been waiting for this moment for days and now that it had arrived he felt that, like most things you wished for, the wishing was always a greater emotional ride than actually having the moment arrive.

"Harry, I know that you killed Wang."

Markle took a cigarette from a pack on the desk, lit it and inhaled deeply, smiling as he let the smoke roll out of his mouth and nose. Harry the dragon slayer had become the dragon.

"It seemed like the right thing at the time," he said, pushing his glasses back on his nose.

"The lesson of Vietnam," said Calvino.

"You want another drink before dinner?" Calvino shook his head.

"You don't mind if I have another one?"

The assassination plot had spun out many more questions than anyone in Bangkok, Saigon and Hanoi could answer.

Who was involved? Marcus had been the ring-leader. But had he acted alone, out of a sense of betrayal, or were there other forces who had rendered assistance for other purposes? Drew Markle had sent the answer with Mark Wang with instructions to deliver the diskette to Harris. Wang never got the chance. Harry took out Wang in Bangkok.

"I did it as a favour to Marcus," said Harry.

"Marcus had promised to look after my brother in Saigon. He was on the Net. We exchanged e-mail almost every day, he let me know how Drew was doing. Real friendly things. Personal messages. We took no precautions. Like having sex with someone you trust, there's no need to suit up, right? Well, it's wrong in sex, it's wrong in friendship. Marcus didn't use any encryption. A high-risk act right up there with unprotected sex. You can get unlucky because any hacker can read messages from the Net. Marcus must have thought that he had covered his tracks. His message had bounced off the four walls of the web, filtered through the Finland node, zipped through Amsterdam, and God knows how many times it crossed Europe, before it came to rest. When it turned up in my mailbox, I knew in my gut that this message was from Marcus. He had gone through enough nodes to strip away his identity. But on the Net you can always reconstruct identity, trace back the message to the sender, given enough resources and time. Having gone through Vietnam we should have been paranoid about message interception. Or, at least, I should have been. As I said, Marcus was on the emotional side. e-mail boxes in cyberspace. Sounds impressive, but I'm in the shit. I know it, you know it."

"Does Noi have any idea Wang's family might find what Marcus put in your e-mail box? You know how the Chinese love their revenge, Harry. That's why Pratt was sent to Saigon. To lay off the heat Wang's murder had brought down on the Department. You happen to have killed one very well-connected Chinese businessman."

Harry took a sip from his glass and shook his head.

"You know what Marcus put on the Net? He says a Hong Kong guy named Mark Wang had intentionally infected his niece with HIV. Jackie Ky was sleeping with Drew. Marcus didn't have to be a genius to know that I would take Wang for something like that. Christ, it's my own brother 's life. So I hit Wang. And stripped his computer hard disk and took away the floppies which might have linked him back to Marcus, Drew, or Jackie. It was a precaution that Marcus suggested. It made perfect sense. Fuck, I had no idea about his plot to kill Judson. And I sure as hell didn't know that Marcus was going to kill my brother."

He watched Harry finish his drink and roll a chunk of ice around in his mouth.

"You should have told me, Harry."

"If I had known what Marcus was doing, I would have. I trusted the sonofabitch."

Calvino stared at him through the smoke and ice crunching.

"You have to believe that," said Harry.

"I have done some bad shit in my life. But one thing I've never done is let down a friend. Someone who would die for you. Do you know what I am saying?" He knew what Harry was saying alright. He thought of how Mai had held the gun on Marcus in the dark room rimmed out with green neon light. How he had awakened in hospital and seen that Pratt had spent the night looking over him like a guardian angel. Harry was right, thought Calvino. He believed that Harry Markle was telling him the truth. God, he needed not to question that belief right at that moment. Vietnam had always been a place where people shifted in and out of maximum amoral overdrive. What to believe was one of those issues which never disappeared; on one side were the ideas bigger than any one tribe, ideas so big that a lot of different people could believe that they were worth fighting and dying for, ideas that could unite many tribes into a whole fabric of shared belief of good and bad, right and wrong, just and unjust.

The big ideas were no more. Just like Marcus, they had gone into oblivion. What had Vietnam left behind? Generations of people who questioned whether any idea was big or important enough to die for, to make others suffer for. In the shattered ruins of the old ideas emerged the god of consumption. Harry had escaped into cyberspace; others were following him. A wall of medals for ideas buried in the past, a computer terminal and screen to establish contact with the survivors from those old times and plans to create a rescue mission to the future. Harry had believed that Marcus had let go of the past and had gone back to Vietnam for a fresh start. Maybe Marcus had, but something happened to pull him back to the past. Once back in-country, it happened without Marcus knowing at first, as the old residue of repugnance, resentment, hatred and anger, smouldering hot, lay just under the surface and the heat sucked Marcus down until all of the last twenty years had burnt off and it was again April, 1975 and he was waiting to be pulled out. Only this time he knew that he would be betrayed and he had time to plan an action to strike first.

"How much time do you think I've got?" asked Harry Markle.

"Pratt laid Wang's murder on Marcus. That's what he wrote in his report, the one he filed with the Department, and that was the report the Department sent to Wang's family in Hong Kong. The report also said Marcus had used all kinds of diversions and false trails to divert attention, to implicate others. They might buy it."

"Or they might not."

"It's what you've got to live with, Harry."

"Looking over my shoulder for the rest of my life."

The only domino theory that ever fit the reality of Vietnam was the domino of betrayals. Men like Judson had been misled and betrayed by their commanders, who had been betrayed up the chain of command. On the way back down that chain of command, Judson had betrayed Marcus, and later Marcus betrayed Harry Markle. And at the end of the day, Harry had betrayed himself, thinking that somehow he alone was immune from being struck by the last domino to fall. It always hits the next guy, the one next to you. This time it was coming for Harry, and even though he was drunk, he could feel the shadow of that final self- betrayal closing in.

§ § § §

BY the time they went downstairs for dinner Harry Markle was pretty drunk. He had polished off half a bottle of Mekhong and smoked a joint as thick as his gorilla's thumb. In Vietnam, the men in the field were divided between boozers and dopers but, after the war, the distinction blurred when the boozers added pot to their daily maintenance program and dopers found a cheap whisky to clean the taste of grass from their mouth. Harry's kids were seated at the table spooning rice onto their plates and reaching toward a plate of chicken legs. Noi set down a large bowl of prawns, the steam and smell of garlic rolling off the surface. Her sister, Meow—the Thai nickname meaning "cat"—came out of the kitchen carrying a plate of vegetables. Calvino had been introduced to Meow briefly before Noi had taken him upstairs to Harry's office. Her presence had come as a surprise; no one had warned him in advance that she was coming to dinner. That had been Harry's idea: a romantic ambush. Calvino's law was that all romance was ambush, a surprise attack, no warning, no chance to escape from the direct hit. He tried not to look annoyed though he was. It wasn't Harry or Noi's fault; they didn't know about Mai. He hadn't told them. It would have been pointless to have done so, until now, when he realized that Noi assumed that he had come to dinner to meet the elusive Meow— the cat who had not shown up at the Fourth of July picnic. She had slipped into the shophouse before him, merging with the rest of the family as she did her part to make him feel comfortable, as if she naturally fit into the domestic scene. That was always the best kind of ambush, around food, around kids and around friends— the last place where one expected to be felled by the opposite sex.

"Did Harry tell you that we signed a lease for a shop at Seacon Centre?"

Harry grinned and winked.

"Yeah, he mentioned it," lied Calvino.

"Noi is the one with ambition in our family," said Harry. From the expression on Calvino's face he knew that he had connected.

"She's opening that New Age drugstore."

"You talked about it at the Fourth of July picnic," said Calvino, who had sat down at the table.

Meow sat opposite him and was peeling a prawn with her fingers.

"I'm sorry I missed the picnic," she said in good English.

"I heard something about you having a bad star alignment," said Calvino.

"Some things are difficult for a *farang* to understand about us," she said, dipping the naked prawn into a small bowl of sauce.

"What Meow means," interrupted Noi, "is that when you grow up with *mor doo,* you know, fortune tellers, it is not something you shake off. It stays with you. You go to university and study science and then you go to visit the mor doo to find out..."

"If you should open a shop at Secon Centre," said Harry, finishing her sentence.

"Exactly," said Noi.

"It's normal," said Harry, slurring the words.

"Are you alright, honey?" Noi asked him.

"I'm just a little drunk," he said.

"Nothing new in that. Nothing wrong. Right?"

She didn't say anything, inhaled deeply. Smiling, she picked up the large spoon cradled on the plate of vegetables and began to fill Calvino's plate.

"You see the special treatment, Vinee?"

"Shut up, Harry. He only has one arm to use."

Meow had finished the one prawn and started to peel another one as she looked up at Calvino. An awkward smile crossed her face. Blind dates were hell with all that pressure to make conversation with someone you don't know but everyone else at the table knows and speaks to in a kind of short-hand code. She was nervous, feeling that she had a duty to please her sister.

"Who do you think are more beautiful? Vietnamese or Thai girls?"

Calvino looked up from his plate of rice, vegetables and a prawn he couldn't peel.

"More beautiful?" he asked, his ears ringing and hot, as if the explosion in Marcus's room had just gone off.

"Some men think Vietnamese girls make better wives than Thai girls. You were in Vietnam, what do you think Khun Vincent?" asked Meow.

His chin dropped and he stared at the table. All eyes were on him, watching, waiting, wondering why this man in a shirt and tie had tears streaming down both cheeks.

"Did I say something wrong?" asked Meow.

She was in a state of near panic.

Calvino looked up. "I'm sorry, Noi. But I have to go now. It's nothing you said. It's just that I'm not feeling so good."

He pushed his chair back. Even the kids had stopped eating as they watched Uncle Vincent rise from the table and walk toward the door. Noi started after him but Harry grabbed her by the arm and pulled her onto his lap.

"Harry, what's happened to Vincent? That's not like him."

They watched the door close behind him.

"He discovered Vietnam," said Harry. "Or Vietnam discovered him and won't let go."

Calvino took in a long breath outside the shophouse door as Harry's daughter locked the metal gate from the inside. Across the street he noticed a 500 series Mercedes parked with the engine running, and in front were the figures of two men. The tinted glass made it almost impossible to see who they were. One lit a cigarette and, for a fraction of a second, he could see the man in the driver's seat was holding a pair of binoculars to his eyes and that they were trained on him. His heart skipped a beat looking at the car. Should he bang on the door, run up and warn Harry that men in a Mercedes were outside, watching his house? Maybe they were just a couple of real estate developers, or maybe they were people hired by Mark Wang's family who knew the Thai Police Department were trying to pull them over the table concerning Mark's murder. If he had wanted to play full-time bodyguard for Harry, if the men had been hired by Wang's family, he might stop these two. But there would be two more, and then two more, until finally there was no more Harry. That was the way the world worked, Calvino knew it, and so did Harry Markle.

§ § § § §

AS Calvino walked into the Comfort Zone Bar, a new double shophouse bar stuck in the back corner of Nana Plaza, where many naked girls were dancing to the beat of "I Can't Get No Satisfaction," some of the girls already looked zonked out and moved like they were shuffling underwater towards some distant shore. Royal barge, fisherman's boat, Calvino thought to himself.

A couple swung their legs around the metal poles, moving their pelvis in and out, and watching themselves in the mirror. He leaned his head against the black upholstery and nursed a Mekhong and water. Number 14—her plastic number badge pinned to her bikini bottom—wore a silver peace medallion on a chain around her neck and had a blue swastika tattoo on her right shoulder. The smile suggested glue sniffing, uppers, or heroin—the ice smiles came from a cocktail of drugs, any one of which might stretch the lips back, bare the teeth, for hours and hours, without pain, without effort. Almost immediately, Calvino felt himself ease into the Zone space. He liked the back, where it was dark, where he could be hidden, his arm in a sling, nothing more special than three or four other cripples dotted around the perimeter, watching the ice goddesses dance. The Zone was not just a bar, or a bunch of bars, it was a state of mind. A mental Zone that never turned off, day or night. He looked around the bar, recognizing a face here and there. It was a new bar that had opened while he had been in Vietnam. In the space of a week the Zone changed, shifted; it was constantly on the move. Very few had any idea as to the borders of the Zone; even fewer had knowledge as to who inhabited the Zone. What everyone agreed upon was that the Zone existed. Out there. Somewhere, maybe everywhere, like thousands of neon holograms flashing from the inner depths of souls, projecting every desire, fear, judgement and doubt. Without checkpoints, without any controls other than the nominal patrol, the Zone was a natural force like a volcano existing beyond the ability of man to master.

Pratt leaned against the steering wheel, thinking that he had let his wife go into the Zone. Alone. He knew she could handle herself and that she would find Calvino. Who was waiting inside Nana? He started to worry, the same kind of fear he felt carrying Calvino down the stairs. He had gone into the unknown. Now he had let Manee go into the Zone alone. He had protested, but he knew that she was right. That she was probably the only person on the planet who could bring him out. It was one thing to carry him down those stairs and into Le Loi Boulevard, it was another to deliver him from another kind of wound.

No one knew who the bar owners were—Thai or *farang*, and no one really cared—what mattered was that it was there, open space filled with young women who learned the fine art of feeding off the ice which hung throughout Nana Plaza. The Zone was a space in time without care or emotional risk, offering every pleasure imaginable.

The duo-stages were designed to look like the transporters on the Starship Enterprise. Above the girls were yellow, red, blue and—of course—green lights syn-chronized to the music, flashing and twisting like stars in another galaxy, and the Comfort Zone was a black hole, sucking in all light, all feeling, all emotion faster than the mind could record. The light washed over the customers, balding heads, short-sleeved shirts with tiny bird wings, over countless faces who had come for the show. Neon like the light that had bathed Marcus Nyugen's body as the J&B neon side outside the window turned him into a being from another world. Any minute he thought Marcus might descend from the ceiling. Any minute he thought Mai might come through the door. What he was looking for was enough Zone ice to cool the minute, to pull it over to the curb and write it a ticket for speeding inside the Zone where time stopped.

Two dozen girls or more on each transporter platform waiting for someone to beam them down or up or round and round until the meter registered finished. "I Can't Get No Satisfaction" faded into "One Night in Bangkok" which cranked through the speaker system filling the internal universe with sound. All around the bar were middle-aged men. Some had advanced decades beyond middle age, white haired, large stomachs, wrinkles and loose skin as if they had mutated into some other kind of being visiting from another solar system. Out of the darkness a *farang* slid onto the cushioned bench.

"You had that one, Vinee?" asked the voice. "Number 46."

A Calvino looked at the profile of the bearded face. He recognized him from the Zone. Lambert was his name and he was a broker during the day.

"No," said Calvino.

"You should try her, she's good. You need snow shoes to get through all that ice. For thirty minutes she gets into it. That's the only downside. She's yours for twenty-nine minutes and fifty-nine seconds and then some switch kicks in and she is pure ice."

"Never had her."

"She's worth it," he said, drinking from a bottle of Singha Gold cooled inside a condom.

"What happened to the arm? Looks like you got on the wrong end of a gang of katoeys. Yes? No?" asked Lambert.

"No, it wasn't a gender bender who did this," said Calvino. "I fell down some stairs."

"Yeah, sure, man," said Lambert.

Half of the girls had climbed down from the transporter

platforms, wearing only G-strings and high-heeled shoes, they fanned out among the customers on barstools and those farther back against the wall, seated on cushions. They had beamed down. Invasion of the ice goddesses. They had been on stage, looking to make eye contact, someone to pay the bar fine and take them out of the Comfort Zone Bar and into one of the short-time hotel rooms above the Plaza. That was the drill, walking stairs from one Zone to the other, ice forming as they walked, holding hands with a trick, smiling, flipping back long, black hair and almost skipping, that ice walk of the young who are holding the hand of the old, the infirm, the crippled, those with the single desire to forget the past, to turn back the clock, those who were looking for one more chance to scale the mountain of their youth. Time warped as the teenagers ran wild and naked around the Zone, cadging drinks from punters—ice picks—finding others to buy them out—ice torches. The ice could be hacked, torched, blown up, but the next morning it was as thick as the first time he saw her dancing on the transporter, before she had beamed down and scooped him up, wrapped him around her little finger. A mamasan ran around with a wooden dildo the size of a billy-club, banging the side of the platform, the stage, bar stools and rubbing it against the crotch of bar girls.

He thought about Mai and the pain was nearly unbearable as he watched the naked girls dancing on the stage. Cold, it felt cold inside. He knew it was the air-conditioning turned up full blast; the girls danced as if in a wind tunnel and if they stopped for a moment they would turn to ice. And Calvino knew the purpose of the Zone was to freeze all feeling. Tears of anger sometimes spilled inside the Zone, and they were almost always those of a dancer who had not learned how to form enough Zone ice to shelter behind. Calvino was an old hand, he knew that the right girl was a virtual ice machine, she froze you in time, numbed out the core of the pain, the memories of loss, and of death.

§ § § § §

MANEE had made Calvino promise that he would bring her husband back. She had told him that she had a real bad feeling about his going off to Saigon. The oath she had required from Calvino was one of serious consequence; she wanted Pratt back, no excuses, no explanation, and she wanted him back in one piece. And, in the end, it had been Pratt who had brought him out. As she walked through the door of the Comfort Zone, Pratt waited on Soi Nana behind the wheel of the family car. As he watched his wife walk toward Nana Plaza, he turned over in his mind the threat the Wang family had made: expose every last contour of the Zone to the outside world, let them see how deeply implicated the Police Department was at every level of the industry. Maybe that would have been a good thing, he thought. Under that intense spotlight of international judgement, the will might have been found to dismantle the Zone, to disconnect from the Force, to end a way of life. Some said the Zone destroyed lives, others said it saved lives. There were no neutral voices in or out of the Zone. Calvino had once told him that the Zone was a refuge against madness. "It's in Shakespeare. As You Like It." Calvino and Manee, to make a confession or to win an argument, often resorted to Shakespeare as an ally. Later, when he looked up As You Like It, he found the madness quote, "Love is merely a madness, and, I tell you deserves as well a dark house and a whip as madmen do; and the reason why they are not so punished and cured is, that lunacy is so ordinary that the whippers are in love too."

§ § § § §

MANEE had gone in and out of several bars, asking for Calvino. He was easy to describe: the Italian looking *farang* with his arm in a sling and his heart on a life-support system. The girls on Nana knew who she was talking about and guided her to the Comfort Zone Bar. She parted the plastic strips which hung like a curtain over the entrance and walked straight through the crowd, found Calvino in the corner, his hand cupped around his glass. He was staring at the lights in the ceiling. He was sitting alone.

"Vincent, it's time to go home," she said.

At first he thought that he was dreaming one of those strange Zone dreams where voices appeared without bodies, and bodies appeared without voices, then he saw it was Manee.

"What are you doing here?"

She stepped up and sat down on the bench next to him. He was embarrassed that she was in the Zone, seeing him like this, with the lights, the girls, the Zone men leering, grabbing, poking, laughing and staggering back and forth from the toilet.

"We've come to take you home, Vinee," she said.

"Pratt's outside in the car. I insisted on coming. It was my idea. I know how much you miss her. I know if something had happened to Pratt...I don't know what I would've done."

"I thought about you and Pratt a lot. I wanted that thing you two have managed to find, Manee."

"You can wish all you want but you won't find it inside this place."

It had been Marcus who had said that the lesson of the world was that brutality was the rule. This was the rule that explained the Zone. The refuge where people pretended to escape in an ice-like coldness of the soul, a place beyond brutality. He turned toward her, trying to make out the expression on her face.

"Manee, where will I find it?"

"You want me to tell you the truth or do you want me to lie to you?"

He didn't respond, his eyes glancing at the stage before they found their way back to Manee.

"I know you care or you wouldn't be here, Manee. But the truth is that she's dead."

"The truth is that you are alive. She taught you one great thing, Vinee. She taught you, that you can commit to one woman. You, Vincent Calvino, actually found that you can love a woman and plan for more than one night at a time..."

"I don't want to love without her."

"It's up to you. Pratt once told me something I never forgot. He has seen many people die. Once you're dead, that doesn't mean the end. That you are no more. What comes afterwards? We believe it is rebirth. And what we put in motion this life determines what happens in the next. It doesn't matter whether you believe like us or not, Vinee. What does count for something is that you go on trying, hoping and looking for love with someone else. That matters. That is the greatest respect you can pay to her. Look around this bar, it's filled with men who have stopped trying. That's not you, Vinee."

"You don't understand, Manee. You just don't."

"Let me ask you this. Would she have understood what you are doing now? Would you want her to understand you in this way?"

"No," he whispered. "She wouldn't."

"To come here is to turn away from who she was and what she meant to you. As I said, Vinee. It's up to you to decide. Where to go, what to do, who to be with. No one will stop you or question you. That is the way things are in Thailand. But only you have to look in the mirror and ask where is the dignity in my life? Do I have the courage to let go and start again? Or do I just keep falling and falling?"

Manee stepped down from the bench and walked several steps past the platforms filled with naked girls. She stopped and looked back because there was something else she wanted to say. But she saw there was no need. Calvino was following one step behind her. On the way through the main entrance she noticed one thing that she told herself would stay with her for a very long time, something she told Pratt in bed that night: he didn't look back.

When Pratt saw them coming toward the car he thought he saw something in Calvino's face that suggested the beginning of a cure.

Calvino left the Zone.

Many others had left before, but they came back to dance around the mouth of the volcano, feeling the heat, the gravity, letting the Zone suck them back into ice. Somehow, Pratt had believed in connections to other worlds and, in one of those worlds, a girl named Mai was still working to change the forces of gravity in her man's life.

CPSIA information can be obtained
at www.ICGtesting.com
Printed in the USA
LVHW03s1241160718
583907LV00008B/148/P